Fourth Edition

THE TECHNIQUE
OF
ORCHESTRATION

Kent Kennan
Donald Grantham

The University of Texas at Austin

 Prentice Hall, Englewood Cliffs, New Jersey 07632

Library of Congress Cataloging-in-Publication Data

Kennan, Kent Wheeler, (date)
    The technique of orchestration / Kent Kennan, Donald Grantham.—
4th ed.
      p.   cm.
    Includes bibliographical references.
    ISBN 0-13-900366-5
    1. Instrumentation and orchestration. I. Grantham, Donald, (date)
    II. Title.
MT70.K37 1989   89-22903
781.3′74—dc20   CIP
                                               MN

Editorial/production supervision and
interior design: *Carole Brown*
Cover design: Marianne Frasco
Manufacturing buyer: *Raymond Keating*

© 1990, 1983, 1970, 1952 by Prentice-Hall, Inc.
A Division of Simon & Schuster
Englewood Cliffs, New Jersey 07632

Printed in the United States of America

10 9 8 7 6 5 4 3 2 1

ISBN 0-13-900366-5

PRENTICE-HALL INTERNATIONAL (UK) LIMITED, *London*
PRENTICE-HALL OF AUSTRALIA PTY. LIMITED, *Sydney*
PRENTICE-HALL CANADA INC., *Toronto*
PRENTICE-HALL HISPANOAMERICANA, S.A., *Mexico*
PRENTICE-HALL OF INDIA PRIVATE LIMITED, *New Delhi*
PRENTICE-HALL OF JAPAN, INC., *Tokyo*
SIMON & SCHUSTER ASIA PTE. LTD., *Singapore*
EDITORA PRENTICE-HALL DO BRASIL, LTDA., *Rio de Janeiro*

Contents

v

Preface

The changes in this fourth edition fall chiefly into two categories: revisions prompted by changes in current orchestral practice, and new material designed to clarify or amplify the subject at hand. In the latter category, a brief new chapter (21) gives basic information on nonorchestral instrumental groups—concert bands, wind ensembles, marching bands, jazz bands, and chamber groups. Also, the Bibliography and the list of recommended recordings in "Suggestions for Using This Book" have been revised; new items have been added and others that are now out of print have been deleted—with the exception of certain especially important out-of-print books that are likely to be found in libraries—and material on the effective use of multiple stops in string writing has been added in Chapter 3.

As in the earlier editions, the emphasis is on the practical fundamentals of orchestration. No attempt has been made to give a detailed account of the construction of instruments, and historical background is given only where it seems essential to an understanding of modern instruments or of scores of an earlier period.

Because many orchestration classes include students who will be working with high-school orchestras, certain problems involved in scoring for such groups are mentioned from time to time, and a short chapter is devoted to that subject.

Knowledge of various styles of scoring must be gained principally through a direct study of scores. Consequently, that aspect of orchestration has been left largely in the hands of the individual teacher, to be undertaken as scores of different periods are studied in class. Some thoughts concerning this phase of the work are included in the "Suggestions for Using This Book" section.

As successive editions of *The Technique of Orchestration* have appeared (over a period of nearly forty years), it has become increasingly difficult to give proper credit to the many persons who have helped with it. We wish to reaffirm our gratitude to the colleagues (past and present) and others who have contributed information and valuable suggestions. In the case of the present edition our particular thanks go to Gayle and Wayne Barrington, Whit Dudley, Robert Duke, Tony Edwards, Richard Floyd, George Frock, Gordon R. Goodwin, William Kraft, Louis Lane, Richard Lawn, Karl Miller, and Dan Welcher.

KENT KENNAN
DONALD GRANTHAM
Austin, Texas

Suggestions for Using This Book

Changes in the order of material in this book are possible. Some of these are the following:

Chapter 11 (Problems in Transcribing Piano Music) can be taken up earlier, most logically following Chapter 4. Use of that order has the advantage of preparing students almost from the start for certain problems they are sure to encounter in working from piano music. If time is limited, instructors who feel that it is more important to move on to a study of the other instruments than to make actual assignments based on Chapter 11 may wish only to go over the material of the chapter in class; further study of this aspect may be undertaken later as time allows.

Chapters 13 and 14, on percussion instruments, can be introduced after Chapter 9. The same is true of Chapter 15, which is chiefly about the harp.

The section in Chapter 4 on string harmonics, sometimes a difficult subject for students, is probably best taken up later as a separate project after they have had more time to become familiar with the workings of stringed instruments and to absorb the more basic information.

Chapter 18, on infrequently used instruments, is intended chiefly as a reference in the more advanced stages of orchestration study and may be omitted in a first-year course—except for the material on saxophones, which should be covered if Chapter 19 on scoring for high-school orchestra is assigned—and which is likely to be useful in any case.

Because much of the most important material on orchestration can be learned through a study of symphonic scores, it is important to equip students for score reading as quickly as possible. With that end in mind, we recommend moving fairly rapidly through the first nine chapters of this book rather than dwelling very long on any one of them. It is always possible to return to individual instruments or sections for more concentrated work once students have acquired enough knowledge of all the instruments to undertake score reading.

As far as the choice of music for score study and listening is concerned, we feel that shorter works are preferable—at least in beginning orchestration courses, where time is generally at a premium. Students can grasp the essential characteristics of Mozart's orchestration about as well from the Overture to *The Marriage of Figaro* as they can from the C Major Symphony (*Jupiter*), for example, and the choice of shorter works allows for the study of more scores of various styles within the allotted time. As a minimum program of score study, one work from each of the following groups is suggested:

1. Haydn, Mozart, Beethoven
2. Berlioz, Wagner, Tchaikovsky, Rimsky-Korsakoff, Dvořák
3. Debussy, Ravel
4. Strauss, Mahler
5. Stravinsky, Bartók
6. Schönberg, Webern

The many scores that might be used for class study and listening include:

> Mozart, Overture to *The Marriage of Figaro*
>
> Beethoven, *Leonore* Overture No. 3; *Egmont* Overture; *Coriolanus* Overture
>
> Weber, *Oberon* Overture; *Der Freischütz* Overture
>
> Berlioz, *Roman Carnival Overture*
>
> Tchaikovsky, *Romeo and Juliet*
>
> Rimsky-Korsakoff, *Capriccio Espagnol; Russian Easter Overture*
>
> Wagner, Prelude to *Die Meistersinger;* Prelude to *Parsifal;* Prelude and Love Death from *Tristan und Isolde;* Overture to *Tannhäuser*
>
> Debussy, *Prelude to The Afternoon of a Faun*
>
> Ravel, *Boléro; Le Tombeau de Couperin; Mother Goose* Suite
>
> Strauss, *Till Eulenspiegel; Don Juan; Death and Transfiguration*
>
> Mahler, *Das Lied von der Erde*
>
> Stravinsky, *Firebird* Suite; Variations; *Movements; Agon*
>
> Bartók, Concerto for Orchestra
>
> Schönberg, Five Pieces for Orchestra, Op. 16
>
> Webern, Six Pieces, Op. 6; Five Pieces, Op. 10

In this list, shorter works of the composers represented have been chosen wherever possible. Longer or more involved works that are particularly instructive for score study include:

Berlioz, *Fantastic Symphony*

Mussorgsky-Ravel, *Pictures at an Exhibition*

Tchaikovsky, Symphonies No. 4, 5, and 6

Franck, Symphony in D minor

Brahms, the Symphonies

Dvořák, Ninth Symphony (*New World*)

Mahler, the Symphonies

Debussy, *Ibéria; La Mer; Nocturnes*

Ravel, *Daphnis and Chloe* Suite No. 2

Stravinsky, *Petrouchka; The Rite of Spring;* Symphony in Three Movements

Prokofieff, Fifth Symphony

Hindemith, Symphony: *Mathis der Maler*

Bartók, *The Miraculous Mandarin*

Schönberg, Variations for Orchestra, Op. 31

Copland, Third Symphony

Lutoslawski, Third Symphony

Ligeti, *Melodien*

Suggestions for listening are given at the end of many chapters in this book. These involve passages from symphonic music that make prominent use of the individual instruments or groups discussed in the respective chapters.

Also valuable for listening purposes are the following, which may be presented as they become pertinent to the material being studied.

Britten, *The Young Person's Guide to the Orchestra.* Variations and a fugue on a theme of Purcell illustrate the various instruments. Columbia M 31808, New York Philharmonic Orchestra, Bernstein conducting; Telarc CD80126, London Philharmonic Orchestra, Previn conducting; RCA RCD 1-2743, Philadelphia Orchestra, Ormandy conducting; others.

The University of Delaware Videodisc Music Series, Disc 2, Side 2 (1986). This videodisc has the great advantage of allowing students to see as well as hear the instruments demonstrated. Available from the University of Delaware, Newark, Delaware 19717.

Inglefield, Ruth K., and Lou Anne Neill, *Writing for the Pedal Harp.* Berkeley: University of California Press, 1985. A small record at the back of the book demonstrates basic harp technique and many special devices.

Jennings, Lucile, *Writing for the Modern Harp.* A video tape (¾ inch or VHS) available on rental or by purchase from Ohio University, Telecommunications Center Marketing Department, Athens, Ohio 45701. Issued in 1974.

Rehfeldt, Phillip, *New Directions for Clarinet.* Berkeley: University of California Press, 1978. A small record at the back of the book demonstrates present-day possibilities in writing for the clarinet.

Also, there is a cassette supplement to the present text that contains selected examples from it played by the University of Texas Symphony

Orchestra under the direction of Dr. Cornelius Eberhardt. The tape includes:

> The arrangements of the two-measure fragment from *Jesu, meine Freude* (Bach harmonization) for strings (Chapter 3), for woodwinds (Chapter 6), and for brass (Chapter 9)
>
> Chords for the various sections and for orchestra (Chapter 10)
>
> Scorings illustrating rearrangement of pianistic figures (Chapter 11)
>
> The different scorings of the Brahms Intermezzo excerpt and the one of the Beethoven Sonata excerpt (Chapter 12)

Examples of individual instruments are not included on that cassette, one reason being that that aspect has been covered elsewhere. Furthermore, in most schools it is possible to arrange live classroom demonstrations of many of the instruments.

The cassette may be ordered from the University of Texas Press, Box 7819, Austin, Texas 78712.

In planning this book, we had in mind a year's course in orchestration. When the book is used for a one-semester course, even a cursory covering of all the material in it will probably not be feasible. The decision as to what material to stress and what to pass over lightly or omit altogether must rest with individual teachers and will be determined by the particular needs of their students.

Actual music to be used for the exercises in scoring is not included in this volume but is available in *Orchestration Workbooks I, II,* and *III,* also published by Prentice-Hall, Inc. These do not represent a graded series of progressive difficulty from *I* to *III;* rather, they all involve roughly the same types of scoring projects but for the most part contain different music, in order to allow instructors some choice and to provide variety from year to year.

Austin Symphony Orchestra
Sung Kwak, Music Director

Introduction

Although orchestration involves many artistic choices, students must acquire a certain amount of factual information at the start. Under this heading come the following:

Names of instruments and orchestral terms (including Italian, French, and German equivalents because many scores are printed in these languages)

Order of instruments on the page

Ranges of instruments

Proper notation, including transpositions and special clefs

General technical abilities and limitations of each instrument (although this does not necessarily involve the ability to *play* the instruments)

Principles of combining and of balancing instruments

Characteristics of various "schools" of scoring

This material can be learned from classroom explanations, from books, from talks with or demonstrations by orchestral players, and from a close study of orchestral scores.

But there is another type of information, which can be learned only by careful and frequent listening (along with score reading) over a considerable period of time. This category includes a knowledge of these things:

The characteristic tone quality of each instrument

The sound of various instruments in combination

The sound of special effects

The point here is that tone colors cannot really be described adequately in words. It is all very well to read in an orchestration book that the clarinet is "dark" in its lower register, but until the sound in question has actually been heard and impressed on the "mind's ear," a student has no real conception of that particular color for purposes of orchestration. Not everyone seems to be equally endowed with aural memory and aural imagination, but these qualities can be sharpened by practice.

Once this information has been acquired, it must be applied in actual exercises in scoring—such as transcriptions of piano or organ music or of music for instrumental groups. Students who are composers will want to go on and write directly for orchestra. That is the ideal situation, for the musical ideas are conceived with the orchestral instruments in mind. But not all students can be composers; furthermore, the ability to *transcribe* for orchestra is one of the most usable and important skills to be gained from an orchestration course.

It is assumed that students who are studying orchestration from this book have already had a thorough training in harmony. Our experience indicates that poor scoring on the part of students is more often the result of a failure to understand harmonic and general musical structure than of a faulty knowledge of orchestration. Unless the principles of good voice-leading, spacing, and doubling are applied in an arrangement, no amount of clever orchestration will produce satisfactory results; and without an understanding of harmonic content and form, intelligent scoring is impossible. In orchestrating, it is of the greatest importance to think in terms of *lines* rather than in terms of isolated notes. Otherwise the total result will be confused and the individual players' parts will be unmusical and unrewarding to play.

Finally, it cannot be stressed too strongly that accurate workmanship, attention to detail, and a practical approach are all parts of successful orchestration. Anyone who has witnessed an orchestra rehearsal where time is wasted and tempers strained because of mistakes in the players' parts knows how costly and serious inaccuracy can be. As for attention to detail, there are a thousand small points involved in scoring—points that may seem trivial but that taken all together make the difference between scoring that comes off in performance and scoring that does not. This all ties in, of course, with a practical approach, which involves the ability to achieve the maximum effect with the simplest means. Orchestration is not a nebulous sort of business conditioned sheerly by "artistic inspiration" but to a large extent an intensely real and down-to-earth technique.

Although the terms *orchestration* and *instrumentation* are sometimes used synonymously, musicians generally make a distinction in meaning between them, which is observed in this book. Orchestration has to do with the actual process of scoring music for orchestra. Instrumentation, on the other hand, usually refers to a study of individual instruments—such aspects as their construction, history, and capabilities. Sometimes the word is also used in connection with the list of instruments required for a particular piece of music, as when we speak of "the instrumentation" employed in an orchestral work. Of course, anyone who sets out to learn orchestration must in the process learn a good deal about instrumentation. Although the two terms certainly overlap, it has aptly been pointed out that instrumentation is a science, while orchestration is to some degree an art.

TABLE 1.1
Instruments in the Orchestra

		SMALL OR CHAMBER ORCHESTRA	LARGER ORCHESTRA
WOODWIND SECTION	Piccolo		1
	Flute	1	2–4
	Alto Flute		1
	Oboe	1	2–4
	English Horn		1
	E♭ Clarinet		1
	Clarinet	1	2–4
	Bass Clarinet		1
	Bassoon	1	2–4
	Contrabassoon		1
BRASS SECTION	(French) Horn	1 or 2	4–6
	Trumpet	(1)	2–4
	Trombone	(1)	3
	Tuba		1
PERCUSSION SECTION	Percussion	2*	4* or more
	Harp	(1)	1–2
STRING SECTION	1st Violins	4–8	10–16
	2nd Violins	3–6	8–14
	Violas	2–4	6–12
	Cellos	2–3	6–12
	Double Basses	1–3	5–10

*These figures indicate the number of percussion players including the timpanist.

In order to gain a general perspective before concentrating on individual instruments and sections of the orchestra, we are going to take a brief look here at the orchestra as a whole. "Orchestra" in this case means the symphony orchestra, but even that term is lacking in precision. It has been applied to groups as small as the "chamber" orchestra and as large as orchestras that include "woodwinds in fours" and a massive brass section (the latter type characteristic of the music of Strauss and Mahler, for example). In between these extremes lies the orchestra most often seen in the concert hall today.[1]

Table 1.1 lists the orchestral instruments and shows how many of each are generally available in small and in larger orchestras. Of course the fact that an instrument is "available" does not mean that it will necessarily be used in any given score. For instance, many scores do not call for an English horn, a bass clarinet, or a contrabassoon, and the alto flute and E-

---

[1]The American Symphony Orchestra League classifies orchestras on the basis of their budgets and uses the following categories: "major" (over $4 million annually), "regional," "metropolitan," and "civic."

flat clarinet are employed even more rarely. In some cases it is possible for one player to play two different instruments (of the same family) alternately. For example, the second flutist may be asked to "double" on piccolo, the second clarinetist on bass clarinet, and so on. If there are three oboists, one might play English horn at certain points—or throughout. Each woodwind family normally has at least one player who is proficient at doubling on one of the "auxiliary" woodwinds. This doubling possibility is partly responsible for the variable figures ("2–4") after certain woodwinds in the table. The other factor is simply the fact that scores vary in their requirements. Table 1.1 presumes a maximum of four players in each woodwind group; that is, one should not normally expect to have four flutes *plus* a piccolo and an alto flute, for example.

For economical as well as musical reasons, orchestras larger than the largest one indicated in the table are only rarely called for.

Each section may play by itself or be combined with one or more of the other sections. Sections that are combined may take the same musical material or different material. Sometimes only one instrument of a section is used, along with part or all of another section. If all the instruments of the orchestra, or most of them, play, the combination is known as a *tutti* (the Italian word for "all").

The fourth section, the percussion, is often used for rhythmic support of other instruments but can also perform on its own to good effect.

The order in which the instruments are listed in Table 1.1 is a standard one that is always employed in modern scores. If an instrument is not included in a score, it will not be listed on the page, but those instruments that *are* used will follow the standard order. In most scores, all the instruments to be used are listed on the first page, whether they play at that point or not, but on succeeding pages, instruments that do not play may be omitted from the listing. When a solo instrument is involved (as in a concerto), its part is normally placed directly above the strings. The same is true of piano, celesta, and choral parts. The examples in Chapter 16 show the appearance of a page of orchestral score.

Figure 1.1 shows the most usual seating plan for the orchestra today. However, numerous variants of this plan are possible. For example, the positions of the second violins and the cellos are sometimes interchanged; the timpani may be placed at the *left* rear; and the harp is sometimes placed on the right side near the front. In any case, the woodwinds are arranged with the first flutist next to the first oboist and the first clarinetist next to the first bassoonist. A similar relationship pertains between the first horn and the trumpet-trombone group.

Although the historical development of the orchestra is not within the scope of this book, a few brief comments on that subject may help to put the present-day orchestra into better perspective. Before the seventeenth century, composers for instrumental groups did not specify particular instruments for the respective parts. Among the first to do so were Giovanni Gabrieli (ca. 1557–1612) and Monteverdi (1567–1643); the latter was also an innovator in the use of special orchestral effects. By J. S. Bach's time it was usual to specify the instruments involved, but little or no distinction (apart from that of range) was made between them or, for that matter, between parts for instruments and parts for voices. Furthermore, there was

FIGURE 1.1

Typical Orchestra Seating Arrangement

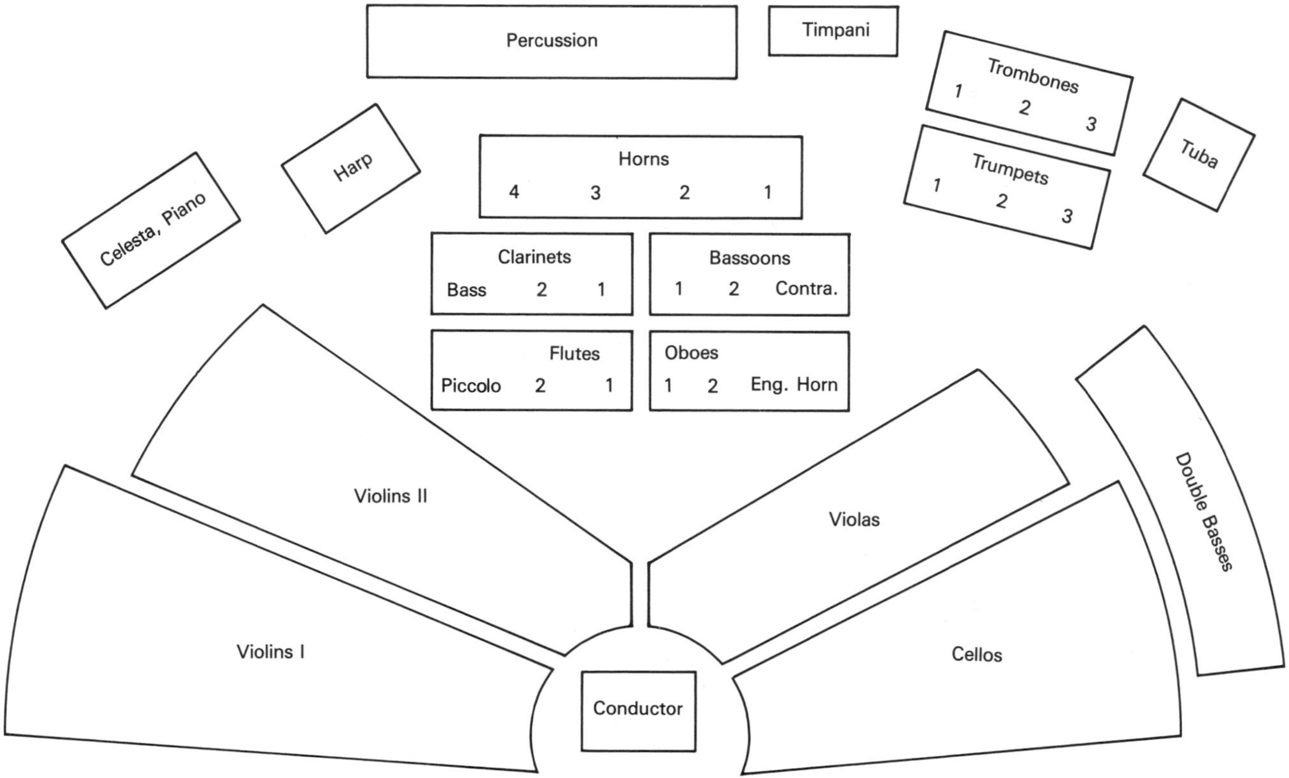

as yet no standardized instrumentation; that concept was not fully in evidence until the Classical period. By the early nineteenth century, the orchestra had evolved into a more or less standard group: two flutes, two oboes, two clarinets, two bassoons, two horns, two trumpets, two timpani, and strings (the latter subdivided as they are today but fewer in number).

A note of explanation is necessary concerning the system used in indicating ranges throughout this book. The limits of the extreme possible range are shown in open notes, the limits of the practical or commonly used range in black notes. The reason for this distinction is that nearly every one of the orchestral instruments has notes at the bottom and/or the top of its range that, because of technical difficulties or doubtful intonation or both, are little used and then only under certain conditions. It must be remembered, though, that there is no sharp dividing line between the practical registers and the extreme possible registers, particularly since players and instruments vary. Consequently it is extremely difficult to fix exact limits for each practical range.

SUGGESTED ASSIGNMENT

Know:

1. the four sections of the orchestra.
2. the names (in English) of the instruments included in each section.
3. the number of each instrument commonly included in the small orchestra and in the larger orchestra.
4. the format used in indicating ranges throughout this book.

2

The Strings

THE VIOLIN

Italian: Violino	*French*: Violon	*German*: Violine
(*plural*) Violini	Violons	Violinen
		(*or* Geige
		Geigen)

EXAMPLE 2.1

Range[1]

The violin's four strings are tuned to the following pitches:

EXAMPLE 2.2

---

[1]All the string ranges given in this chapter may be extended upward by the use of harmonics.

These are known as the "open" strings, that is, the strings as they are when not stopped by the fingers. A chromatic scale upward is obtainable on each string by stopping the string at the appropriate points. Normally a note is

played on the nearest string below it; for example, the note would usually be played on the D string. However, the G string might be chosen in certain cases in order to maintain the particular color of that string throughout a passage or to avoid a change of position. This same principle is sometimes used in connection with the D and A strings. Although notes more than a 10th above the pitch of each open string are seldom used on any one of the three bottom strings, the top string is necessarily called upon for very high notes.

Normally, the choice of string rests with the player, a particular string being indicated only in cases where a choice other than the normal one is involved. The strings are sometimes designated by Roman numerals, starting with the E string as I and working down. Thus, "on the G string" is often indicated by IV placed above the first note to be taken on that string and followed by a dotted line to show how far the direction is to apply. Another way of indicating the same thing is to write *sul G* (literally, in Italian, "on the G") above the passage. The German equivalent is *G Saite, Saite* meaning string.

As for the colors of the various strings, the G string is characteristically full, rich, and rather dark in quality. From about

upward, its tone becomes curiously intense, as if charged with emotion. The D string is less dark and full, the A considerably brighter, and the E especially brilliant and penetrating.

Each of the following examples illustrates the use of a particular string of the violin. Of course not all melodies lie entirely on one string, as these do (with the exception of one or two notes); the great majority, in fact, require changes from one string to another.

EXAMPLES SHOWING THE USE OF PARTICULAR STRINGS OF THE VIOLIN

EXAMPLE 2.3

(a)   E string: *Classical* Symphony

(b)   A string: Third Symphony

Eastman School of Music Publication; Carl Fischer, Inc.

(c)   D string: Second Symphony

(d)   G string: First Symphony

Stringed instruments (Figure 2.1) may be either bowed or plucked. For these two effects the Italian words *arco* (bow) and *pizzicato* (picked or plucked) are used. *Pizzicato* is usually abbreviated to *pizz.* and written above the staff, just before the first note of the passage concerned. When the player is to return to the use of the bow, the word *arco* is written in above the staff. These directions are important and must be included by the orchestrator. However, since the normal method of tone production on stringed instruments is by means of the bow, *arco* need not be included unless there has been a pizzicato passage just previously. For example, if a work starts out with a bowed passage, no arco direction is needed. It is not customary to use dots (to indicate short notes) in pizzicato passages; if the

FIGURE 2.1

Studio Gilmore, Austin, Texas

Double Bass   **Violoncello**

Viola   **Violin**

pizzicato direction is there, the notes will automatically be short to some degree, although (particularly in the case of the double basses and the cellos, with their greater resonance) notes that are not too high can be made to ring somewhat, especially if *vibrato* is used. Under normal circumstances, the easiest notation of time values is employed, rests being omitted wherever possible; for instance,

   rather than   

But the second notation, accompanied by the direction *secco*, might be used if an extremely short, dry pizzicato were desired. And in passages involving longer values where the notes are to be allowed to ring, half notes or even whole notes would be helpful in suggesting that effect. (Usually the direction *vib.* is included in such cases.) As a rule, it is best not to write pizzicato passages for the violin above about (musical notation); higher notes played pizzicato are so thin and lacking in resonance as to be ineffective for ordinary purposes. It is important to remember that there is a limit to the speed with which successions of pizzicato notes can be performed, and that very rapid changes from arco to pizzicato (or vice versa) are awkward, even impossible beyond a certain speed. Changes of this sort that must be made with scarcely any rest between the last arco note and the first pizzicato note are somewhat easier if the last arco note can be taken "up-bow" so that by the end of the bow-stroke the player's hand is close to the strings and in position to play in pizzicato fashion. Lefthand pizzicatos, though not uncommon in solo violin literature, are seldom used in orchestral parts—and then only with an open string. They are useful chiefly in places where there is not time to change from arco to a normal (right-hand) pizzicato. The indication for a left-hand pizzicato is a small cross above or below the note head.

A few names for particular parts of stringed instruments come up frequently in orchestration work (see Figure 2.2). The *fingerboard* is the part of the instrument on which the fingers stop the strings. The *bridge* is a

FIGURE 2.2

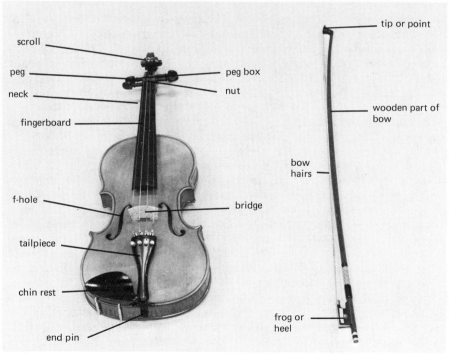

Dorf Photography, Austin, Texas

Violin   **Bow**

small piece of wood that keeps the strings raised and in place above the main body of the instrument. Parts of the bow that are often referred to are the *frog* (or *nut* or *heel*), which is the portion nearest the player's bow hand, and the *point* or *tip* at the opposite end. The wooden portion of the bow is sometimes referred to as the *stick*. Special effects involving these and other terms are discussed later on.

A *vibrato* is normally used in playing stringed instruments and is produced by an oscillating motion of the hand on the fingerboard. Without a vibrato the tone is "white" and lacking in expressiveness and warmth (although this very sound is occasionally used for a particular effect in orchestral music). Because a vibrato cannot be produced on an open string,[2] players usually avoid the open strings in slow, *espressivo* passages where the difference in tone quality would be too apparent. A further disadvantage in such cases is that the open strings tend to ring and to be louder than stopped tones. The alternative to playing an open tone is to take the same pitch as a stopped tone on a lower string, though this is obviously not possible with the lowest open string of each instrument. The symbol for an open string is an O above the note (not to be confused with the symbol for a natural harmonic, which is smaller and perfectly round). The numbering of the fingers in string writing may be mentioned in passing because it is invariably confusing to pianists. The index finger is 1; the middle finger is 2; and so on. Since the thumb does not figure in the stopping of the strings, no symbol is needed for it.

Frequently string players speak of taking a passage "in first position" or in some other position. A few examples will serve to explain this concept of position, which is basic to string technique. If the player's left hand is placed on the D string with the first finger on E and the other fingers ready to play F, G, and A (or F♯, G, and A, or other chromatic variations of these basic pitches), he or she is said to be "in first position on the D string." In first position on the A string, the player's first finger would rest on B (or B♭, or in rare cases B♯). For second position on the E string, the first finger would rest on G; for third position on the G string, it would be on C, in each case with the other fingers on (or over) the three notes immediately above. The first, third, and fifth positions are easier and more natural than the second and fourth and are consequently chosen more frequently. Positions higher than the fifth are seldom used on the three lower strings (except in solo writing), but higher positions are often needed on the E string. Although players can shift rapidly from one string to an adjacent one or from one position to another, sudden or repeated jumps *across* strings make for awkward string writing, as do sudden or repeated changes from one position to a distant position. Figure 2.3 shows a fingering chart for first position on the violin.

A point to remember, especially in writing for players of limited ability, is that the higher the player goes on a string, the closer together the notes lie on the fingerboard and the harder it is to play perfectly in tune. Because higher positions are not so often necessary on the three lower strings, the chief point of difficulty is in passages high on the top string.

---

[2]Except by artificial methods, usually involving sympathetic vibration between the open string and another string fingered with vibrato at the pitch of the open string.

FIGURE 2.3

Fingering Chart for First Position on the Violin

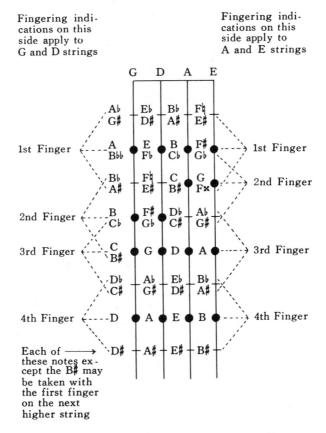

FINGERBOARD OF THE VIOLIN

These can be written with safety for a professional group, but they are an almost certain invitation to disaster in a school orchestra. As a general rule it is safest not to go beyond third position in scoring for school groups. (See Chapter 19 for further comments on this subject.)

Double, Triple, and Quadruple Stops

Although the violin is predominantly a single-line instrument, it is capable of playing two, three, or four notes at a time, provided that each note can be taken on a separate string and that the pitches involved can be fingered at once. If any of the notes can be played on open strings, that will make the fingering problem much easier for the player. It is obvious that two pitches cannot be played at the same time on the same string. For

example, 𝄞 is impossible as a double stop on the violin because both notes would have to be taken on the G string. But [musical notation] is quite

easy since the A can be played on the G string and the F♯ on the D string, the bow being drawn across both strings at once. The double stop

[musical notation] is even easier, because the D can be played on the open D string

and the B on the A string. Of course the notes of a double stop must be playable on *adjacent* strings. The following may be considered practical upward limits for double stops involving intervals up to an octave (practical, that is, for the professional orchestra violinist of average ability):

EXAMPLE 2.4

Of these intervals, 6ths are probably the most successful as double stops. Octaves, 5ths, and 4ths present a certain problem of intonation since the slightest deviation from the correct pitch in either note is more apparent to the ear than it would be in such intervals as the 6th and 3rd, where the mathematical ratio between notes is more complex. Perfect 5ths, by the way, are played with one finger stopping both strings (assuming that open tones are not involved). Unisons, though rare, are possible and are sometimes introduced for the sake of added resonance and volume. They almost always involve an open string; that is, they are generally written on

one of these three pitches: [musical notation] For example, in [musical notation] one

of the A's would be played on the open A string, the other on the D string.

Double stops involving intervals larger than an octave are also possible in certain cases. Sometimes even such widely spaced double stops as

[musical notation] are used. Unwieldy as this may look to the pianist's eye, it is

actually very simple, for the A is an open note and the D presents no problems. For purposes of orchestral writing, quick successions of double stops are generally impractical, though short successions of 6ths or 3rds are not out of the question. Usually, however, such passages are better arranged *divisi* (with the string group divided).

As for triple and quadruple stops, those that include at least one open string are the easiest and the most resonant, but certain other chord arrangements that contain no open note are also possible. Because of the curvature of the bridge, four notes cannot be played at exactly the same time. However, in quadruple stops the bow can be drawn so quickly over the strings that the effect is that of a four-note chord only slightly arpeggiated or broken. Examples 2.7 and 2.8 show the more commonly used three-note and four-note chords playable on the violin. (Cecil Forsyth, in his book *Orchestration* points out that a complete catalog of all the chords possible on the violin would amount to nearly 1500 combinations!) The method used here in listing chords that contain no open notes may need a word of explanation. Instead of writing out all the possibilities in connection with each chord pattern, we have merely indicated them in the following manner:

EXAMPLE 2.5

This particular example means that three-note chords arranged in this pattern are playable on every half-step within the limits shown:

EXAMPLE 2.6

This and other upward limits given must not be thought of as hard and fast points above which the chords become impossible. All the patterns are possible in still higher positions, but at that level they become so difficult as to be impractical for normal orchestral use. The limits shown here are therefore intended merely as guides for practical usage. Notice that the predominant intervals in these chord arrangements are 5ths and 6ths.

THREE-NOTE CHORDS FOR THE VIOLIN (PARTIAL LIST)*

EXAMPLE 2.7

(Chords containing two open notes)

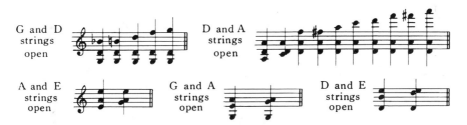

This list has been limited to major and minor triads and dominant-type seventh chords (or incomplete forms of these chords).

(Chords containing one open note)

(Chords containing no open note)

Note: *Accidentals are written separately for each chord.*

FOUR-NOTE CHORDS FOR THE VIOLIN (PARTIAL LIST)

Example 2.8

(Chords containing three open notes)

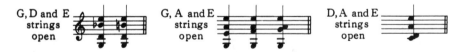

(Chords containing two open notes)

16

A and E strings open

G and E strings open

(Chords containing one open note)

G string open

E string open

(Chords containing no open note)

Note: *Accidentals are written separately for each chord.*

Although double stops may be used effectively in sustained chords and at a low dynamic level, there is not much point in writing triple and quadruple stops except in fairly loud passages, usually in sharply detached chords where an extra degree of volume or accent is wanted. It is, however, possible to sustain the top note or the two top notes of a three-note or four-note chord:

EXAMPLE 2.9

Even inner notes may be sustained, though that possibility is not of much practical use. Since the main objective in triple and quadruple stops is usually added resonance, those that contain one or more open tones are ordinarily the most effective, besides being the most comfortable to play.

Certain other string effects, although not technically triple or quadruple stops, depend on the same principle. For instance, in these passages,

EXAMPLE 2.10

the player's fingers remain fixed on the quadruple stop  while the bow produces the particular effect called for.

Examples 3.12(b) and (h) illustrate the use of "multiple stops" (a term that may conveniently be used to apply to double, triple, and quadruple stops).

EXAMPLES OF PASSAGES FOR THE VIOLIN

EXAMPLE 2.11

(a) Symphony No. 40, K. 550

(b) Third Symphony

(c) Overture to *Oberon*

(d) *Capriccio Espagnol*

♩.= 66 *sempre non div.*   Rimsky-Korsakoff

(e) Fifth Symphony

♩=66   Tchaikovsky

fff con desiderio e passione

(f) *Death and Transfiguration*

Allegro   Strauss

ff marcato

(g) *The Rite of Spring*

Vivo   Stravinsky

THE VIOLA "c" clef

Italian: Viola   *French:* Alto   *German:* Bratsche
          Viole   Altos   Bratschen

EXAMPLE 2.12

Range   Open Strings

Much of what has been said about the violin applies to the other stringed instruments as well. In the case of the viola, the chief differences to be considered are (1) its greater size as compared with the violin; (2) its characteristic tone color; (3) its range; and (4) the use of the alto clef.

Although the viola and the violin look similar from a distance, the viola is somewhat larger and heavier,[3] and the distance between notes on the fingerboard is slightly greater than on the violin. Also, due to its larger size the viola is more limited than the other strings in its upper register because of the difficulty of getting the left hand over the body of the instrument.

There is an attractively reedy and nasal quality to the sound of the viola, especially on the top (A) string. The middle two strings are more neutral and less penetrating in timbre, while the bottom string (C) is dark, rich, and even a bit ominous at times.

For those who have not used the C clefs before, a note of explanation is necessary here. The alto clef, , puts middle C on the middle line of the staff. The open strings of the viola, then, are C, G, D, and A, reading from bottom to top. Since the viola's normal register is from an octave below middle C to about a 12th above it, the use of the treble clef would require frequent ledger lines below the staff, while writing in the bass clef would involve an even more forbidding array of ledger lines above the staff. The alto clef provides a solution to the problem by placing middle C in such a location that the average viola part can be kept within the staff. If the part goes unusually high and stays there for some time, the treble clef is used. As a rule, it is not wise to change clef for the sake of one or two notes; players prefer to read a few ledger lines occasionally rather than shift their thinking from one clef to another. Viola parts intended for high school use should not go above about a G (just above the staff in treble clef).

Too often in orchestral scoring the violas are given rather undistinguished parts: chordal figurations, sustained harmony tones, afterbeats, and the like. (This is particularly true in older music.) They are capable, however, of doing everything the violins can do, discounting differences of range, of course. As we move on to a view of the string group as a whole, it will become more apparent how valuable the viola is as a bridge between the violin and the cello.

The same patterns available as multiple stops on the violin are possible on the viola a 5th lower. However, quadruple stops in the higher positions are a bit more difficult and less effective than on the violin and are better avoided. Examples 2.13 and 2.14 show the more usable triple and quadruple stops on the viola.

---

[3]There is more variation in size among violas than among the other stringed instruments. Many violas are slightly larger than the one shown in Figure 2.1.

EXAMPLE 2.13

(Chords containing two open notes)

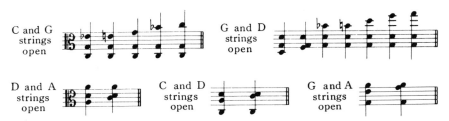

(Chords containing one open note)

(Chords containing no open note)

Note: *Accidentals are written separately for each chord.*

This list has been limited to major and minor triads and dominant-type seventh chords (or incomplete forms of these chords).

EXAMPLE 2.14

(Chords containing three open notes)

(Chords containing two open notes)

(Chords containing one open note)

(Chords containing no open note)

Note: *Accidentals are written separately for each chord.*

EXAMPLE 2.15

(a) Prelude to *Tristan und Isolde*

(b) *Romeo and Juliet*

(c) Fifth Symphony

(d) *Till Eulenspiegel*

(e) *Daphnis and Chloe* Suite No. 2

THE VIOLONCELLO (CELLO)

Italian: Violoncello   *French:* Violoncelle   *German:* Violoncell
         Violoncelli   Violoncelles   Violoncelle

EXAMPLE 2.16

Range   Open Strings

The complete name violoncello (not violincello) has been more or less abandoned today in favor of the shortened form, cello. Although the instrument (see Figure 2.1) is too large to be held as the violin and viola are and must rest on the floor (secured by an adjustable peg at the bottom), it operates on basically the same principles as the smaller stringed instruments, except for some differences in fingering necessitated by the fact that the notes are farther apart on the fingerboard. The open strings have the same letter names as the open strings of the viola but are an octave lower.

The normal clef for the cello is the bass clef. However, in order to avoid the use of many ledger lines in passages that lie in the upper part of

the compass, the tenor clef, ⬚, is often used. This clef places

middle C on the fourth line and must not be confused with the alto clef, which is never used by the cello. If the part goes so high as to require the continuous use of ledger lines even in the tenor clef, then the treble clef will probably be substituted. One might argue that bass and treble clefs would be sufficient. That is perfectly true. But when a passage lies between the F below middle C and the F above middle C, for example, the tenor clef will keep the notes on the staff, whereas either bass or treble clef would require ledger lines. In any case, tradition and common practice dictate that the cello shall use the tenor clef for most of its higher passages. An old and fortunately obsolete custom ruled that when the treble clef was used immediately following the bass clef, the notes in the treble were to be written an octave higher than the sounds desired. Such a system appears completely pointless. It is mentioned here only because it occasionally turns up (as late as Tchaikovsky, Dvořák, and Mahler) and proves confusing to the uninitiated score reader.

The cello has a reputation, amply deserved, for mellowness and warmth of tone. The two bottom strings (the C string in particular) are rich and full-bodied; passages played on them have a way of sounding grave and somehow reflective. The D string is brighter, with a warm and ingratiating quality, while the A string possesses a vibrant, singing tone all its own. Melodies played on it take on a strongly *espressivo,* almost passionate, quality that becomes more intense and poignant as one goes higher on the string. The upper limit of use is particularly hard to fix here. Virtuoso solo work occasionally calls for notes even higher than the top G given as the highest possible note, but for orchestral use it is best not to write above

 . In scoring for school orchestras, a safe upper limit is the A a

third lower.

Much of the time, the cellos constitute the bass voice of the string group (often with the double basses sounding an octave lower). However, they may be used as a tenor or baritone voice or even on the melody if it does not go too high.

There are two small limitations concerning double stops on the cello: Avoid 2nds and octaves unless one of the notes is open. Triple and quadruple stops based on the following patterns are all practical as long as the top

note is no higher than .

EXAMPLE 2.17

This is by no means an exhaustive list but includes the chord arrangements most frequently encountered in orchestral cello parts.

The cello section is frequently called upon to play broken-chord patterns such as the following, which (like those in Example 2.10) are simply multiple stops in which the notes are sounded consecutively instead of at approximately the same time.

EXAMPLE 2.18

(a) *Scheherazade*

(b) Symphony in D minor

Cello

ff

(c)   Fourth Symphony

EXAMPLES OF PASSAGES FOR CELLO

(See also the double bass examples, which include passages for cellos and basses sounding in octaves.)

EXAMPLE 2.19

(a)   Third Symphony

(b)   Fifth Symphony

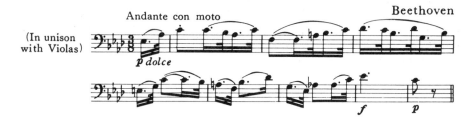

(c)   Fourth Symphony

(d)   *Don Juan*

(e) Third Symphony

Con moto   Harris

THE DOUBLE BASS

| *Italian:* Contrabasso | *French:* Contre basse | *German:* Kontrabass |
| Contrabassi | Contre basses | Kontrabässe |

EXAMPLE 2.20

Sounding an 8ve lower.

Range   Open Strings

The double bass is known by a variety of other names: contra bass, string bass, bass viol, or simply bass. ("Bass violin" is an amateurish misnomer.)

We now encounter for the first time an instrument that does not sound as written. The double bass sounds an octave lower than written, or, to state the case conversely, the notes must be written an octave higher than they are intended to sound. A glance at the lower range of the instrument will explain the need for such an arrangement. If the part were written at actual or "concert" pitch, ledger lines would be in continuous use, and the result would be cumbersome to write and awkward to read.

The double bass in standard use today has four strings, which are tuned in 4ths rather than in 5ths. The five-string bass, which is still much used in Europe but is rarely seen in the United States, tunes its fifth string to a C below the low E. In the United States, the device commonly used for making these low notes possible is an extension to the fingerboard of a four-string bass. The bottom string can then be tuned down to C instead of E. In most professional orchestras, at least two or three basses have this extension, and in some orchestras the whole bass section is equipped with them. School orchestras, on the other hand, seldom include a bass with an extension. Fortunately, notes below the low E do not occur very often; where they do, they can often be played an octave higher without any serious damage to the effect. This "extended" low register of the instrument is valuable for dark color effects and for finishing out phrases that dip below the low E. But as a general rule, the double bass sounds much better when it is not kept too low. It has more incisiveness, more sense of definite pitch, in its upper and medium registers. Then, too, it has a way of sounding low even when the part appears to be moderately high. The tenor clef or the treble clef may be used in very high passages.

Because of its great size and the ponderousness of its technique, the instrument has some limitations of performance as compared with its smaller relatives. For one thing, it is less agile. Though rapid running passages are possible, they should not be too long or too frequent. Besides being strenuous for the player, they are apt to sound "fuzzy" and unsatisfactory. In order to ease the technical problem and make for a clearer effect, the basses are sometimes given a simplified form of what the cellos—and possibly the lower woodwinds—are playing:

EXAMPLE 2.21

Of course it is not necessary or even advisable that the basses play constantly; in fact, their effectiveness is generally in inverse ratio to the amount they play. Therefore, a possible solution if the passage at hand seems unsuited to their technique is simply to give them a rest.

One point to remember in writing for the double bass is that triple and quadruple stops are completely out of the question. A few double stops—those involving one or two open strings—are possible. Usually, however, it is better to divide the section when two notes must be played by the basses. Most of the other effects discussed in connection with the violin, viola, and cello are possible on the double bass. Pizzicato passages are frequent and especially effective because they provide support without heaviness and give a welcome relief from the bowed sound.

The basses are seldom called upon to play alone. Their tone tends to be a bit dry and lacking in focus, and they do not have the *espressivo* possibilities of the cellos. But they frequently take melodic passages an octave below the cellos. Their lower register is dark, almost ominous, in quality, while the upper two strings are somewhat clearer and brighter in color.

EXAMPLES OF PASSAGES FOR DOUBLE BASS

(Since the double bass sounds an octave lower than written, passages in which the cellos and basses are written in unison will sound in octaves.)

EXAMPLE 2.22

(a) Fifth Symphony

(b)   Symphony in B minor (*Unfinished*)

(c)   "The Elephant" (from *The Carnival of Animals*)

(d)   *Death and Transfiguration*

(e)   *Daphnis and Chloe* Suite No. 2

So far we have discussed only the more elementary material on the individual stringed instruments. It should be apparent even from this brief discussion, however, that writing for strings is a special technique. What looks easy to the pianist may prove surprisingly awkward for the string player, while there are fine string parts that would be totally impractical for woodwind or brass instruments. There is a good deal to be learned not only about combining the stringed instruments to make up a string orchestra but also about matters of bowing and special effects. These are the subjects to be taken up next.

SUGGESTED ASSIGNMENT

Know

1. open strings and ranges (possible and practical) of the stringed instruments.
2. correct notation in alto and tenor clef.
3. transposition used by the double bass.
4. indications for the use of a particular string.
5. general principles involved in writing double, triple, and quadruple stops.
6. Italian, French, and German names for the stringed instruments.

SUGGESTED LISTENING

Because passages for the violins are so abundant and familiar and because the violins are heard prominently in the music for suggested listening given at the end of Chapter 4, they are not included here.

Violas

Wagner, Prelude to *Tristan und Isolde*, meas. 90.[4]
Tchaikovsky, *Romeo and Juliet*, letter G; Fifth Symphony, 3rd movt., letter E.
Strauss, *Don Quixote*, meas. 18, etc.; *Till Eulenspiegel*, meas. 179 (*Gemächlich*).
Ippolitov-Ivanov, *Caucasian Sketches: In the Village*.
Ravel, *Daphnis and Chloe* Suite No. 2, figure 158.
Bartók, *Music for String Instruments, Percussion and Celesta*, beginning; 3rd movt., meas. 6.

---

[4]Throughout the "Suggested Listening" sections of this book, only the *beginning* point of each passage is indicated, by means of a measure number or a rehearsal letter or figure.

William Schuman, *American Festival Overture*, 5 bars after figure 80.
Dominick Argento, *In Praise of Music*, 4th movt.

Cellos

Beethoven, Third Symphony (*Eroica*), beginning.
Schubert, Symphony in B minor (*Unfinished*), 1st movt., 2nd theme.
Brahms, Third Symphony, 3rd movt.; Fourth Symphony, 2nd movt., meas. 41;
  Piano Concerto No. 2, 3rd movt., beginning.
Saint-Saëns, "The Swan" from *The Carnival of Animals* (solo cello).
Wagner, *Tristan und Isolde*, beginning of Prelude; *Love Death*, meas. 9.
Glinka, Overture to *Russlan and Ludmilla*, 2nd theme, meas. 81.
Strauss, *Don Quixote*, Variation 5.
Elgar, *Enigma Variations*, Variation 12.
Mahler, Fourth Symphony, 3rd movt., beginning and at figure 9.
Roy Harris, Third Symphony, beginning.
Howard Hanson, First Symphony, beginning.
Villa-Lobos, *Bachianas Brasileiras* No. 1, for eight cellos.
Bloch, *Schelomo* (virtuoso writing for solo cello with orchestra).
Penderecki, *De Natura Sonoris* No. 2, meas. 52.

Double Basses

Since the double bass section seldom takes a musical idea entirely by itself, most of
the examples that follow involve octave or unison doublings with other instruments.

Beethoven, Fifth Symphony, 3rd movt., beginning; also beginning of Trio; Ninth
  Symphony, 4th movt., meas. 8.
Franck, Symphony in D minor, beginning.
Verdi, *Otello*, beginning of Act IV, scene iii.
Saint-Saëns, "The Elephant" from *The Carnival of Animals*.
Goldmark, *Rustic Wedding* Symphony, beginning.
Strauss, *Also Sprach Zarathustra*, fugue in the "Von der Wissenschaft" section (in-
  volves four desks of basses, each desk playing a separate part); *Death and Trans-
  figuration*, 16 bars after letter D.
Mahler, Fourth Symphony, 3rd movt., figure 9 (basses playing *pizzicato* notes); First
  Symphony, 3rd movt., beginning (solo bass with mute).
Stravinsky, *The Rite of Spring*, 1 bar after figure 121; *Pulcinella*, 7th movt. (duet
  between trombone and solo double bass).
Prokofieff, *Lieutenant Kije*, II. Romance.
Respighi, *Pines of Rome*, beginning of Part IV ("Pines of the Appian Way") (bottom
  string tuned down to low B).
P. M. Davies, *A Mirror of Whitening Light*, 1 bar after C.

3

The String Orchestra

The strings may well be considered the most important section of the orchestra for a number of reasons:

1. As a group they possess an enormous pitch range: from the highest note of the violin to the lowest note of the double bass.

2. Strings are very versatile technically. Rapid scale passages, slow *cantabile* melodies, short detached notes, long sustained tones, skips, trills, and chordal figurations are all practical and effective.

3. The vibrancy and warmth of the string tone make it especially useful. The strings can produce a particular *espressivo* quality unobtainable in the other choirs of the orchestra. And the tone is one that does not pall easily.

4. There are fewer problems of *blend* in the string section than in the other sections of the orchestra.

5. The *dynamic* range of the string section is unusually wide. Although neither strings nor woodwinds can equal the brass in the matter of sheer power, a full string section is able to produce a good, resonant *fortissimo*. At the other end of the dynamic scale, the string choir can reduce its tone to an almost inaudible *pianissimo*.

6. Unlike the woodwind and brass instruments, which must be given rests from time to time in order to allow the players to breathe and rest their lips, the strings are able to play continuously for longer periods if necessary. This is not to say that they should be asked to play indefinitely without resting, but the problem is not nearly so acute as in the case of the wind instruments.

7. The strings are sometimes spoken of as "the backbone of the orchestra." This description is based in part on the points listed above but also on traditional

usage. Since the early days of the orchestra, the strings have been called on to carry the greatest burden of the playing. That is, if the number of measures played by the woodwind, brass, and string sections in a large number of scores were counted, in most works the strings would be found to play the greatest number of measures, with the woodwind section ranking second and the brass third.

The number of players in each string group is not specified in scores, except in rare cases where an extra-large string section or a minimum number of players is called for. Ordinarily the full complement of strings is implied: 16 first violins, 14 second violins, 12 violas, 10 cellos, and 8 to 10 double basses. But in actual practice many orchestras do not include this number of string players, as Table 1.1 shows. When scores written especially for "small orchestra" are played, the size of the string section is reduced. Also, because the orchestra of Haydn's and Mozart's day included fewer string players than our modern orchestra does, many conductors prefer to use only a portion of each string group in performing music of the Classical period.

Normally the members of each string group play a single melodic line in unison. But it is possible to divide each group into two or more parts, each part playing different notes. In that case the Italian word *divisi*, usually shortened to *div.*, is placed next to the passage, most often above the staff. In the case of division into more than two parts, the number of parts is indicated as follows: *div. a 3* or *div. a 4*, etc. (See Appendix A for the equivalents of these terms in other languages.) Ordinary *divisi* passages (two parts) are very frequent; more than two parts are less often used, and the use of more than four is apt to be risky if one is writing for anything less than a full string section or for players of limited ability.[1] In ordinary *divisi* writing, the two parts can usually be written on the same staff. If they involve the same time values, a single stem may be used for both—provided, of course, that the *div.* indication is present so that the two notes will not be taken for a double stop. But if the time values in the two parts are different, then separate stems will be necessary: that is, stems up for the upper part, stems down for the lower part. When the two parts cannot conveniently be written on the same staff (for example, when they cross repeatedly), two staves are used. In that case, the *divisi* direction is sometimes put at the edge of the page, preceding the divided part. (All these points are illustrated in the examples of string scoring that follow.) With division into three or more parts, the parts may be arranged in whatever way is most convenient—two or more to a staff or each part on a separate staff. Any or all of the string groups may be divided, though the basses are divided less often than the other string groups. After a *divisi* passage, when the string group is to play in unison again, the expression *unisono*, shortened to *unis.*, is used. *Non divisi (non div.)* is commonly written above passages that could be played *divisi* but are meant to be played by the use of multiple stops.

---

[1]Some contemporary scores, by Ligeti and Penderecki among others, make use of heavily divided strings. This approach is discussed in Chapter 17 on "Special Devices" and shown in Example 17.11.

Dynamics must be indicated below each staff. This is extremely important and sometimes difficult to impress upon the beginning orchestrator. Whereas pianists can gain a complete idea of the music they are playing from the page and can adjust dynamics and the weight of individual voices accordingly, orchestral players see only their own parts. They cannot tell from the page whether they are playing an important musical idea that should be brought out or a subordinate voice that must be kept in the background. Therefore, they must be told exactly how loudly to play at all times. It is quite possible that while one person is playing *ff,* another instrument in the orchestra will be marked *mf* or even *pp* in order to achieve the proper effect. Crescendos, diminuendos, and any other dynamic changes, along with such directions as *espressivo* or *marcato,* must likewise be written in beneath each part they apply to.

Since matters of *tempo* normally apply to all the instruments at the same time, one tempo marking at the top of the page, above the woodwinds, and one lower down, just above the strings, are usually sufficient in the score. But these tempo indications (including any *ritardandos, accelerandos,* or similar markings) are included by the copyist in each part, when the players' parts are extracted from the score.

A brief reminder on a few points of notation is pertinent here. Notes below the middle line of the staff have stems up; those above the middle line have stems down; notes *on* the middle line may have stems either up or down. In groups such as eighths or sixteenths, the direction of the stems is determined by the position of the majority of the notes in the group. Notice that in orchestral writing, instrumental rather than vocal notation is used (see Example 3.1).

EXAMPLE 3.1

(a)

not

(b)

Notice, too, that it is unnecessary to have a separate barline for each staff. Simply draw one long barline through all the parts of each section. Be sure to line up the parts so that the notes which are to sound together are in a straight line, vertically, on the page. Whole notes go at the beginning of the measure, but whole rests should be placed in the middle. Nowadays,

the whole rest ▬ may be used with any meter signature to indicate

a full measure of rest.

On the first page of a score, the names of instruments are normally written out in full; after that, abbreviations are commonly used. In the case of strings, those most often seen are: "Vl." or "Vln." or just "V." for violin (followed by I or II for first or second); "Vla." for viola, or "Vle." (the Italian plural abbreviated) for violas; "V-Cello" or "Vc." for violoncello; and "D. Bass." "D.B.," "C.Bass," or "C. B." for double bass. The usual method of bracketing the violins and the whole string section can be seen in the examples that follow.

POSSIBLE ARRANGEMENTS IN SCORING FOR STRING ORCHESTRA

In order to make our first work in scoring for strings as uncomplicated as possible, a short phrase from a Bach chorale harmonization[2] has been chosen as an example:

EXAMPLE 3.2

Certain obvious arrangements of the strings suggest themselves immediately: first violins on the melody, second violins on the alto part, violas on the tenor, and cellos on the lowest voice. The double basses may either rest or be given the same *written* part as the cellos, which means that they will sound an octave lower than the cellos. Using the latter choice, the scored version would look like this:

EXAMPLE 3.3

* (down an octave)

---

[2]This chorale excerpt is from an *a cappella* motet. Of the arrangements shown in Examples 3.3–3.11, only Example 3.3 corresponds to Bach's own practice as seen in his cantatas.

This is the most frequent arrangement of the strings and one that will sound very satisfactory either with or without double basses.

The range of a voice is obviously a factor in deciding what instrument should take it. For example, in this Bach excerpt the tenor line could not be taken by violins because it goes down to an F♯, one half-step lower than the violins can play. Nor could the bass voice be taken by viola because of the notes that fall below the viola's low C.

Since no dynamics or tempo indications are included in the original Bach version, we have had to supply our own. Dynamic markings could be anything from *ppp* to *fff*, depending on the mood and general conception we give to the excerpt. Various dynamic levels have been used in the scorings shown and a tempo marking of *Adagio* chosen arbitrarily. We might decide that the music should be either *legato* or *molto marcato;* but that question will have to be put aside temporarily, for it involves problems of bowing, which are taken up in Chapter 4.

Suppose we feel that the chorale melody (the upper part) in *Jesu, meine Freude* should be brought out a bit in relation to the other voices. The effect could be achieved very easily by marking the first violins a little louder than the other instruments. Or we could arrive at an effect of greater weight and resonance on the melody by giving it to both first and second violins. In that case, we have a new problem: The three remaining voices must somehow be taken by *two* sections, the violas and the cellos. (It seems best to use the double basses only for the part they played in the first version.) The obvious solution here is to divide either the violas or the cellos to give two parts. If we divide the violas, the arrangement is as follows:

EXAMPLE 3.4   *Include Dynamics*   *✶/*

With a full viola section this version would sound satisfactory; but in school and other nonprofessional groups, viola sections are apt to be "understaffed," and when they are divided in half there is simply not enough body in each half to balance the rest of the strings. In such a case, the balance might be improved by marking the violas a degree louder than the other sections.

The other solution is to divide the cellos:

✶ indicate strings are separated **36** *or else tiruso as being double stops*

EXAMPLE 3.5

In this version the division is somewhat compensated for by the fact that the upper cellos are in their high, vibrant register where they will come through rather prominently. If this upper part stayed high, it might well be written in tenor clef, in which case separate staves would be used for the two halves of the cello section, as in Example 3.6.

In case the particular color of violas were wanted on the melody, such an arrangement could be used. Because the tenor part in our example is too low for violins, the alto is the only line left that they could play; and as first and second violins together would be too heavy for the alto, either first or second violins could be given rests. There is nothing wrong with letting a section rest, but a more effective solution might be to put violas and first violins on the melody (in unison) for greater weight and for mixed color:

EXAMPLE 3.6   (usable with an inexperienced group)

37

Half the cellos doubled in unison with violins on the melody would add poignancy and intensity to the tone. That would take the upper half of the cellos rather high, but not unreasonably so for a professional group. It should be pointed out, though, that this arrangement of the strings is by no means a common one and that in many pieces of music it would be inappropriate or impractical (or both) to give the cello the melody, particularly at its original pitch. In fact, the high cello part in Example 3.7 is open to question as being too lush and romantic in this context; it is included here more with the idea of exploring various possibilities than with any implication of stylistic appropriateness. (There is, however, much debate about what *is* stylistically appropriate in scoring music of earlier periods.)

EXAMPLE 3.7

Of course it would be possible to use all the cellos on the melody, but in that case the double basses would have to play the bass at its original pitch by themselves. While that arrangement might be satisfactory if the bass section were large, it is much safer to retain half the cellos on the bass line and to write the double bass part so that it will sound an octave lower. One might suppose that dividing the double basses in octaves (on the bass and its doubling an octave lower) would work out well. In actual practice it does not; the effect is disappointing and is almost never used in orchestral scoring.

VERSIONS USING OCTAVE DOUBLINGS OF THE THREE UPPER VOICES

In having the double basses play the bass voice an octave lower than in the original, we amplified the original version slightly. Similarly, the top voice (when it is the melody) may be doubled an octave higher than in the original. The effect is somewhat more brilliant. It is also possible to fill in the octave at the top by doubling the alto and tenor voices an octave higher as well. These two versions are shown in Examples 3.8 and 3.9, respectively.

EXAMPLE 3.8　　　　　　　　　　　　　**EXAMPLE 3.9** if the original octave is kept.

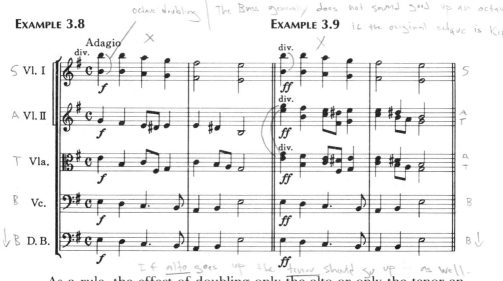

If alto goes up the tenor should go up as well.

As a rule, the effect of doubling only the alto or only the tenor an octave higher is not good because of the gaps of open 4ths and 5ths that often result. In other words, in scoring a four-voice composition of this sort it is normally best to double both alto and tenor or neither at the octave. Doubling of inner voices an octave *lower* than the original is usually out of the question because of the muddiness that results when voices are spaced close together low in a chord.

In some music, the same objection applies to a doubling of the melody an octave lower. In our Bach example, however, the effect of doubling it at the lower octave is not too thick; in fact, that arrangement actually improves the spacing by filling in some unnecessarily wide gaps between the tenor and bass voices. This possibility is demonstrated in Examples 3.10 and 3.11.

Example 3.11 also makes use of upper-octave doublings of the soprano, alto, and tenor voices. As in the preceding versions, the double basses

EXAMPLE 3.10 Double melody (octave below)　　**EXAMPLE 3.11**

not very common

have been written to sound an octave lower than the bass in the original. Although the layout of the divided violin sections is different in Examples 3.9 and 3.11, respectively, the sound of the combined violin sections will be approximately the same in each case.

The last version is obviously the fullest, the most resonant. This is not to say that it is therefore preferable to the others, however. There are generally many effective ways of scoring a given passage, and the way chosen will be the one that seems the most telling and appropriate in context.

Example 3.12 shows excerpts from symphonic literature that involve the string section prominently. In (c), (d), and (g) only the strings are playing; in the remaining examples other instruments not shown here are also playing, but in each case the strings give a fairly complete idea of the musical substance. In (b) note the use of multiple stops in which the top note is held. In (c) and (g) the effect is extremely rich and warm, partly because of the harmonic fullness afforded by the division of one or more string groups, partly because the melody is taken by violins playing high on their G string. Concerning (d), the speed of the notes is about the maximum at which successive pizzicato notes can be played comfortably. Example (e) makes use of the very high register of the violin, where the quality is bright, singing, and intense. In (f) harmonic background is supplied through some characteristic and effective string arpeggios based on multiple-stop patterns. In (h) the effect is heavy and savage. Woodwinds, horns, timpani, and bass drum are also playing.

EXAMPLES SHOWING VARIOUS POSSIBILITIES
IN ARRANGING THE STRINGS

EXAMPLE 3.12

(a)   Symphony No. 41, K. 551 (*Jupiter*)

(b) Fifth Symphony

Note: *In order to avoid the slight arpeggiation necessary in playing the quadruple stops here, most conductors have the violins divide in such a way that only* double *stops are involved. Especially in the eighth-note chords, a sharper, cleaner effect results.*

(c) Fourth Symphony

(d) Fourth Symphony

(e) Second Symphony

(f)   Ninth Symphony (*New World*)

(g)   Ninth Symphony

(h)   *The Rite of Spring*

It is essential to have some fluency with multiple stops played by the entire string orchestra in order to write idiomatically for strings. (The subject of multiple stops for the individual stringed instruments was addressed in Chapter 2.) Certain scoring situations—for example, an orchestral *tutti* involving loud, separated chords—demand the use of multiple stops in order to achieve proper balance with the other sections and to provide a full and convincing string presence. It is also much easier to plan accompaniment figurations and bravura solo string passages if one understands how to use the appropriate multiple stops. The following discussion provides basic information about a few common multiple-stop patterns that can be successfully employed by violin, viola, and cello.

An experienced orchestrator will immediately recognize the following triple stop for violin as one easily produced: . The D and A would be played on open strings and the F♯ would be fingered on the E string. Furthermore, if the stop were transposed one half-step higher or lower, it would still be feasible, even though no open strings would be involved. This stop is one of three commonly used patterns that will work with all pitches fingered and on all stringed instruments except the double bass. Example 3.13 illustrates these patterns.

EXAMPLE 3.13

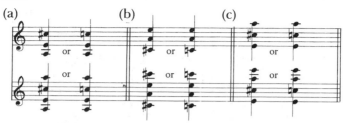

(a)   (b)   (c)

Note the following points. First, the stops are (1) in root position, (2) in first inversion, and (3) in second inversion. Second, the quadruple-stop pattern simply adds a top note to the triple-stop pattern. Third, only the intervals of 5ths and major and minor 6ths are used. And last, the chords may be either major or minor. For the best effect the top note should be no more than a 7th above the highest open string. (The quadruple-stop pattern in Example 3.13(c) is shown at that pitch level only for purposes of comparison with the triple-stop pattern. It is much more resonant and better in tune at a lower pitch level.)

Using only these patterns, it is possible to score many primary and secondary triad progressions (in either major or minor keys) and particularly those found at loud final cadences that require maximum brilliance and fullness from the string orchestra.

EXAMPLE 3.14

First Symphony

46

Example 3.15

Fourth Symphony

Dvořák

The two other patterns seen in Examples 3.14 and 3.15 are practical because of the presence of an open string. Incidentally, the arpeggiation symbol in the Dvořák example is unnecessary and very rarely used.

Accompanimental figuration is easily derived from the given patterns (see Examples 3.12[f] and 2.18[c]), as is grateful and idiomatic solo writing:

Example 3.16

Capriccio Espagnol

Rimsky-Korsakoff

Use of these patterns is by no means limited to music of the common-practice period, as a glance at Ligeti's *Melodien* (Example 16.11) reveals. The following colorful passages from Debussy's *Ibéria* (suggestive of guitar strumming) are likewise based primarily on these patterns.

EXAMPLE 3.17

Ibéria

When scoring multiple stops for the full string orchestra, a few points should be remembered: (1) because of the wide spacing of the stops, the chords often use an interlocking arrangement (see Chapter 10, pages 173 and 180); (2) assuming common-practice style, avoid parallel fifths or octaves between the highest- and lowest-sounding pitches of two consecutive chords in the string orchestra (parallelisms involving the *inner* voices in two adjacent chords are less objectionable and rarely audible); (3) if possible, have the lowest note of the cello stop take the bass line; (4) the strings can sustain only two notes at a time.

REMARKS ON SPACING, DOUBLING, AND VARIOUS TEXTURES

Students about to embark on their first project in scoring for strings will need to keep in mind some points concerning spacing and doubling. Also, because we refer to the overtone series in connection with spacing and with string harmonics and at many other points later on in connection with wind instruments, a short commentary on that subject is in order here.

All musical instruments make use of a vibrating body (a string, an air column, etc.), which vibrates not only as a whole to produce the main tone or "fundamental," but in halves, thirds, fourths, and so on. These fractional vibrations produce pure sounds of higher pitch and much weaker intensity than the fundamental, the pure sounds normally being heard as part of the composite tone. Example 3.18 shows a fundamental (C) with its first fifteen overtones.

EXAMPLE 3.18

Note: *Notes that do not correspond closely with tones of our equally tempered scale are shown in black.*

The terms *partials* and *harmonic series* are often used in connection with overtones, but they include the fundamental, whereas the term *overtone* does not. The first overtone, then, is the second partial. In Example 3.18 the notes have been numbered on the basis of partials; that is, the fundamental is numbered 1, and so on. Certain partials come out more strongly on some instruments than on others, with consequent differences among the respective tone qualities of the various instruments.

Normally spacing of harmony is modeled in a general way on the harmonic series: the wide intervals are put at the bottom, the smaller intervals in the upper part of the chord. Usually it is best to leave a clear octave at the bottom, although if the chord is not too low it may be possible to begin with a 5th at the bottom:

EXAMPLE 3.19

If notes are put close together in the lower portion of a chord, a thick, muddy effect results; therefore, avoid putting the 3rd of the chord too low—say below ♭𝄢 (assuming the chord to be in root position).

In scoring music written originally in open spacing, it is often a wise idea to fill in the gaps between the upper parts by means of octave doublings, in effect to convert the open structure to close. For example,

EXAMPLE 3.20

might become

While open spacing is frequently used for the strings and is not out of the question for the other instruments, close spacing is generally more effective in the orchestra.

Even in music written in close structure it sometimes becomes necessary to add a "filler" part: that is, an extra voice introduced in order to fill in gaps between voices (most often between tenor and bass). Such a voice may double other voices part of the time, then branch off to fill in gaps where necessary; or it may take an independent line of its own, doubling chord tones at times but not actually playing the same line as any of the other voices. In the following excerpt from "America" a possible filler part is shown in small notes:

EXAMPLE 3.21

However, students should avoid fillers except in cases of absolute necessity. Such parts are usually not very strong or interesting from a linear standpoint, and if used indiscriminately they tend to detract from the clarity of the other voices and to bring about a muddy texture. Besides, beginning orchestrators often have difficulty in maintaining good voice-leading in the orchestral parts, and the addition of an extra voice that may rove at will only complicates the problem.

Sometimes the top voice of a closely spaced chord is doubled an octave higher, leaving a gap of an octave at the top (as in Example 3.8). In such cases the effect is good, and there is no objection to the octave gap.

As a rule, when a primary triad (I, IV, or V) is in first inversion, the bass should not be doubled in the upper parts. The same applies to seventh chords in any inversion:

EXAMPLE 3.22

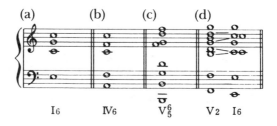

Of course the bass may always be doubled an octave *lower*. Notice that in (d), above, proper voice-leading demands that certain notes be doubled in the tonic chord. When an "active" tone (such as the seventh scale degree) is taken by a particular instrument, the resolution of that tone must obviously occur in the same instrument.

It should perhaps be added that this material on spacing and doubling does not always apply in twentieth-century music. Certain composers, Stravinsky in particular, have achieved fresh and intriguing effects by a deliberate use of unusual spacings and doublings (see Example 17.1).

What has been said here so far applies chiefly to harmonic (chordal) music. Homophonic and especially polyphonic textures will involve different approaches. These musical situations are discussed at some length in later chapters, but a few comments on them at this point may be helpful.

In scoring homophonic music it is normally desirable that the melody stand out from the background. This may be achieved by presenting it in a contrasting color, by giving it extra weight, by marking it louder, by doubling it in octaves, or by using a combination of any of these means. Homophonic music for the piano often involves idiomatic accompaniment figures (such as wide arpeggios), which may have to be changed to patterns better suited to the instruments concerned; and certain notes may have to be sustained in the orchestral version to approximate the effect of the piano's damper pedal. In general, wide gaps between the notes played by the two hands should be filled in, at least partially.

In polyphonic music, the chief objectives are balance between voices (or a calculated emphasis on one, when that is appropriate) and linear clarity. The most effective way to make the voices stand out sharply from each other is to give them to instruments of different timbres. But that approach is not always necessary, nor is it always possible (as, for example, in scoring for one section of the orchestra alone). Concerning doublings, the upper voice can generally be doubled an octave higher and the bottom voice an octave lower without damaging the clarity of the texture; occasionally the upper voice may be doubled an octave lower. Lower-octave doublings of the inner voices are usually out of.the question because of the thickness and the overlapping of the bass that may result; even upper-octave doublings of these voices may produce linear confusion.

SUGGESTED ASSIGNMENTS

Music for suggested listening is listed at the end of Chapter 4.

A. Know:

1. number of players in each string group (in a full orchestra).
2. order and arrangement of the strings on the page.
3. customary abbreviations of names of stringed instruments.
4. directions for the division of a string group into two or more parts.
5. proper placing and use of indications for dynamics and tempo.
6. principles of good spacing and doubling.

B. Select a short four-voice chordal excerpt and score it six different ways for strings. Bowing need not be indicated.

Bowing
and Special Effects

The term *bowing* may mean the actual motion of the bow over the strings, or it may mean the indications in a string part that tell the player how the music is to be bowed. Using the word in the latter sense, bowing includes (1) slurs, one over each group of notes to be taken in the same bow; (2) down-bow marks (⊓) or up-bow marks (V) at points where the use of one or the other is preferable; (3) such indications as dots or accent marks over the notes to suggest the type of bowing appropriate; and (4) actual words, such as *spiccato*, to indicate the exact type of bowing to be used. The directions *arco* and *pizzicato*, which are discussed in Chapter 2, might also be listed under the heading of bowing.

When beginning students of orchestration are asked to include bowing in their scores, their usual reaction is, "Why not let string players worry about that? They know more about it than we do." There are several answers. One is that a passage may be given a number of different interpretations depending on how it is bowed; although the players may know more about bowing than the budding orchestrator, without bowing marks they cannot tell just what effect the orchestrator intended. In other words, bowing is an integral part of the music and should not be left to chance. A glance at any orchestral score will confirm the fact that slurs to indicate bowing are always included as a matter of standard practice. It may be objected that the conductor or the players will probably make some changes in the bowing anyway. That is true, even in the case of standard symphonic literature. Nevertheless, the original bowing gives an idea of the basic conception of the music. Another answer is that planning the bowing for all the groups of the string section at the same time brings about a very important uniformity of effect that would be hard to achieve if each group were allowed to choose its own bowing.

There is a point that needs to be clearly understood at the beginning: in string music the slur does not normally indicate broad phrase outlines as it often does in piano music. Instead it is used to show which notes are to be taken on the same bow. For instance, in Example 4.1 the first four notes are taken on one bow; then the bow reverses direction to take the next two notes and again to take the last three.

EXAMPLE 4.1

(a)

The same passage might have been bowed in several other ways, three of which are shown here:

(b)   (c)   (d)

In (d), where no slurs are shown, the player would use a separate bow (that is, change the direction of the bow) for each note. It should be emphasized that no break in sound need occur when the bow changes; however, a separation between notes *may* be made if desired.

It is desirable to "balance" the up- and down-bows *in a general sort of way*. For example, it would normally be inadvisable to bow Example 4.1 as follows:

(e)

The tendency of the player would be to give too much emphasis to the singly bowed note in an effort to "use up" enough of the bow to get back in position for the next bow.

There are a few scores in which phrasing rather than bowing is indicated at certain points in the string parts, usually in long, sustained melodic lines. In such cases the bowing to be used is decided upon by the conductor or the players. Occasionally phrase marks are included in addition to bowing slurs in order to ensure an even, connected effect, but the vast majority of scores rely solely on bowing slurs to project the musical structure of the string parts.

Some factors that influence bowing are the dynamics and tempo involved, the general effect desired, and such technical considerations as the need for a down-bow or an up-bow at certain places.

As for dynamics, the amount of bow used up varies in a general way with the volume of tone produced. Consequently the player can take more notes per bow in a soft passage than in a loud one. But that does not mean that all soft passages should be slurred in long groups and all loud passages played with separate bows. It is perfectly possible to change bow frequently in a soft passage, even to the point of playing rapidly moving parts with a bow to a note:

EXAMPLE 4.2

Overture to *The Marriage of Figaro*

And a reasonable number of notes may be taken on one bow even in a *fortissimo:*

EXAMPLE 4.3

Symphony: *Mathis der Maler*

Reproduced by permission of Schott & Co., Ltd., London.

The influence of tempo on bowing is fairly obvious. The faster the tempo, the more notes the player can take comfortably on each bow.

In describing the difference between a slurred effect and a separately bowed effect, it might be said that the first is smoothly flowing, while the second gives a greater sense of articulation to each note. Fast running passages in which each note is separately bowed are particularly vigorous and sparkling. Of course a passage need not be all bowed or all slurred. Interesting combinations of the two effects are illustrated in Example 4.4.

EXAMPLE 4.4

(a)   First Symphony

(b)   Symphony No. 41, K. 551 (*Jupiter*)

In plotting bowing, it is often necessary to bring the player out on a down-bow or an up-bow at a particular point. For example, down-bows are in order for heavily accented notes and are even preferable for strong beats in a measure. On the other hand, an anacrusis (up-beat) is best given to an up-bow in order that the strong beat that follows may be taken down-bow. Crescendos are somewhat easier on an up-bow. A *slurred-staccato* bowing, to be described presently, is mainly an up-bow stroke, whereas the *jeté* (or *ricochet*) is normally performed on a down-bow. The signs for up-bow and down-bow (∨ and ⊓) are put in above the notes only at points where the player would not be likely to choose that bowing automatically. For instance, it is a convention that the first note of a passage will be taken downbow unless an up-bow mark is shown or unless the first note is an upbeat requiring an up-bow. But wherever the proper bowing cannot be anticipated at a glance, it should be clearly indicated at the beginning of the passage. Usually it is superfluous to include alternate down-bow and up-bow signs throughout a passage, for the player must necessarily change from one bow to the other, and the slurs will indicate where to change. The important thing is to start the passage with the right bow, and the rest should follow automatically.

Another small technical point influences bowing: if a jump from one string to a nonadjacent string is involved, the notes in question obviously cannot be taken *legato*.

TYPES OF BOWING

Perhaps no aspect of orchestration offers more chance for controversy than does the labeling of various types of bowing. There is disagreement on this subject not only among the authors of orchestration books but among players themselves. In the first place, the terminology involves a hodgepodge of languages, and there are sometimes two or three different names in each language for a particular type of bowing. To complicate matters still further, descriptions of certain bowings differ from book to book and from player to player. Then too, the period and style of the music influence the interpretation of bowing marks. For example, dots over the notes in a passage by Haydn might call for one type of bowing, whereas the same indication in a contemporary score might suggest another type.

As a result of all this confusion, it is very difficult to write in an authoritative way on the subject of bowing types. Students of orchestration should consult with string players in order to gain a more intimate knowledge of bowing possibilities. The list given here is highly simplified: many combinations and subtle variations are possible.

The chief bowing types may be broken down into two main categories: those in which the bow stays on the string and those in which it leaves the string.

ON-THE-STRING BOWINGS

Legato

Groups of notes are slurred together; the total effect is as smooth as possible.

EXAMPLE 4.5

Don Juan

Strauss

Vl. I

pp dolce espr.

Tie with slur

Détaché

Each note is bowed separately. Although the word *détaché* suggests a break between the notes, that is not normally implied in the term as it is used by most string players in this country today. Successive notes taken *détaché* may be joined together smoothly, or the connection may be made less smooth by emphasizing the articulation that goes with the changing of the bow. An accented *détaché* is possible and effective. *Détaché* bowing can be executed at practically any speed and dynamic level. At slower tempos (especially in a *forte*), full bows may be used; at medium or faster speeds, the middle or upper portion of the bow is normally involved. The point may be used for a delicate effect or, less often, the frog for a heavy one. As a rule, there is no special indication for the use of *détaché* bowing apart from the absence of slurs. But sometimes in older music, particularly in passages where slurred and *détaché* groups alternate, dots are used to signify the *détaché,* as in Example 4.4 (a). A consistent use of *détaché* is seen in Example 4.6.

EXAMPLE 4.6

(a)   Prelude to *Die Meistersinger*

Sehr gewichtig

Wagner

Vls. I & II

ff

(b)   Fourth Symphony

Allegro ma non troppo

Beethoven

Vc.

ff

Martelé (martellato)

The description "hammered," which has commonly been applied to this type of bowing because of the literal meaning of *martelé,* is perhaps misleading; the bow does not strike the string from above but begins and remains on it, moving very quickly and stopping abruptly at the end of each stroke so that there is a clean-cut separation between notes. The *martelé* is most often done at the upper part of the bow but may also be done at the frog to produce a more robust effect. The indication for it may be dots, arrowheads, accents, or a combination. Occasionally the word *martelé* is written in, sometimes followed by a direction for the specific use of the frog or the point (see Appendix A for these terms in other languages). More often, however, the player simply chooses the *martelé* bowing as being appropriate to the music at hand. Obviously, this type cannot be used when the notes move along too swiftly; beyond a certain speed, the stopping of the bow between strokes becomes impossible.

EXAMPLE 4.7

Fourth Symphony

Slurred Staccato

The word *staccato* can be applied generically to any bowing (off-the-string or on-the-string) in which the notes are separated from each other. However, when used as part of the term *slurred staccato* (or *group staccato*), it refers specifically to an on-the-string bowing in which a series of notes is taken (generally up-bow) with a separate "push" for each note. If many notes are involved, the stroke is so difficult as to be impractical for orchestral playing. But in a limited form it figures constantly in orchestral string parts. There are two types, the first primarily an up-bow stroke consisting of three or four notes (occasionally more) that are made to sound separately under the same bow, as at the beginning of Example 4.8.

EXAMPLE 4.8

Eighth Symphony

The second type (Example 4.9) is sometimes referred to as "hooked bowing" or "linked bowing." It can be performed on either an up-bow or a down-bow and consists of two notes (most often in a dotted rhythm) with a separation between them that is produced by a momentary stopping of the bow before it continues in the same direction. Illogically, the notation usually involves either a staccato dot (Example 4.9[a]) or a small line (b) at the end of the slur, next to the *second* of the two notes, although the first is actually the one that is shortened in performance. Sometimes staccato dots are placed on both notes (under a slur), as in (c); and at times the separation between notes is shown by a brief rest (d). Whichever notation is used, the effect will be approximately the same, the only differences being subtle ones. These notations—and combinations of them—can be seen in Examples 4.9(e) and (f).

EXAMPLE 4.9

(e) Fifth Symphony

Prokofieff

(f) Sixth Symphony

Tchaikovsky

Louré (portato, brush strokes)

This bowing is used chiefly in music of a slow, *espressivo* character. Two or more notes (seldom more than four) are taken on one bow, with a separate pressure and a slight initial swelling of the sound on each note. As applied in some music, the *louré* may involve an almost imperceptible break between the notes.

EXAMPLE 4.10

Second Symphony

OFF-THE-STRING BOWINGS

Spiccato

This is normally a light, middle-bow stroke in which the bow bounces off the string, taking one note to each bow. It is used very frequently in orchestral playing but is not generally practical if the dynamic level is to be louder than about *mf*. However, in passages that are not too rapid, a heavier type of spiccato done at or near the frog may be employed in case more sound is wanted. The usual indication for *spiccato* bowing is simply dots; or the word *spiccato* can be written in.

Example 4.11

(a) Second Symphony

(b) First Symphony

The term *sautillé* (from the French verb meaning "to leap"), although often used interchangeably with *spiccato,* is better reserved for a very fast, light, and delicate type of *spiccato* bowing in which the jumping of the bow results chiefly from the resilience of the stick rather than from an individual drop-and-lift motion for each note. *Sautillé* bowing is sometimes described as "an uncontrolled *spiccato.*" (See Example 4.11[c].)

(c) *Midsummer Night's Dream* Overture

Staccato Volante (flying staccato)

This is a type of *spiccato* bowing similar to the *slurred staccato* but *off* the string (thus the classification under *spiccato*). Instead of reversing direction for each note as in the ordinary *spiccato,* the bow picks up a series of short notes, usually on an up-bow. (See Example 4.12.)

Example 4.12

Fourth Symphony

Jeté (ricochet, saltando, sautillé)

In the *jeté* (meaning "thrown" in French), the bow is made to bounce on the string very rapidly with a down-bow stroke in such a way as to sound a group of two to six notes—most often repeated notes. The notation usually consists of dots under a slur.

EXAMPLE 4.13

(a) *Capriccio Espagnol*

(b) *Firebird* Suite

Successive Down-Bows

This device is sometimes used when a very decided break between notes is in order. Since the bow must be lifted and returned to the string between each two notes, the separation comes about automatically. This type of bowing is seldom employed for more than a few notes at a time, and it is not practical when the notes move along too quickly. The effect of successive down-bows is vigorous, sometimes almost savage, especially on the lowest string of each instrument.

EXAMPLE 4.14

(a) *Petrouchka*

(b) Fifth Symphony

Successive Up-Bows

This bowing also produces a clear separation between notes, but it is useful chiefly for a more delicate effect at softer dynamic levels. (Compare Examples 4.14[b] and 4.15[a].)

EXAMPLE 4.15

(a) Fifth Symphony

(b) *Classical* Symphony

SPECIAL EFFECTS

Tremolos

Although tremolos are often included under the heading of bowing types (of the on-the-string variety), they are not actually *types* in the sense that the bowings described in the preceding pages are. The bowed tremolo is, after all, simply an accelerated version of the *détaché,* and the fingered tremolo makes use of ordinary slurred bowing while the fingers produce the distinctive effect. Furthermore, because the function of tremolos is often a coloristic one, there is considerable reason for grouping them with the other devices to be discussed in this section.

Unmeasured bowed tremolo.

EXAMPLE 4.16

In the unmeasured form of the bowed tremolo, the bow is moved back and forth over the string as rapidly as possible. Three bars through the stem are ordinarily interpreted to mean an unmeasured tremolo, though sometimes in very slow tempos four bars through the stem are used to ensure that the notes are not played as measured thirty-seconds.[1] It is best to write in the word *tremolo* (abbreviation, *trem.*) in doubtful cases. The expression *at point* or *punta d'arco* in tremolo passages signifies that the tremolo is to be made at the point of the bow in order to achieve a more delicate sound. In some passages the unmeasured tremolo gives an effect of energy and excitement; at other times, especially when used high and softly, it can produce a shimmering, ethereal effect.

---

[1]Penderecki and others have used the symbol to indicate a fast, totally unrhythmicized bowed tremolo. (See Example 17.13.)

EXAMPLE 4.17

(a) *Tristan und Isolde*

(b) Second Symphony (c) *Prelude to The Afternoon of a Faun*

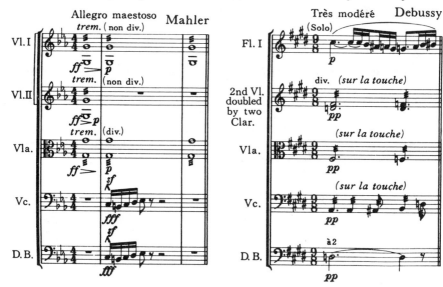

Measured bowed tremolo.

EXAMPLE 4.18

The measured tremolo, as its name implies, calls for a definite number of repeated notes, the number being shown by the notation. One line through a quarter-note or half-note stem means eighth notes; two lines, sixteenths. One line through an eighth-note stem means sixteenths; two lines, thirty-seconds; and so on. Triplets are indicated by the numeral 3 above each note or occasionally by three small dots placed next to the note head. Probably the safest way is to write out the actual notes involved in a measured tremolo for one measure at the beginning of the passage; after that, the simplified notation may be used. This method is shown in Example 4.19(a).

Tremolos (particularly the unmeasured variety) have been so overexploited in romantic music that they have lost a good deal of their effectiveness and had better be used sparingly today.

EXAMPLES OF MEASURED BOWED TREMOLO

EXAMPLE 4.19

(a)   Sixth Symphony

(b) *Fantastic Symphony*

(c)   Symphony in D minor

(d)   Fifth Symphony

With special permission from Wilhelm Hansen, Copenhagen.

Fingered tremolo.

EXAMPLE 4.20

In the fingered, or slurred, tremolo, which is usually unmeasured and which ordinarily involves two notes on the same string, one finger remains fixed on the lower of the two notes while another finger alternately plays and releases the upper note very rapidly so that a kind of trill between the

63

notes results. The bow moves over the string in the normal way rather than quickly back and forth as in the bowed tremolo. The two notes involved are most often a 3rd apart, though intervals up to a diminished 5th are possible on the violin. On the viola, the limit had better be a perfect 4th; and on the cello, a major 3rd. In notating fingered tremolos, each note is given twice the value it should have, mathematically speaking. Presumably, the theory is that the two notes of each pair sound so nearly at once that each note can be given full value.

EXAMPLES OF FINGERED TREMOLO

EXAMPLE 4.21

(a) *Prelude to The Afternoon of a Faun*   (b) *Fingal's Cave Overture*

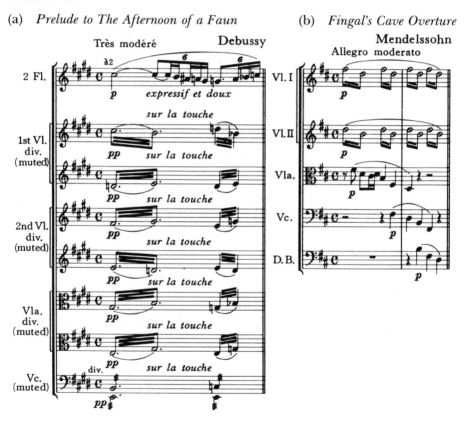

Frequently, fingered tremolos are written as in Example 4.22:

EXAMPLE 4.22

That is, the two notes of each pair are crossed with themselves to insure that both notes will sound on the beat. However, some writers on orchestration question whether this notation (as opposed to that in Example 4.20) results in enough difference in sound to justify its use. The fingered tremolo gives a delicate, rustling effect that is elusive and attractive. It is most often used as a background for solo passages played by woodwinds or horn. Fingered tremolos involving notes on two different strings are possible but not very satisfactory.

Muting

Muted (Italian: *con sordino [sordina]*, abbrev., *con sord.;* French: *[avec] sourdine[s];* German: *mit Dämpfer*). The mute, a small clamp of wood, metal, rubber, leather, bone, or plastic which fits onto the bridge, reduces the volume of tone and gives it a veiled quality. At least two bars of moderate 4/4 time (preferably more) should be allowed for putting on mutes and at least one bar for taking them off. The Heifetz Mute is so constructed that it can be clamped to one of the strings behind the bridge when not in use; it can therefore be put on and taken off more quickly than the ordinary mute. The Tourte Mute takes even less time because it is simply slid up to the bridge from its position behind the bridge—or back to that position. But there is, of course, no assurance that all string players will have one of these two. Usually it is wise to write in the players' parts "Put on mutes" in the rest preceding the muted passage and "Take off mutes" in the rest following it, so that players will be prepared in plenty of time for the passage to follow, which will bear the direction *senza sord.* A little-used effect calls for the mutes to be put on or taken off one desk at a time over a given number of measures. ("Desk" or "stand" is used to describe each group of two players who sit side by side and read from the same music.) The double bass uses a mute less often than the other stringed instruments because the unmuted bass tone can be reduced to a whisper and can be made to blend fairly well with the other strings muted.

Special Bowing Devices

1. At or near the bridge (Italian; *sul ponticello;* French; *sur le chevalet;* German; *am Steg*). The resulting sound is glassy and eerie in quality. The intensity of this distinctive color varies with the proximity of the bow to the bridge. The device is probably most effective when used with a bowed tremolo. Examples can be seen near the beginning of Bartók's Concerto for Orchestra, at measure 219 of the first movement, and at measure 482 of the fifth movement. In the last instance the player is directed to return gradually to the normal sound in the course of measures 529 to 533.

2. Over the fingerboard (Italian: *sul tasto* or *sulla tastiera;* French: *sur la touche;* German: *am Griffbrett*). The sound is softer and less resonant. This is an effect that appears frequently in French impressionist scores (see Example 4.21[a]). The term *flautando* directs the player to bow only slightly over the fingerboard.

3. With the wood—that is, the back of the bow (Italian: *col legno;* French: *avec le bois;* German: *mit Holz*). There are two ways of producing this effect: (1) by striking the string with the wood of the bow (*col legno battuto*); this method, the more frequent of the two, is most often used for repeated-note figures; (2) by drawing the wood of the bow across the string (*col legno tratto*). In either case

the sound is brittle, dry, and lacking in strong pitch definition; little volume is possible. Examples occur in Bloch's *Schelomo* at figure 6, in Bartók's *Music for String Instruments, Percussion and Celesta* at measure 90 of the fourth movement, and at the beginning of Holst's *The Planets*.

The above three effects are all frequently encountered and have been used for a long time in orchestral music; those that follow are likely to be found only in more recent scores.

4. Behind the bridge. The sounds are of indeterminate pitch but vary in pitch according to the string. Notation: X's on the pitches of the specified open strings, along with the desired rhythm.

5. On the bridge (as distinguished from near it). The result is a buzzing sound almost without pitch definition.

6. On the top or side of the mute placed in its usual position.

7. On the tailpiece. Gardner Read remarks that on the cello and double bass this produces "a low groaning noise."[2]

8. On the string behind the tailpiece ("a very shrill and penetrating tone"[3]).

9. On the body of the instrument—the edge of the fingerboard, the belly, or the side.

10. As close as possible to the left-hand fingers on the string (but on the usual side of the fingers).

11. *Behind* the left-hand fingers.

12. Near the nut (between the tuning pegs and the fingerboard).

13. Underneath the strings, in front of the bridge (most workable on the cello and the double bass).

14. With the bow hair flat against the string while pressure is exerted, the result being a rough, raspy tone. (Direction: "scratch tone.")

Other Unorthodox Methods of Producing String Sounds

1. Silent fingering. The player fingers the given notes forcefully without bowing or plucking the strings; faint pitched sounds result.

2. Damping the string. The left hand touches the string, stopping the sound before it dies away naturally. The symbol used to indicate damping (muffling) in harp parts is employed here: ⊕ .

3. Striking the strings with the palm of the right hand. This motion produces the sound of the strings ringing.

4. Tapping the body of the instrument at various places, normally with the

---

[2]Gardner Read in *Contemporary Instrumental Techniques* (see Bibliography). For an extensive listing of special devices (on all instruments), see that book and those on notation listed in the Bibliography. Many composers have invented their own symbols; thus there is a multiplicity of these for each effect. However, certain ones were proposed as "standard" at a conference in Ghent, Belgium, in 1971 and have received some general acceptance.

[3]Read, op. cit.

fingers. (Notation: X's on any line or space, the rhythm desired, and a direction as to where the instrument is to be tapped.)

5. Rubbing the body of the instrument with the palm in a circular motion.

Special Pizzicato Effects

1. The "snap pizzicato." The string is plucked with such force that it rebounds against the fingerboard. The indication is the sign ♪ (or ♀) over each note to be played in this fashion. (Bartók was especially fond of this device.) A variant of it is the "pulled pizzicato" on the cello or double bass; pulled to one side, the string rebounds to the fingerboard.

2. The "nail pizzicato" (indication ◡). This involves using the fingernail rather than the fleshy part of the fingertip to pluck the string. The resulting sound is sharply metallic.

3. "Plectrum pizzicato." The string is plucked with a guitar, mandolin, or banjo pick.

4. "Pinch pizzicato." The string is plucked with *two* fingers.

5. The "buzz pizzicato." After being plucked, the string vibrates against the player's fingernail.

6. "Guitar pizzicato" or "brush pizzicato." The strings are stroked gently by the thumb or several fingers.

7. Multiple stops played pizzicato with a back-and-forth motion of the hand, the indication being either alternating down-bow and up-bow signs or arrows with alternating directions shown. Example 10.14(i) illustrates this effect. Sometimes *quasi guitara* is included. The arpeggiation in pizzicato chords may be accentuated or reduced to a minimum; if the latter effect is desired, *non arpeggiato* should be written in, or a vertical bracket before the chord may be used instead (or additionally).

8. Pizzicato roll or tremolo (measured or unmeasured) on a single note. This is accomplished by plucking the string with two or more fingers alternately.

9. Pizzicato glissando. After the string is plucked, the left hand makes a glissando.

10. Pizzicato behind the bridge. (This sound can also be made with the nail.)

The direction for canceling any of these special effects is *modo ordinario* (or simply *ord.*), meaning "in the ordinary way."

Abnormal Vibrato

Molto vibrato directs players to use more vibrato than they normally would, *senza vibrato* to use none at all. As indicated earlier, the latter direction results in an inexpressive, white tone. The width and/or speed of the vibrato to be used are sometimes specified either by appropriate adjectives (wide, narrow, fast, slow) or by a wavy line above the notes, which shows by the width and height of its upward curves the kind of special vibrato called for. *Normal vibrato* signals the return to the usual method of performance.

Microtones

Long a staple of Asian music, microtones (intervals smaller than a semitone) have figured in recent Western music mainly as the subject of composers' sporadic experimentation. Of the many microtonal possibilities, the quarter tone is the one seen most frequently. Unfortunately there is no standard notation for it. One method—probably the simplest—uses a small upward-pointing arrow above a note for a quarter tone higher, a downward-pointing arrow below a note for a quarter tone lower. (See the horn part in Thea Musgrave's Horn Concerto for examples of this notation.) For other notational possibilities the reader is referred to the books on notation listed in the Bibliography.

Abnormal Tuning

(Italian: *scordatura.*) The player is directed to tune one or more strings higher or lower than usual. The most frequent purpose of this arrangement is to extend the range of an instrument downward, as in Part IV of Respighi's *Pines of Rome,* where half the cellos and half the basses tune their bottom string to a low B. *Scordatura* may also be used to allow a particular pitch to be played as an open note, as in the last measure of Stravinsky's *The Rite of Spring,* where the cellos tune their A string down to a G♯, which is then played as part of a quadruple stop. Or, rarely, the device may be employed for reasons of color: in the second movement of Mahler's Fourth Symphony the score calls for a solo violin with all four strings tuned a whole tone higher than usual, the object being to simulate the sound of a "cheap fiddle."

Glissando

Two notes connected by a line

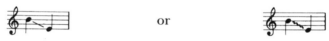

are played in such a way that the notes in between sound as a *glissando:* that is, the finger slides along the string instead of stopping each note separately. The glissando effect may be made very pronounced or may be reduced to an almost imperceptible connection between the notes. In the more moderate form, it is sometimes known as a *portamento* and is often introduced by the player, even where no direction is present, in order to give an extremely legato effect.

Half (of a string group)

(Italian: *la metà;* French: *la moitié;* German: *die Hälfte.*) Occasionally the sound of a smaller-than-normal string group is wanted. In such cases the score may specify that only half of a particular string group is to play ("½ Violins I," or "½ Cellos," etc.). An example as applied to the double basses can be seen at the beginning of Strauss's *Till Eulenspiegel.*

First Desk Only or First Two Desks Only, Etc.

(Desk—Italian: *leggio;* French: *pupitre;* German: *Pult.*) The sound is reduced still further and approaches the solo quality, especially if only one desk is playing.

Solo Strings

When a more intimate, personal quality is desired, strings may be employed in a solo capacity. The direction in such cases is "1 solo violin" or "2 solo violas" (if two different parts are involved) or "4 solo cellos," as the case may be. Such parts are usually written on a separate staff or staves just above the string group to which the solo instrument belongs, although if the rest of the string group is not playing, a separate staff need not be used (in the case of one solo instrument). For a rare instance of twelve solo violins all playing different parts, see Example 17.8.

Some of the special effects mentioned in this section are included in Example 17.11.

NATURAL HARMONICS

Harmonics are simply overtones of the strings. They have a flutelike, silvery quality that can be highly effective as a special color. In orchestral writing they are apt to be used for isolated notes, upper pedal tones, or for short melodic lines in a moderate tempo. Rapid successions of them are difficult to perform and should be avoided.

As explained at the end of Chapter 3, strings, like other sounding bodies, vibrate not only as a whole but in halves, thirds, fourths, and so on at the same time, producing overtones that are normally heard as parts of the composite tone. In Example 4.23 the basic (open) pitch and the fractional vibrations of the cello's C string are shown through the fifth partial. (Of course what is true of this string is true of any other string on any stringed instrument.)

N stands for node, and if the string is lightly touched at one of these points, the fundamental is prevented from sounding, and a harmonic sounds instead. The smaller the fraction, the larger the number of nodal points and the more places a string can be touched to play the harmonic. Compare, for example, the second and fourth partials. The second has only one nodal point because the string is vibrating in halves. The only way to produce this harmonic is by touching that node in the middle of the string. For the fourth partial, the string is vibrating in quarters and would appear to have three nodes that will produce the harmonic. However, the second node falls in the middle of the string; because that division of the string produces the *octave* above the fundamental, only two nodes will produce the fourth partial.

The location of each node is identified in musical notation either by a circle above a note or by a small diamond-shaped note head. The small circle is used for the node at that point where the note would ordinarily be played as a stopped pitch. The small diamond-shaped note identifies the other nodes that will produce the same harmonic. (The actual pitch of the harmonic usually does not appear in this case, although some composers prefer to include it as well.) The string to be used is often indicated below the note—for example, "sul D" or "D string" or "III" in the case of the violin.

Example 4.24 shows the natural harmonics available on each of

Example 4.23

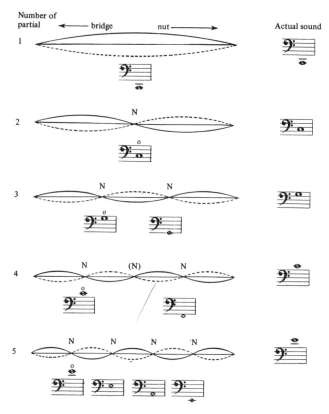

the violin's four strings, along with the notation involved. Notice that in some cases the same pitch occurs as a natural harmonic on two different strings.

NATURAL HARMONICS

Example 4.24

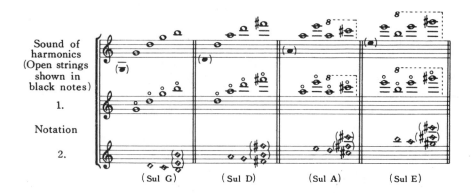

Sound of harmonics (Open strings shown in black notes)

1.

Notation

2.

(Sul G) (Sul D) (Sul A) (Sul E)

Although it may appear difficult to remember the location of all the nodal points, it is actually simple if one remembers two things (1) harmonics indicated with Notation 1 (Example 4.24) must always correspond to the harmonic series of which the open string is the fundamental; (2) diamond-shaped notes, on every string of every stringed instrument, will always have the same interval relationship to the open string (e.g., all fifth-partial harmonics will be produced by diamond-shaped notes a major 3rd, a major 6th, or a major 10th above the open string).

Although natural harmonics as high as the ninth partial for the viola and the twelfth for the cello have been required by Stravinsky, it is exceptional to find natural harmonics higher than the fifth partial for any stringed instrument other than the double bass. Because of its much longer strings, the double bass is capable of producing many useful natural harmonics unavailable to the other stringed instruments. The harmonics that composers most frequently employ for it are those within an octave above or below (sounding) middle C. The natural harmonics for the G string, as well as the two methods of notating them, are shown in Example 4.25.

EXAMPLE 4.25

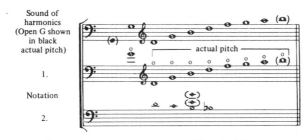

Composers most often choose to notate treble clef harmonics for the double bass at actual pitch, as in Example 4.25, rather than an octave higher, in order to avoid an excessive number of ledger lines. One should include the designation "actual pitch" in such instances to avoid any possible confusion. (Harmonics in tenor or bass clef sound an octave lower than written.)

Example 17.1 features a highly inventive and imaginative use of double bass harmonics. Since all the pitches played by the double basses in this section are harmonics, the composer has dispensed with the small circles that would normally appear above each pitch. Note that the harmonics are written at actual pitch. The reader is encouraged to examine this excerpt and to identify the partial number and the string on which each harmonic is played.

Although harmonics have a way of sounding complicated on paper, they can be made quite clear in a few minutes by means of an actual demonstration with a stringed instrument. Such a demonstration is invaluable when this material is taken up.

ARTIFICIAL HARMONICS

In order to produce as harmonics notes that are not overtones of the open strings, a slightly different procedure is necessary. The string is pressed down firmly by the first finger at a point two octaves below the pitch of the desired harmonic; at the same time, the fourth finger touches the string lightly at a point a perfect 4th higher, which is equivalent to dividing the unstopped portion of the string into quarters. A harmonic two octaves above the firmly fingered pitch results. (This corresponds to the fourth partial produced on an open string.)

To illustrate: if we finger ♯ firmly, then touch the string lightly at ♯ , the note will sound as a harmonic. The usual notation for this would be ♯ , with the lightly touched pitch

2 octaves above given note.

indicated by a diamond-shaped note. (The diamond-shaped note is open, no matter what the value of the lower note is.) As with natural harmonics, the actual sound is not normally shown (though sometimes it is included as well, making three written notes for one sound). A question that students invariably ask at this point is, Why not avoid all these complications by simply writing the passage at actual pitch and marking it "harmonics"? This is what Forsyth calls "the lazy way," and it is not recommended, for it saddles the player with the problem of figuring out the most convenient method for producing each harmonic—a problem that is apt to waste time in rehearsal and one that should rightfully have been solved in advance by the arranger. A similar objection applies to the practice of indicating all harmonics by circles over the notes.

Let us go back now and review the process of writing a note as a harmonic. The orchestrator should first see whether the note is playable as a natural harmonic. If it is, that way is usually easier and therefore preferable. If the note cannot be played as a natural harmonic, the following procedure can be adopted for writing it as an artificial harmonic: measure down two octaves from the actual pitch desired and write that note (with the proper time value), then write an open diamond-shaped note a perfect 4th higher. (Notice that to make a *perfect* 4th, an accidental must often be added.) For example, if the following passage were to be played in harmonics,

EXAMPLE 4.26

we would write:

(b)

Assuming that this passage will be played on the A string, the last note, A, could be played as a natural harmonic and would almost certainly be taken that way by the player even though it is written as an artificial harmonic. This substitution of the "artificial" for the "natural" notation when number 3 of the natural harmonics occurs in a series of artificial harmonics is a license that has come to be more or less accepted.

Artificial harmonics other than those involving the stretch of a 4th are possible but are seldom used. To give just one example: if the player touches the string lightly with the fourth finger a perfect *5th* above the stopped note, a harmonic a 12th higher than the stopped tone results.

Although two artificial harmonics at a time are occasionally called for in virtuoso solo literature for the violin, that arrangement is generally too difficult for orchestral use, with the exception of two artificial harmonics a perfect 5th apart, which can be played as a double stop by pressing down two adjacent strings firmly with the first finger and touching the two strings lightly a perfect 4th higher with the fourth finger.

What has been said about harmonics on the violin applies equally to the viola. Artificial harmonics are more difficult for the cello and out of the question for the double bass except in the higher positions; they appear more frequently for these instruments in virtuoso solo work. Natural harmonics are easy for both, however.

EXAMPLES OF NATURAL HARMONICS

EXAMPLE 4.27

(a) *Capriccio Espagnol*

(b) Concerto for Orchestra

(c)   *Pictures at an Exhibition*

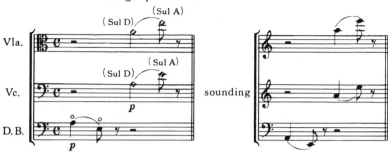

(d)   *The Rite of Spring*

Note: *These harmonics are performed by sliding the finger lightly over the C string between middle C and c^3. The harmonics shown result automatically.*

EXAMPLES OF ARTIFICIAL HARMONICS

EXAMPLE 4.28

(a)   *Ibéria*

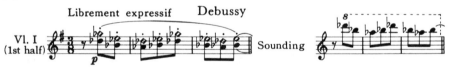

(b)   *Capriccio Espagnol*

SUGGESTED ASSIGNMENTS

A.   Know:

1. the various types of bowing, the names commonly used for them, and the indication for each.
2. special effects obtainable on strings and the names for them.
3. principles involved in writing harmonics (natural and artificial).

B. The following are suitable as exercises in scoring for string orchestra. Include bowing indications (slurs and any other markings necessary).

1. a chorale harmonization.
2. Bach, Sarabande from First *French* Suite.
3. Bach, Fugue XVI from *The Well-Tempered Clavier*, Vol. I.
4. Bach, Fugue in G minor from *Eight Little Preludes and Fugues for the Organ*.
5. Bach, Fugue VII from *The Art of Fugue*.
6. Bach, Fugue IX from *The Art of Fugue*.
7. Mozart, Sonata in B-flat major, K. 498a, 3rd movt.
8. Beethoven, Sonata, Op. 2, No. 1, 2nd movt., meas. 1-16.
9. Beethoven, Sonata, Op. 2, No. 2, 2nd movt., meas. 1-8.
10. Beethoven, Sonata, Op. 10, No. 2, 3rd movt., meas. 1-32.
11. Beethoven, Sonata, Op. 10, No. 3, 3rd movt., meas. 1-16.
12. Beethoven, Sonata, Op. 28, 2nd movt., meas. 1-8.
13. Schubert, Sonata, Op. 147, 2nd movt., meas. 1-28.
14. Schubert, Sonata, Op. 164, 2nd movt., meas. 1-16.
15. Schumann, "Träumerei" from *Scenes from Childhood*.
16. Schumann, "Curious Story" from *Scenes from Childhood*.
17. Brahms, *Romanze*, Op. 118, No. 5.
18. Tchaikovsky, "Morning Prayer" from *Album for the Young*.
19. Scriabin, Prelude No. 1, Op. 74.
20. Prokofieff, Gavotte, Op. 12, No. 2.
21. Bartók, "Syncopation" (*Mikrokosmos*, No. 133, Vol. V).
22. Bartók, No. 12 from *Fifteen Hungarian Peasant Songs*.
23. Hindemith, "Interludium" between "Fuga Decima" and "Fuga Undecima" from *Ludus Tonalis*.

SUGGESTED LISTENING

Strings

Vivaldi, Concertos.
Corelli, Concerti Grossi.
J. S. Bach, Suites for Strings; Brandenburg Concertos Nos. 3 and 6.
C. P. E. Bach, Symphony No. 3 in C major.
Handel, Concerti Grossi.
Mozart, *Eine kleine Nachtmusik;* Divertimentos.
Tchaikovsky, *Serenade for Strings*, Op. 48.
Strauss, *Metamorphosen*.
Schönberg, *Verklärte Nacht*.
Bloch, Concerto Grosso for string orchestra (with piano).
Bartók, *Music for String Instruments, Percussion and Celesta*.
Vaughn Williams, *Fantasy on a Theme by Thomas Tallis*.
Stravinsky, *Apollon Musagète*.
Barber, *Adagio for Strings*.
William Schuman, *Symphony for Strings*.
Copland, Third Symphony, 3rd movt., beginning.
Persichetti, Symphony for Strings.
Penderecki, *Emanationen* for Two String Orchestras; *Threnody for the Victims of Hiroshima*.
David Amram, *Autobiography for Strings*.
Ned Rorem, *Pilgrims*.
Tōru Takemitsu, *Requiem*.

5

The Woodwinds

THE FLUTE

Italian: Flauto   *French:* Flûte   *German:* Flöte
Flauti   Flûtes   Flöten

EXAMPLE 5.1

It is often difficult for the orchestration student who does not play a wind instrument to understand the wide differences in power and quality between the various registers of each woodwind. To complicate matters still more there is no general principle that applies to all the woodwinds in this respect; some are thick and heavy in their bottom register, thin and light at the top, while others reverse this relationship. In the case of the flute (see Figure 5.1) the bottom octave is weak and somewhat breathy, but it has a velvety, sensuous charm that is shown off to good advantage in such scores as Debussy's *Prelude to The Afternoon of a Faun.* Since little volume is possible in this low register, accompaniment must be kept light if the flute is to come

through. From  the tone becomes progressively brighter

and stronger. The notes above this have considerable strength and a haunt-

FIGURE 5.1

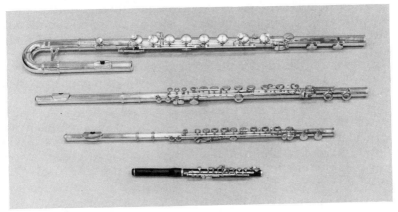

Dorf Photography, Austin, Texas

Bass Flute
Alto Flute
Flute
Piccolo

ing, silvery brilliance. However, from [musical notation] upward the tone tends to be shrill, and the notes are less easy to produce. This extreme upper register should not be used at softer dynamic levels. Some orchestration books list C as the top note possible on the flute; but since the C♯ and D above this can actually be played and are called for in certain scores, it seems reasonable to include them in the "possible" range. On the other hand their quality and intonation are apt to be inferior. Consequently they are not suitable for sustained tones but are useful chiefly for finishing out phrases that extend momentarily above the high C. Some flutes are built to include a B below the bottom C, and that note is occasionally called for in scores. Obviously it is better avoided unless one is sure of having a flute with the low B extension on hand.

The flute is equally at home in sustained melodies and in florid passages. Because of its lightness and grace, it is especially good at airy, scherzolike parts and ornate "filigree" work. Rapid repeated notes, double-tonguing, triple-tonguing, flutter-tonguing (to be discussed later), rapid scales, and arpeggios are all practical and effective on the instrument. All trills are possible except the following: [musical notation]. Those on or above [musical notation] are more difficult, require the use of alternative fingerings, and are of doubtful quality in some cases. There is, then, little the flute cannot do from a technical standpoint in either a legato or a staccato passage. Although its smaller counterpart, the piccolo, has the distinction of being the most agile of the woodwinds, the flute is a very close second.

An important point to remember is that the flute requires a great deal of breath in playing and that plenty of rests are therefore desirable. Of course it is possible for the player to take a breath very quickly (between phrases, for example), but too much of that sort of thing without a rest is tiring. Rests give the flutist—or *flautist,* to use the traditional name—a chance not only to breathe more comfortably but to relax the lips.

The normal fingering for the notes above the second C♯ on the flute involves the use of harmonics. But the term *harmonics* as applied to the flute refers only to those harmonics not normally used. These are occasionally called for, the indication being the same as that for certain string harmonics—a small circle above the note. They have an odd, "white" quality useful for a particular effect but tend to be flat in pitch. Example 17.1 includes a succession of harmonics for two flutes. Now and then flutists play one or two notes as harmonics in passages where the normal fingering would be awkward.

Just as the double bass is written an octave higher than it sounds in

EXAMPLES

EXAMPLE 5.2

(a) Third Symphony

(b) "Dance of the Reed Flutes" (*Nutcracker* Suite)

(c) First Symphony

(d)   *Daphnis and Chloe* Suite No. 2

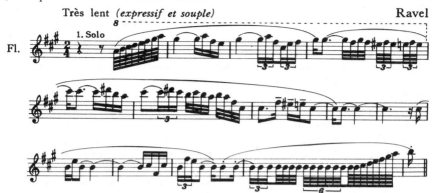

Note: *See also the flute parts in the excerpts from Debussy's* Prelude to The Afternoon of a Faun *given in Examples 4.17(c) and 4.21(a).*

THE PICCOLO

Italian: Flauto Piccolo   *French*: Petite Flûte   *German*: Kleine Flöte
(*or* Ottavino)

EXAMPLE 5.3

Sounding an
8ve higher

order to keep the part more nearly within the staff, the piccolo is written an octave lower than the sounds desired in order to avoid too many ledger lines above the staff. Even so, players must often cope with three or four ledger lines; but they become accustomed to reading these and seem to prefer them to an *8va* sign over the notes written an octave lower.

The piccolo is without doubt the most agile instrument of the orchestra, able to perform incredibly fast runs, skips, arpeggios, and elaborate figurations of all kinds. On the other hand, it is not often used for slow *cantabile* passages, though certain contemporary scores contain solos of a quiet, sustained nature that are surprisingly effective.

The bottom octave of the instrument is so weak and breathy as to be nearly useless in heavily scored passages. In fact, there is not much point in having the piccolo play at all in a *tutti* unless it is above a written

or so, for it will not have enough strength or brilliance to make any difference. Notes below this are usable when the background is not too heavy. It should be noted that the written piccolo range does not include the low C and C♯ possible on the flute. The second octave, from   , is

79

clear and bright, whereas notes above that are more piercing. From the high A upward, the notes tend to be shrill, and the B♮ and C are extremely difficult to produce. They are better avoided except in cases where a phrase extends momentarily into this very high register.

Obviously the piccolo's most valuable talent is its ability to add a brilliant edge to a melodic line. It frequently doubles other woodwinds (or even strings) an octave higher. Now and then it is written to sound in unison with the flute to reinforce the flute's top tones. Like most brightly colored instruments, it cannot be used too continuously without losing in effectiveness; furthermore, if overused, it may give an unintentional "military band" feeling because of its long association with band music.

The fingering for piccolo is the same as that for flute, and the third flute player of an orchestra often doubles on piccolo, playing either a flute part or a piccolo part, as required; this player may change from one instrument to the other several times in the course of a work, as directed by the composer or arranger. Of course such changes require at least two or three measures of rest, preferably more. This arrangement is often described at the beginning of scores by the expression "Flute III interchangeable with piccolo." If only two flutes are used, the second flute player may double on piccolo. Occasionally the piccolo part is listed *below* the flutes in the score in cases where the player is to change to flute III. But most often it is listed at the top of the page, and in many scores a player is assigned exclusively to the piccolo part. One hazard involved in changing from flute to piccolo (or vice versa) is that whichever instrument has been laid aside temporarily will be cold when it is picked up again; as a result it will probably be flat in pitch and a bit sluggish in general responsiveness. Players like to have a few measures of rest in which to warm up the new instrument before actually playing.

EXAMPLES

(Sounding an octave higher)

EXAMPLE 5.4

(a)   *Háry János* Suite ("Viennese Musical Clock")

(b)   *Petit Poucet (Hop o' My Thumb)* from *Mother Goose* Suite

(c)   Seventh Symphony

Note: *See also Example 6.15(b), which includes a prominent and effective piccolo part.*

THE ALTO FLUTE

Italian: Flauto   *French:* Flûte en sol   *German:* Altflöte
contralto

EXAMPLE 5.5

Sounding a perfect 4th lower.

Because the alto flute has the same written range as the C flute but sounds a 4th lower, its "concert" range extends down to the G below middle C. The bottom octave of the instrument is its most distinctive—rich and somewhat dark, though easily covered—whereas the top octave is not quite so effective as the others. There is normally not much point in using the highest register anyway; the C flute can ordinarily take such passages more successfully. All that was said earlier about the technical possibilities of the flute applies here, although the alto flute speaks a bit less quickly. Being a larger instrument than the C flute, it requires more breath; consequently rests are particularly important in parts for it.

The alto flute appears conspicuously in Ravel's *Daphnis and Chloe* and in Stravinsky's *Rite of Spring*, among other works. It is finding increasing favor with today's composers, perhaps most notably in chamber works and those for small orchestra.

A word of forewarning: in British scores the alto flute is sometimes listed as "bass flute." This is obviously an undesirable practice, since there is an actual bass flute for which the latter name is specifically needed. (The bass flute is discussed in Chapter 18.)

EXAMPLES

EXAMPLE 5.6

(a) *Amériques*

(b) *Daphnis and Chloe* Suite No. 2

(c) *Night of the Four Moons, I*

THE OBOE

Italian: Oboe	*French*: Hautbois	*German*: Oboe
Oboi	Hautbois	Oboen
		old spelling: Hoboe(n)

EXAMPLE 5.7

The oboe, along with the English horn, bassoon, and contrabassoon, belongs to the double-reed branch of the woodwind family (see Figure 5.2); it

FIGURE 5.2

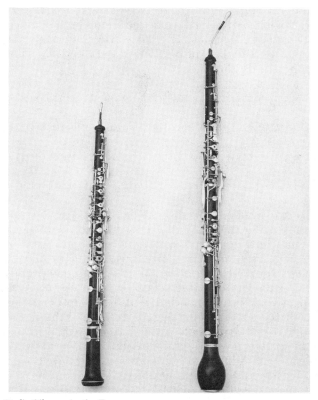

Oboe   **English Horn**

is a descendant of the 17th-century shawm (or "pommer" or "bombard" or a variety of other names). Its spicy, somewhat nasal tone is one of the most distinctive of orchestral colors—one that has a way of cutting through other colors and of standing out against any background. For this reason, the oboe is an ideal solo instrument. It can be poignant or lighthearted, and it is especially well suited to melodies of a pastoral nature. Although not as agile as the flute or the clarinet, it can perform with considerable speed and flexibility, either legato or staccato. This is not to imply that it is valuable only in a solo role, for it is also useful in combination with other instruments. However, one must be careful about giving it a subordinate voice in a lightly scored passage, for its incisive tone may come through too prominently for background. Another point to remember is that the highly colored oboe timbre becomes tiresome if used for too long at a time.

Below about ♭ the oboe tends to sound a bit thick and coarse, and notes in that bottom register are difficult to produce softly. For that reason, these bottom notes, particularly the low B♭, are better avoided in any passage where the oboe is to be heard prominently. Parts that dip down into this lowest register but quickly get away from it are not objectionable; the main point is not to stress these very low notes in solo work. Occasionally, however, they are used intentionally to achieve a special effect, as in Stravinsky's *Symphony of Psalms,* where they give an ultrareedy, primitive flavor, and in Prokofieff's *Peter and the Wolf,* where they serve admirably to personify the duck.

From [♮] is the oboe's most useful and characteristic register. Above that the tone becomes thinner and less pungent, though quite usable up to about [♮]. The notes above this are generally impractical for orchestral use; the high A, in particular, is extremely difficult.

All trills are available except the half-step trill on the bottom B♭, though trills involving the top F and G are better avoided.

Double-tonguing and triple-tonguing, which are very difficult on the oboe, are rarely used, but the instrument is capable of playing fairly rapid repeated notes even with single-tonguing. As intimated earlier, it should not be expected to play extremely fast or intricate passages. Unlike the flute, it requires very little expenditure of breath in performance. But the player has a different problem, that of *holding in* the air until the next breathing point while using only a small amount of it in playing. Consequently sufficient rests are as essential in oboe parts as in flute parts, if for a different reason. In addition to being an uncommonly taxing instrument, the oboe is a sensitive and somewhat unpredictable one as well. Notes must be humored and cajoled; the reed is delicate and must be "just so"; temperature and atmospheric conditions can produce unexpected and disastrous results. In short, the oboe is something of a temperamental *prima donna,* but an indispensable one in the orchestra.

EXAMPLES

EXAMPLE 5.8

(a) Third Symphony

(b) Seventh Symphony

(c) Second Symphony

(d) *Ibéria*

THE ENGLISH HORN

Italian: Corno Inglese   *French:* Cor Anglais   *German:* Englisch Horn

EXAMPLE 5.9

Sounding a perfect 5th lower

In the same way that the oboe evolved from the treble member of the shawm family, the early forms of the English horn (Figure 5.2) were descendants of the alto shawm. In the seventeenth and early eighteenth centuries these forms were known variously as "tenor oboe" and "oboe da caccia" ("hunting oboe," although no connection between the instrument and the hunt has ever been established). It was not until some time after 1750 that the name *English horn* came into use. Instrument makers apparently decided to ease the problems involved in playing the long, straight tenor oboe by making it curved, and Carse[1] points out that because curved or coiled instruments were then frequently referred to as horns, that might explain the second part of English horn. But the "English" part remains a mystery. There has been some speculation that because the instrument was angled, it may have been called *cor anglé* in French and that *anglé* became confused with *anglais* because of the similarity in pronunciation. Carse finds that argument unconvincing, however, because there appears to be no real evidence that the name *cor anglé* was actually used before *cor anglais* came into standard use.

The modern instrument, which is straight rather than angled, differs from the oboe chiefly in being longer and having a bulbous distension at the end of the bell as well as a curved bocal, a small metal pipe connecting the instrument to the reed. The tone is akin to that of the oboe but more sonorous and melancholy. Possibly because of this serious quality, the English horn is seldom called on to play fast, technically complicated music,

---

[1]Adam Carse, *Musical Wind Instruments.*

and it is not a particularly agile instrument by nature. The part for it is written a perfect 5th higher than the sounds desired.

Although the low B♭ is obtainable on the oboe, the lowest written note on the English horn is a B♮, sounding E below. Now and then one comes across an instrument that has the low B♭ (concert E♭) but not often enough to justify writing the note as a general practice. The bottom notes of the English horn are not only usable but highly effective; strangely enough, they do not seem to suffer from the coarseness that afflicts the lowest tones of the oboe. There is seldom any need to take the English horn above the

written note , even though notes up to a 5th higher are possible.

Moreover, the instrument loses some of its characteristic color in its top-most register and is consequently less effective there.

EXAMPLES

(Sounding a perfect 5th lower)

EXAMPLE 5.10

(a)   Ninth Symphony (*New World*)

(b)   Symphony in D minor

(c)   *La Mer*

THE CLARINET

Italian: Clarinetto	*French:* Clarinette	*German:* Klarinette
Clarinetti	Clarinettes	Klarinetten

EXAMPLE 5.11

In B♭, sounding a
major 2nd lower.
In A, sounding a
minor 3rd lower.

In the past, clarinets pitched in various keys were used. Of these, the two chief survivors today are the clarinet in B♭ and the clarinet in A, the first being the more commonly used of the two (see Figure 5.3). Both are transposing instruments; that is, they are not written at actual pitch. In the case of the B♭ clarinet, the part must be written a major 2nd (a whole step) higher than the sounds desired, while the part for the A clarinet is written a minor 3rd higher than the sounds. For the benefit of students who have not had experience with transposing instruments, let us elaborate a bit on this system and give some examples to show how it works.

The B♭ clarinet is so labeled because B♭ is the sound that results when

FIGURE 5.3

Dorf Photography, Austin, Texas

Bass Clarinet   **B♭ Clarinet**   **E♭ Clarinet**

written C is played. That is, when a B♭ clarinet player sees ♯ on the page, he or she uses the fingering that will produce the sound ♯. Consequently, if we want the B♭ clarinet to *sound* ♯, we must write ♯. On the A clarinet, the note A is the sound that results when written C is played. Therefore, if the sound ♯ is wanted on an A clarinet, we must write ♯, a minor 3rd higher.

In dealing with transposing instruments, remember that the key of the instrument is the *sound* that results when written C is played.

Example 5.12 shows how a passage (given first at actual pitch) would be written for B♭ and A clarinets, respectively.

EXAMPLE 5.12

Actual sounds

Notation on
B♭ Clar.

Notation on
A Clar.

Notice the inclusion of key signatures. Example 5.13 gives the key signature that would be used by each of the two instruments in each of the · major keys. The term *concert key* means the actual or sounding key. The word *concert* is also applied to notes; for example, "concert G," means the actual sound G as opposed to the written G on a transposing instrument, and we use the general term, *concert pitch*.

EXAMPLE 5.13

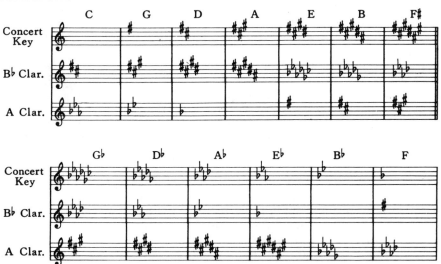

In dealing with transposing instruments we encounter two types of transposition: (1) the "reading" type, the kind that is involved when we are reading a score and have the problem of converting *transposed* pitches to *actual* (or concert) pitches, and (2) the "writing" type, in which we must convert *actual* pitches to *transposed* pitches. (The difference between the two types is, of course, only one of direction.) If this distinction is understood at the outset and kept in mind, a good deal of confusion can be avoided.

Considering the complications that the transposition system involves for both orchestrator and score reader, a very natural question at this point is, "Why must it be used at all?" Although a complete answer to that question would entail excursions into technical points of acoustics and fingering, certain general reasons for the use of the system can be cited here. As far as resonance and good intonation are concerned, the B♭ and A clarinets are superior to the now obsolete C clarinet. Since they started out as transposing instruments and have been treated as such ever since, a change to another method of notation now would be all but impossible. (Certain composers make a practice of writing the parts for clarinets and other transposing instruments at actual pitch in the score; but even in such cases the individual parts for the players are written in transposed form.) An advantage of the transposition principle as applied to clarinets is this: it allows for a pattern of fingering common to clarinets of different sizes; the player need not learn a new fingering in order to perform on an alto or bass clarinet, for example. Instead it is the notation that changes in each case.

As a general rule key signatures involving flats are easier for the instruments pitched in flat keys, whereas instruments such as the A clarinet find the sharp keys a bit more comfortable. However, the B♭ clarinet is frequently called on to play in keys up to three or four sharps, whereas the simpler flat keys are perfectly practical for the A clarinet. The advantage of having the two instruments available is that if a part would involve awkward fingering on one, it can nearly always be played with relative ease if assigned to the other. In general, the B♭ clarinet is first choice; the A clarinet is selected chiefly in cases where the B♭ instrument would have to play in a difficult key or where the low concert C♯ is required.

By way of illustration, suppose that we are to score a piece in the key of E♭ major, concert. If we use the B♭ clarinet, its part will be written in F major (an easy key for the instrument) whereas the A clarinet would be written in the more difficult key of G♭ major or, enharmonically, F♯ major. Obviously the B♭ instrument is the better choice here. But suppose that the music to be scored is in A major, concert. The B♭ clarinet would call for a signature of five sharps, whereas the A clarinet would be written in C major. In such a case the A clarinet would be the better choice. Of course there are certain keys that are suitable to either instrument. For example, in music in G major concert, the B♭ clarinet could play in A major about as easily as the A clarinet could play in B♭ major. However, the B♭ instrument would probably be chosen here, simply because it is the more commonly used and more generally available of the two.

Sometimes parts are best written enharmonically. For instance, if we are using B♭ clarinet and we come to a section in B major, a transposition of the part up a major 2nd would bring us out in the key of C♯ major (seven sharps), whereas the enharmonic equivalent, D♭ major (five flats), would be a great deal easier from a reading standpoint and should of course be chosen. Notice that such enharmonic respellings alter the interval used in the "transposition by interval" method.

Although changes from B♭ clarinet to A clarinet (or vice versa) in the midst of a work are possible and are occasionally called for, they are not recommended. The clarinet that has been lying unused will be cold and will consequently tend to be flat in pitch and sluggish in its general response until it has had time to warm up. There is, by the way, a slight difference in tone quality between the B♭ and the A instruments, but it is scarcely apparent to any but the most sensitive ear.

What has been said here about the use of the A clarinet does not apply in school orchestras. There the B♭ clarinet is used exclusively. The problem of difficult key signatures never arises because the concert keys are chosen with an eye to keeping the B♭ instruments in the easier keys.

The bottom octave or so of the clarinet is called the *chalumeau* register. It has a dark, hollow quality. Notice that although the written range of both B♭ and A clarinets is the same, the A clarinet can go a half step lower in sound than the B♭ instrument since the low written E sounds D on the B♭ clarinet and C♯ (or D♭) on the A clarinet. The middle (or "throat") register, roughly from to , is rather neutral in quality and not too strong, while the octave above this (sometimes known as the *clarion* register) is clear and bright. Above about the tone becomes more shrill and good intonation more difficult to achieve. Although on paper the clarinet's "possible" range extends up to a high C above this, these very high notes are seldom usable for practical purposes. Occasionally the very shrillness of the upper register is used for humorous or grotesque effects, as in Stravinsky's *Petrouchka,* where the high notes of the clarinet imitate the sounds of a peasant's reed pipe as he plays while his bear dances.

Of all the woodwinds, the clarinet is the most sensitive in the matter of dynamic range and control. It can reduce its warm, round tone to an incredibly soft whisper and can achieve the subtlest nuances of color and phrasing. These capabilities make it an ideal solo instrument for *espressivo* melodies. In agility it nearly equals the flute; it can perform rapid runs and arpeggios, skips, trills, and legato or staccato effects. However, because it is a single-reed instrument, it is somewhat limited in its ability to play rapid repeated notes.

In treatises on the clarinet, much has been made of the "break," a point on the instrument at which an awkward change of fingering is involved,[2] and of the register associated with it, which includes some notes of slightly inferior quality. From the standpoint of the fingering problem, the actual break occurs between the written notes [musical notation: "and"] or [musical notation: "and"]

Passages that pass through this area in either direction cause no particular difficulty; it is only when a part involves a continuous use of these notes that the part becomes unduly awkward. As for tone quality, the three written notes [musical notation] (particularly the B♭) are the weakest on the instrument and are better not stressed in solo passages. Because of modern improvements in clarinet construction, the break is now much less of an obstacle than it once was. In fact, clarinet players today seem rather unconcerned about this difficulty.

Likewise, certain trills that were once listed as "awkward" or "better avoided" in clarinet writing are now quite usable. In fact, all trills are now practical on the instrument.

Although it is not the intention here to go into the historical background of instruments, it is worth noting that the clarinet did not begin to be accepted as a member of the symphony orchestra until Mozart's day; only four of the Mozart symphonies contain clarinet parts.

---

[2]In connection with this point at which the player begins to repeat the fingering pattern, it might be mentioned that the clarinet, being cylindrical, "overblows" at the 12th, whereas the oboe and the bassoon, which are conical, overblow at the octave. (The flute, although cylindrical, behaves like an open pipe and consequently overblows at the octave.)

(All examples are given as written in the score. Those for B♭ clarinet will sound a major 2nd lower, those for A clarinet a minor 3rd lower.)

EXAMPLE 5.14

(a) Sixth Symphony

(b) First Symphony

(c) Overture to *Tannhäuser*

(d) *Capriccio Espagnol*

THE E♭ CLARINET

EXAMPLE 5.15

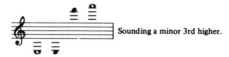

This is a small clarinet (see Figure 5.3) that has found great favor with military bands but less with orchestras. One reason is that its tone lacks the mellow warmth of the B♭ and A instruments and tends instead to be a bit hard and inelastic. On the other hand this very quality has now and then been exploited with striking effect in orchestral writing, as in Berlioz's

Fantastic Symphony (the section entitled "Dream of a Witches' Sabbath"), in Strauss's *Ein Heldenleben* (in the "critics" section), and in Ravel's *Daphnis and Chloe* Suite No. 2. Because its practical upward compass in actual sounds is slightly higher than that of the Bb and A clarinets, it can take passages that would be uncomfortably high for them. However, unless both instrument and player are first-rate, there is a danger that high passages for the Eb clarinet may be unpleasantly shrill or out of tune or both. The part is placed *above* that of the Bb or A clarinets in the score.

Strauss and others have written for a small clarinet in D, which has the same written range as the Eb clarinet but sounds a major 2nd higher than written. The D clarinet is all but unknown in the United States, and the few parts for it (such as the important one in *Till Eulenspiegel*) are usually played on the Eb instrument.

EXAMPLES

(Sounding a minor 3rd higher.)

EXAMPLE 5.16

(a) *Fantastic Symphony* (V. "Dream of a Witches' Sabbath")

(b) *El Salón México*

(c) *Pli Selon Pli*, V. "Tombeau"

THE BASS CLARINET

Italian: Clarinetto   *French:* Clarinette   *German:* Bassklarinette
　　　　Basso　　　　　　　　　Basse

EXAMPLE 5.17

(a)

Sounding a
major 9th lower

or

(b)

Sounding a
major 2nd lower

*Pitches down to the low written C (concert B♭) are possible on some bass clarinets.

The bass clarinet (Figure 5.3) differs from the clarinet not only in being larger but in having a curve near the mouthpiece and an upturned bell, the whole shape being a little like that of a saxophone. Although at one time there was a bass clarinet in A, it is now extinct. Therefore, the B♭ instrument must be used and the part transposed when the player has a part written for bass clarinet in A.

In approaching the notation of the bass clarinet, we come across a rather confusing convention: when written in the treble clef as it commonly is today, the instrument sounds a major 9th lower than written; but in earlier scores it was sometimes written in the bass clef, in which case it sounds a major 2nd lower than written. To give an example of the two

methods of notation, the concert pitch 𝄢 ○ would be written

𝄞 ○ in the treble clef, whereas the same sound would be written

𝄢 ○ in the bass clef.[3] Although the first method is the one now in

---

[3]These two types of notation are sometimes known, respectively, as the "French system" (treble clef) and the "German system" (bass clef). However, these names must not be taken too literally; there are instances of bass clef parts in French music and of treble clef parts in German music.

regular use, players and score readers must, of course, be able to read parts written either way; occasionally both systems were used at different places in the same score, as in Example 5.18(c).

In its bottom octave the bass clarinet is extremely dark, almost sinister, in quality. The color becomes progressively less somber above that until, in the top octave, it is a bit strained and white. There is little point in writing for the instrument in this top register, for other instruments can take these notes with better effect. But in its middle and lower registers the bass clarinet is valuable not only for doubling bass and tenor parts but in a solo capacity. Wagner was particularly fond of using it as a solo instrument to give a sense of gloom and impending tragedy. Other composers have exploited what Forsyth calls its "goblinesque" quality, a certain attractive grotesqueness. Although not quite so agile as the clarinet, it can move with considerable speed, and it shares the clarinet's phenomenal control of volume and dynamic nuance.

In some scores, the bass clarinet is interchangeable with the second or third clarinet: that is, the two parts are played by the same person. This is obviously a sensible arrangement where both instruments are not needed at once and particularly where there is only a small part for the bass clarinet or for the second or third clarinet.

Bass clarinets built to include the written D, D♭, and C below the low E♭ are available but not widely used. It is possible to add these notes to a bass clarinet not built with them initially by means of an extension attached to the bottom joint. Such an extension, which must be fitted at an instrument factory, may be either removable or a permanent part of the instrument.

A B♭ contrabass clarinet, sounding two octaves and a major 2nd below the written pitches, is sometimes used in bands.

EXAMPLES

(Sounding a major 9th lower when
written in the treble clef, a major 2nd lower when written in the bass clef.)

EXAMPLE 5.18

(a)   Third Symphony

William Schuman

(b) Symphony in D minor

(c) *The Rite of Spring*

THE BASSOON

Italian: Fagotto	*French:* Basson	*German:* Fagott
Fagotti	Bassons	Fagotte

EXAMPLE 5.19

Although the bassoon (Figure 5.4), like the oboe, is a double-reed instrument, its tone is much less nasal and less highly colored than that of the oboe. In fact, its characteristic quality is a relatively neutral one that is apt to be largely absorbed by any other orchestral color it is doubled with. For example, if bassoon is doubled with cellos (as it very frequently is), the cello tone will predominate but will have more body and focus than it would alone.

In the bottom octave or so of the bassoon, the tone is dark and full, even a little gruff in the bottommost notes, which are difficult to produce *pianissimo*. The next octave is middle ground, neither notably dark nor light in color, but probably the most used register of the instrument. The notes

FIGURE 5.4

Zintgraff, San Antonio, Texas

Bassoon   **Contrabassoon**

in the top octave become progressively thinner until above about A 440
they take on a pinched, complaining quality. Stravinsky, with his penchant
for exploiting extreme registers, uses these top notes in a wonderfully
effective bassoon solo at the beginning of *The Rite of Spring.* But such
passages are extremely difficult, and it is better to let A or B♭ suffice as an
upward limit. When the part goes too high to be comfortably written in the
bass clef, the tenor clef may be used.

The bassoon is sometimes spoken of as "the clown of the orchestra."
Bassoonists resent the title, and with good reason. For although certain
passages (especially *staccato* passages) have a way of sounding comical on
the instrument, it can perform many other types of music effectively, including sustained melodies of a serious nature.

Technically, the bassoon is quite agile and is capable of making wide
and sudden leaps. Because it does not have a great deal of power and
because its color is so readily absorbed by that of other instruments, it is
easily covered by the rest of the orchestra and should not be pitted against

too heavy a background in solos. Probably its most frequent function is that of reinforcing other instruments in the bass or tenor registers.

Trills below  are difficult, the one on D♭ to E♭ being impossible. Also avoid  unless the instrument is known to have a special trill key.

EXAMPLES

Example 5.20

(a) Fifth Symphony

(b) Fourth Symphony

(c) *The Sorcerer's Apprentice*

(d) Concerto for Orchestra

THE CONTRABASSOON OR DOUBLE BASSOON

Italian: Contrafagotto   *French:* Contre-basson   *German:* Kontrafagott

EXAMPLE 5.21

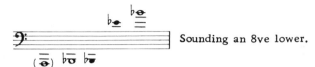

Sounding an 8ve lower.

As might be expected, the contrabassoon is one of the more ponderous instruments of the orchestra, in both appearance and sound (see Figure 5.4). Because of its great size it must rest on the floor in performance. Its tone is somewhat rough and thick; very soft effects are difficult to achieve, especially in the lower register. As a result, the instrument is valuable chiefly for adding volume and incisiveness to the bass parts in loud, heavily scored passages. Occasionally it is used in other ways; for example, to add a somber tinge to low melodic lines or as a solo instrument to produce a rather grotesque effect. There is seldom reason to use it in its upper register; bassoons or bass clarinet are better equipped to play these notes. Like the double bass, it is written an octave higher than it is to sound.[4]

Most school orchestras and even many semiprofessional orchestras do not own a contrabassoon or, if they own one, do not have a competent player on hand. Consequently it is always something of a gamble whether the part will really be played, unless one is sure of getting a major orchestra to perform the score.

Although Beethoven and Brahms wrote contrabassoon parts that went as high as (written) ♩, notes above ♩ are somewhat difficult. Heckel now makes a contrabassoon that is capable of playing the low A one half step below the B♭ usually given as the bottom note. (Incidentally, this A is the lowest note on the piano.)

Rapid, intricate parts are not well suited to the technique of the contrabassoon. Its part should be fairly simple and should contain plenty of rests.

In Example 5.22(c) the contrabassoon is doubled in unison by the harp and three octaves higher by clarinet and vibraphone—surely one of the most unusual and inventive doublings in orchestral literature!

---

[4] In a few scores (Wagner's *Parsifal* and Debussy's *Ibéria* and *La Mer,* for instance) the contrabassoon part is written at actual pitch.

(Contrabassoon parts sounding an octave lower)

EXAMPLE 5.22

(a) *The Sorcerer's Apprentice*

(b) "Beauty and the Beast" (from *Mother Goose* Suite)

(c) Fourth Symphony

WOODWIND REGISTERS

(Written notes)

EXAMPLE 5.23

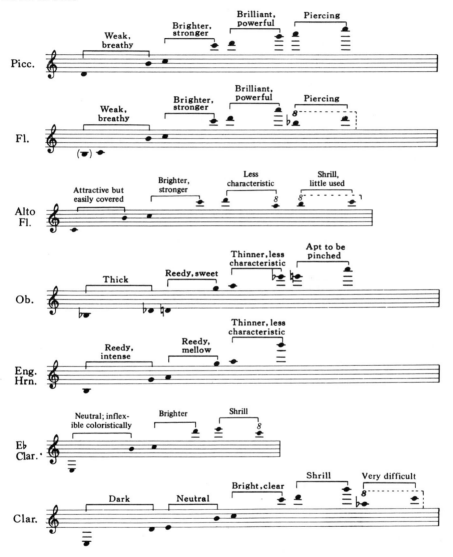

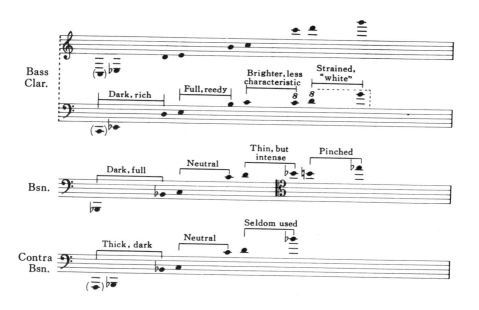

SUGGESTED ASSIGNMENTS

A. Know:

1. ranges (possible and practical) of flute, oboe, clarinet, and bassoon.
2. ranges (possible and practical) of piccolo, alto flute, English horn, Eb clarinet, bass clarinet, and contrabassoon.
3. transpositions where involved.
4. colors and relative strengths of the various registers of each woodwind.
5. particular abilities and limitations of each woodwind.

SUGGESTED LISTENING

Piccolo

Tchaikovsky, Fourth Symphony, 3rd movt., meas. 194.
Pierné, "Entrance of the Little Fauns" from *Cydalise.*
Debussy, *Ibéria.* Part I ("Par les rues et par les chemins") many passages.
Ravel, *Mother Goose* Suite: II. "Petit Poucet," figure 7; III. "Laideronette, Impératrice des Pagodes," figure 1: *Daphnis and Chloe* Suite No. 2, figure 183.
Kodály, *Háry János* Suite, Part II ("Viennese Musical Clock") and Part IV ("The Battle and Defeat of Napoleon").

Shostakovich, Seventh Symphony, 1st movt., figure 14; Ninth Symphony, first movt., 3 bars after figure 6.
Copland, Third Symphony, 3rd movt., 3 bars after figure 69; figure 71; 2 bars after figure 78; 3 bars after figure 83, etc.
Schuller, *Seven Studies on Themes of Paul Klee*, 4th movt.

Flute

Bach, Suite in B minor for flute and strings; Brandenburg Concertos Nos. 2, 4, 5.
Beethoven, Third Symphony, last movt., meas. 190, also meas. 292.
Mendelssohn, Fourth Symphony (*Italian*), last movt., meas. 6.
Brahms, First Symphony, last movt., meas. 38.
Tchaikovsky, Piano Concerto in B♭ minor, beginning of 2nd movt. (*Andantino*).
Dvořák, Ninth Symphony (*New World*), 1st movt., figures 5 and 12.
Bizet, *Carmen*, Entr'acte between Acts II and III.
Debussy, *Prelude to The Afternoon of a Faun*, beginning and many other passages.
Ravel, *Daphnis and Chloe* Suite No. 2, 3 bars after figure 176.
Stravinsky, Variations, meas. 59.
Bartók, *Concerto for Orchestra*, 2nd movt., meas. 60.
Kennan, *Night Soliloquy* for flute, strings, and piano.
Messiaen, *Chronochromie*, meas. 50.

Alto Flute

Varèse, *Amériques*, beginning (solo).
Ravel, *Daphnis and Chloe* Suite No. 2, after figure 187.
Stravinsky, *The Rite of Spring*, figure 27.
Holst, *The Planets*, V. beginning; 3 meas. after figure II; 13 meas. after figure V.
Shostakovich, Seventh Symphony, figure 97.
Sessions, Fifth Symphony, 2nd movt., meas. 187 (in combination with two C flutes).
Crumb, *Night of the Four Moons*, beginning (solo). Chance to hear alto flute in context of a smaller ensemble.
Stravinsky, Variations, meas. 61.
Henze, Sixth Symphony, 5th movt., 9 bars after Z.

Oboe

Bach, Brandenburg Concertos Nos. 1, 2.
Beethoven, Third Symphony, 2nd movt. (*Marcia Funebre*) meas. 8; Sixth Symphony, 3rd movt. (*Scherzo*) meas. 91; Seventh Symphony, 1st movt., meas. 300.
Schumann, Second Symphony, 3rd movt. (*Adagio espressivo*) meas. 8.
Brahms, Violin Concerto, beginning of 2nd movt.
Mahler, *Das Lied von der Erde*, beginning of 2nd movt., beginning of 6th movt.
Debussy, *Ibéria*, Part II (*Les parfums de la nuit*) beginning, also 4 bars before figure 40.
Ravel, *Le Tombeau de Couperin*, Trio of the *Rigaudon; La Valse*, figure 18.
Strauss, *Death and Transfiguration*, measure 30; *Don Quixote*, 8 bars before figure 3.
Shostakovich, First Symphony, beginning of 3rd movt.
Bartók, *Concerto for Orchestra*, II. ("Giuoco delle Coppie"), meas. 25.
Schuller, *Seven Studies on Themes of Paul Klee*, 5th movt.

English Horn

Berlioz, *Fantastic Symphony,* beginning of 3rd movt. ("Scène aux champs").
Wagner, *Tristan und Isolde,* beginning of Act III.
Franck, Symphony in D minor, 2nd movt., near beginning.
Dvořák, Ninth Symphony (*New World*), 2nd movt., near beginning.
Debussy, *Nocturnes:* I. "Nuages," meas. 5; *La Mer,* figure 16.
Sibelius, *The Swan of Tuonela.*
Stravinsky, *The Rite of Spring,* section entitled "Ritual of the Ancestors," figure 129; *Petrouchka,* 9 bars after figure 72.
Respighi, *Pines of Rome,* 4 bars before figure 19.
Rorem, *Air Music,* IX.

E♭ Clarinet

Berlioz, *Fantastic Symphony,* V. "Dream of a Witches' Sabbath," figure 63.
Ravel, *Daphnis and Chloe* Suite No. 2, figure 160, 3 bars after figure 201.
Prokofieff, Fifth Symphony, many passages.
Bartók, *The Miraculous Mandarin,* many passages.
Varèse, *Amériques,* many passages.
Copland, *El Salón México,* 1 bar after figure 27, 5 bars after figure 29.
Boulez, *Pli Selon Pli,* V. "Tombeau," many passages.
Tippett, Third Symphony, figure 217.

Clarinet

Beethoven, Fourth Symphony, 2nd movt., meas. 26; Sixth Symphony, 2nd movt., meas. 69.
Weber, Overture to *Oberon,* meas. 64.
Schubert, Symphony in B minor (*Unfinished*), 2nd movt., meas. 66.
Tchaikovsky, Fifth Symphony, beginning; 2nd movt., meas. 66; 3rd movt., meas. 28; Sixth Symphony, 1st movt., meas. 163, also meas. 326.
Debussy, *Ibéria,* meas. 8.
Rachmaninoff, Second Piano Concerto, 2nd movt., near beginning.
Stravinsky, *Petrouchka,* figure 100.
Prokofieff, *Peter and the Wolf,* figure 11 ("The Cat").
Bartók, Concerto for Orchestra, 2nd. movt., meas. 45.
Britten, *Four Sea Interludes* from *Peter Grimes,* I. "Dawn."
Schuller, *Seven Studies on Themes of Paul Klee,* 7th movt.

Bass Clarinet

Wagner, *Tristan und Isolde,* Act. II, "King Mark's Song."
Tchaikovsky, *Nutcracker* Suite: "Dance of the Sugar Plum Fairy."
Strauss, *Don Quixote,* Variation III.
Stravinsky, *Petrouchka,* figure 65 ("The Moor dances").
Khachaturian, Piano Concerto, 1st movt., meas. 390; 2nd movt., beginning and meas. 220.
William Schuman, Third Symphony, Part II, meas. 157.

Bassoon

Beethoven, Fifth Symphony, 2nd movt., meas. 205.
Tchaikovsky, Fourth Symphony, 2nd movt., meas. 77; Sixth Symphony, beginning; last movt., meas. 30.
Rimsky-Korsakoff, *Scheherazade,* 2nd movt., meas. 5.

Mussorgsky-Ravel, *Pictures at an Exhibition*, beginning of Part II ("The Old Castle").
Dukas, *The Sorcerer's Apprentice*, figure 7.
Stravinsky, *The Rite of Spring*, beginning; *Petrouchka*, 4 bars after figure 68 (end of Moor scene); *Agon*, "Bransle Gay."
Shostakovich, Ninth Symphony, last movt., 10 bars after figure 67.
Carter, *A Symphony of Three Orchestras*, meas. 40.

Contrabassoon

Mahler, Ninth Symphony, last movt., meas. 28 (see Example 17.2).
Ravel, *Mother Goose* Suite: IV. "Les Entretiens de la Belle et de la Bête," figure 2.
Dukas, *The Sorcerer's Apprentice*, figure 42.
Stravinsky, *Petrouchka*, 9 bars after figure 72.
Bloch, *Schelomo*, last 5 bars.
Tippett, Fourth Symphony, figure 108.
Argento, *A Ring of Time*, 3rd movt., figure 9.

6

The Woodwind
Section

The proportions of woodwind sections of different sizes were discussed in Chapter 1, and that material should be reread before going on with this chapter. As indicated, the woodwind section in a professional orchestra consists, at a minimum, of two flutes, two oboes, two clarinets, and two bassoons ("woodwinds in pairs"), plus any or all of the auxiliary woodwinds—piccolo, alto flute, English horn, E♭ clarinet, bass clarinet, and contrabassoon—as needed. Woodwinds in threes may be used instead. And whatever the size of the section, the possibility of having one player in each woodwind group double on an auxiliary instrument should be remembered.

In scoring for high school or nonprofessional orchestras, it is safest to write for woodwinds in pairs unless one is sure of having auxiliary woodwinds on hand.

As mentioned earlier, the orchestra of the Classical period did not regularly include clarinets. For example, the woodwind section used in the early Haydn symphonies consisted of one or two flutes, usually two oboes, and one or two bassoons. But by Beethoven's time, woodwinds in pairs (including clarinets) had become the accepted arrangement.

Table 1.1 shows the standard order in which instruments are listed on the page. This consistency of arrangement is obviously a great help to the eye of the conductor or the score reader. The only possible variation in order is the placing of the piccolo part below that of flutes I and II in cases where flute III is interchangeable with piccolo.

As a rule, each pair of woodwinds is written on the same staff. When the two instruments are playing different parts, the upper notes are normally taken by the first of the pair, the lower notes by the second. As with *divisi* string parts on one staff, a single stem for both notes may be used as long as the time values in both parts are the same, but separate stems must be used if the time values are different:

EXAMPLE 6.1

(Notice the proper notation of the interval of a 2nd—with the two stems lined up.) If the parts cross briefly, both can still be written on the same staff; the abnormal arrangement of the parts is shown by the direction of the stems. But if they involve continuous crossing or are so independent as to be awkward on one staff, it is better to use separate staves.

We now come to a point that should be noted very carefully, for it is one that students seem to have a hard time remembering. Whenever two wind instruments are written on the same staff and a single melodic line is involved, an indication *must* be included to show whether the passage is to be played by the first instrument of the pair, by the second, or by both. Otherwise the part is ambiguous. If the first is to play, either of the following systems may be used:

EXAMPLE 6.2

The arrangement in Example 6.2(a) is the easier and more commonly used of the two. Similarly, if the second instrument is to play, the part could be written in either of these ways:

EXAMPLE 6.3

Sometimes "1°" and "2°" are used to designate the first and second of each pair. These are abbreviations of the Italian words *primo* and *secondo*, corresponding to our "1st" and "2nd."

In case the passage is a solo, the word *solo* should be written in at the beginning of it. Solos are most often given to the first of each pair. Occasionally the solo indication is used even when the passage in question is not the chief melodic idea but must be played in such a way as to give it a certain prominent or important quality. If both instruments of a pair are to take a melodic line in unison, the passage can be written in either of the following ways:

EXAMPLE **6.4**

(a)   (b)

(Literally, *a2* means "to two" in Italian.) Here, again, the way shown in Example 6.4(a) is the usual one; the double-stem system used in Example 6.4(b) is normally reserved for passages where both instruments play in unison for just a few notes, as in the following:

EXAMPLE **6.5**

If a melodic line to be played by both instruments in unison is of solo quality, the word *soli* may be written in at the beginning of it. The direction "a2," by the way, is never used for passages in which the two instruments play *different* parts; in such cases no indication is needed since it is quite obvious that both instruments are playing.

Although the terms *divisi* and *unisono* are appropriate in band music where a whole section of flutes or clarinets is to divide or unite, in an orchestra these terms are used only for strings, never for winds.

When one instrument of a pair is already playing and the other enters, it is customary to label the entering voice as being 1. or 2. and to show at what dynamic level it should enter. All dynamic markings must be shown beneath each staff, of course, just as with strings. Occasionally a second dynamic marking is shown *above* the staff when the first of the pair is to play at a different dynamic level from the second.

TONGUING AND SLURRING

In performing on a wind instrument it is possible to articulate each note with a separate *tu*[1]—in which case the note is said to be "tongued"—or to slur it with the note that precedes or follows. Where no slur mark is pre-

EXAMPLE **6.6**

Third Symphony

Brahms

Allegro con brio

Ob

p grazioso

---

[1]Or variations of this syllable, such as *du, ta,* and *da,* depending on the instrument, the register, and the effect involved.

sent, the note is to be tongued. For instance, in Example 6.6 the first two notes are slurred together, the next two are slurred, the next four are slurred, the next note is tongued separately, and so on. But there is no break in sound between the last note of each slurred group and the note that follows; the general effect is *legato*. For an even smoother, more *legato* effect, the whole passage could have been slurred together. Or if an articulated effect had been wanted, the passage might have been written entirely without slurs (each note tongued separately). And there are possibilities other than the one shown that involve alternate slurring and tonguing. When repeated notes occur, they must be tongued (though not necessarily sharply) in order to sound with a fresh attack. For example:

EXAMPLE 6.7

However, slurs plus dots or slurs plus a line above or below each note are sometimes used to indicate a "soft tonguing," even with repeated notes:

EXAMPLE 6.8

The notation in Example 6.8(b) would imply a kind of pressure on each note, with less separation between notes than in the case of the dots.

In some scores, phrasing rather than slurring is shown in the woodwind parts. But since phrasing and slurring are indicated in exactly the same way, players are frequently in doubt as to which is which. All things considered, it seems best to show slurring. If necessary, breathing points between phrases may be indicated by the same symbol used in vocal music: '.

A question that often arises is, When strings and woodwinds play the same melodic line, what is the relationship between bowing in the strings and slurring in the winds? There is no hard and fast rule to follow here. In some cases the slur marks in the woodwinds will correspond to the bowing slurs in the strings, and certain composers use this approach more or less consistently. Certainly a general unity of *effect* is desirable; for example, a sharply *marcato* passage would undoubtedly call for separate bows in the strings along with separate tonguings in the woodwinds. But there are many cases in which the actual slurrings in the two sections will not be the same. Sometimes, for instance, several measures of a wind part will be slurred together, whereas the strings will need to change bow a good many times within the course of these measures.

In double-tonguing the player rapidly alternates *tu* and *ku:*

EXAMPLE 6.9

109

In triple-tonguing the pattern is *tu tu ku* (or *tu ku tu*), which is suited to music involving triplet figures. Both types of tonguing are useful in articulating passages that are so fast that single-tonguing would be impractical. Both are easy and effective on the flute but impractical on the clarinet and bassoon. Although most orchestration books speak of them as being out of the question for the oboe as well, some skilled oboists are able to achieve them.

Flutter-tonguing (German: *Flatterzunge*), once an exotic special effect, has become almost commonplace today. To produce it the player executes a rapid roll with the tongue. The result is a kind of whir that may be applied either to sustained tones or to melodic lines. Strauss and Stravinsky, in particular, were fond of using it for very rapid scale passages. The indication is usually the same as that for unmeasured tremolos in the strings (three lines through the stem) plus the word *flutter-tongue* written in. Sometimes, especially in very fast passages, the indication *flutter-tongue* alone suffices. The effect is well suited to the flute and piccolo, possible (though less easily produced and rarely used) on the clarinet, and extremely difficult on the oboe and the bassoon.

There are two matters involving attack and release in wind instruments that need to be mentioned. The first is the *fp* or *sfp* effect, in which the tone is started with a strong attack and then reduced in volume immediately. After that, it may be sustained at a constant dynamic level or allowed to diminish even more (*fp, diminuendo*) or made to increase in volume (*fp, crescendo*). In any case, the *fp* marking indicates an effect rather than a particular degree of volume and may be used at any dynamic level, from very soft to very loud. This device is, of course, not the exclusive property of the woodwind and brass sections, for the strings and the percussion also make frequent use of it.

The other matter is a point of notation that arises constantly in orchestral scoring. In piano and vocal music, sustained tones followed by a rest are usually written 𝅗𝅥 ▬ or 𝅗𝅥. 𝄾 or 𝅝 | ▬, etc. A more usual plan in the orchestra is to write 𝅗𝅥 ♪ 𝄿 𝄾 or 𝅗𝅥. ♪𝄿 or 𝅝 ♪ 𝄿 𝄾 ▬, the sustained tone being tied into the beginning of the next beat. If the first notation is used, players tend to differ as to the exact point at which they release the note (since it is difficult to cut off the sound on the last fraction of a beat), and a ragged effect is likely to result when a group is involved. The second notation gives an easier and more definite cutoff point and consequently leads to a cleaner, more unified release. Of course there are cases where, for harmonic or other reasons, it would be inappropriate to tie the notes into the next beat; but for the most part this system is preferable not only in woodwind writing but in the strings, brass, and percussion as well.

Muting possibilities in the woodwinds are few and seldom used. Because of the flute's construction, muting is not possible. The clarinet can reduce its tone to the merest whisper anyway and consequently has no need for a mute. With the oboe it is possible to achieve a muted effect (chiefly on the notes 𝄞 o ———to——— o) by inserting a chamois or cloth into the bell.

110

However, this system has a tendency to throw certain notes out of tune. An example of muted oboes can be found in the closing measures of Stravinsky's *Petrouchka*. Muting of the bassoon can be accomplished in the same fashion or with an actual mute, and although this effect is seldom called for specifically in scores, some bassoonists employ a mute in very soft passages to reduce the volume of tone in the lower register of the instrument, especially between 𝄢 and 𝄢 One disadvantage of this arrangement is that it makes the bottom B♭ unplayable.

SPECIAL EFFECTS

In recent years many new performing techniques on woodwinds have been developed. Some of these techniques will be presented next, with the knowledge that certain ones will soon be absorbed in the mainstream of orchestral usage—as such earlier "novelties" as flutter-tonguing have been—and that they will then no longer belong in the "special" category. Because it is not possible to give a satisfactory description of the sound of these effects, it is suggested that readers who have a particular interest in them arrange for demonstrations.

Multiphonics.   The most frequent method of production calls for the use of special fingerings and embouchure techniques that cause a note and one or more of its partials to sound simultaneously. However, because the same fingering may produce different results on different instruments, it has so far been impossible to set up a standard set of fingerings. Attempts to do so, such as those in Bruno Bartolozzi's *New Sounds for Woodwind,* have been controversial. Some composers simply indicate that a multiphonic sound is desired at a certain point and let the player work out a satisfactory sonority. A different way of producing multiphonics involves playing one note and humming another. The two pitches that result may, in turn, produce sum or difference tones. For comments on this effect in connection with the horn, see the Special Effects section in Chapter 8.

Microtones.   These may be specified as a quarter tone, a third tone, and so on, lower or higher than the "true" pitch or simply lower or higher, the player determining the degree. They have long been used in non-Western music and in jazz, where they are often introduced by the player even when there is no indication for them in the music. They are achieved by various means (depending on the instrument) involving the mouth, tongue, throat, mouthpiece, reed, special fingering, or—in the case of the flute—the angle of the instrument in relation to the player's mouth. (Suggestions concerning the possible notation of quarter tones were given in the Microtones section of Chapter 4.) Sometimes the player is directed to start with the normal pitch and then make the tone progressively sharper or flatter. (The "bend" technique frequently seen in commercial music is an example of the latter.)

Key slaps.   These include pad slaps and fingers slapping the open holes of flutes.

Key clicks. The keys are operated noisily so that the clicking is audible.

An abnormally fast or abnormally slow vibrato. Also, a change from one type of vibrato to another; or a complete absence of vibrato (*senza vibrato*).

Special attacks, releases, or changes in the quality of sustained tones. These are produced by forming an indicated consonant or vowel with the mouth while playing. Symbols from the International Phonetic Alphabet are preferred for this purpose (e.g., [k] for a particular attack effect, [t] for a particular release effect, [ɛ] for a particular sustained sound). This device is most effective on the flute. Sometimes the flutist is directed to make a kissing sound at the mouthpiece.

Air tones. Air is simply blown through the instrument, producing either a distorted pitched tone or no tone at all.

Breath tones. These are a type of air tone limited to the flute and piccolo.

Whistle tones. A very small stream of air is directed into the flute, producing a soft, *sotto voce* effect.

Playing on the head joint of a flute or piccolo (detached from the rest of the instrument). Obviously, little variation in pitch is possible unless some small cylindrical object that will fit into the end of the mouthpiece is moved in or out.

Speaking, whispering, or singing through the instrument. In *Night of the Four Moons* George Crumb indicates "Speakflute," an effect (marked "ghostly") in which the words are whispered over the flute mouthpiece while the player fingers given pitches. "A faint pitch echo should sound under whispering," say the directions. A *tongue click* is also called for. See Example 5.6(c).

"Smack" tones. These are possible only on the double-reed instruments and involve an unorthodox, noisy application of the mouth to the reed.

Playing on the reed of a double-reed instrument alone. The result is a crude squawking sound, although some changes in the tone can be produced by cupping the hands around the reed in various positions.

Subtones. These are playable on the clarinet and saxophone and are useful in achieving an extremely soft tone (though one that is easily covered) in the lower register. The direction is simply *subtone* or *sotto voce*.

Timbral variation. On woodwinds, the same pitch can often be obtained by two different fingerings, each producing a slightly different quality. Specific fingerings are therefore sometimes indicated for the sake of introducing color variety. The same principle applies to *timbral trills,* in which the same pitch is produced alternately and rapidly by two different fingerings. Because there are technical limitations involved in this effect, consultation with a player is advised.

Double trills.   In some cases, a trill can be produced by both hands at once. Again, technical considerations make consultation with a performer a necessity.

SCORING FOR WOODWINDS IN PAIRS

The same chorale excerpt used earlier for examples of string scoring has been selected for purposes of illustration here:

EXAMPLE **6.10**

At the start we will focus on a woodwind section consisting of two flutes, two oboes, two clarinets, and two bassoons. First, let us examine the ranges of the voices and see what instruments can take them (ruling out for the moment the possibility of transposing the excerpt). The bass can be taken only by the bassoon, for that voice goes too low for any of the other instruments. The tenor can be taken by the other bassoon or by a clarinet (the latter in its dark *chalumeau* register). The alto, with its B at the end, is too low for most flutes, and even if we were sure of having a flute with the low B on it, that register of the instrument is so weak that good balance would be very hard to achieve. Although the alto is within the range of the oboe, the oboe's low B tends to be a bit coarse in quality; consequently the clarinet would be a better choice for that voice. The soprano can be taken by flute, oboe, or clarinet, though it would be relatively weak on the flute. Here are some possible scorings:

EXAMPLE **6.11**

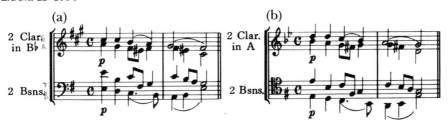

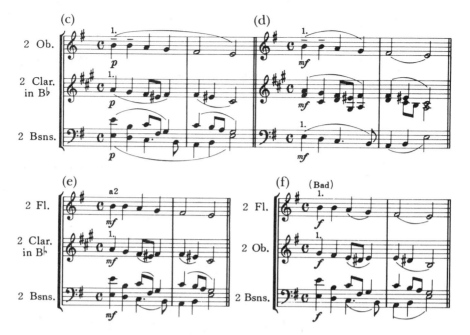

Versions (a) and (b) would sound alike. In (b) clarinets in A have been used instead of B♭ clarinets, and the bassoons have been written in the tenor clef.

Versions (c) and (d) differ from the preceding ones in that the top voice in the oboe will stand out sharply from the other voices below. Any separate color on a part will tend to produce that result, but the distinctive oboe tone has a particular way of asserting itself.

In version (e) two flutes are used on the melody to give more body in the weak lower register of the instrument and to bring about better balance.

Version (f) has been included as an example of what *not* to do. The oboe would outweigh the flute in that register and would be too prominent in character for an inner voice. The doubtful quality of the low B has already been mentioned.

Various slurrings have been used here for purposes of illustration.

Assuming that there is no reason why we must retain the original key, transposition will give us a good many new possibilities. By placing certain of the instruments higher in their range, we can arrive at better resonance and blend (see Example 6.12).

One undesirable feature of (a) and of some of the other versions in Example 6.12 is the fact that the oboes play the interval of a 4th in a sustained chord (at the end). This is not a good plan as a rule because the incisive oboe color accentuates the "bareness" of the 4th; 6ths or 3rds sound much better. But if we are to give the two top voices to the oboes here, there seems to be no way of avoiding the 4th except by changing the original voice-leading in the cadence and (in [a], for example) having the second oboe go from F♯ up to G (instead of down to D), thus omitting the 5th of the chord.

EXAMPLE 6.12

The objections that applied to version (f) in Example 6.11 do not apply to (c) in Example 6.12 because the oboe is in a sweeter, thinner register and because the flute is better able to assert itself in this higher version. Even so, the flute has been marked one degree louder than the other instruments to make doubly sure that it comes out clearly on the melody.

Version (d) in Example 6.12 involves the use of mixed colors (flute plus oboe) on the two top parts, whereas we have used mostly pure colors previously. Notice that two clarinets and two bassoons are indicated here for the sake of proper balance. It would have been possible to mix clarinet and bassoon colors on the tenor and bass parts, also.

So far we have used only the original four-voice structure, with no octave doublings. Doublings of the soprano or of all three upper voices an octave higher will allow the flutes and clarinets to play in a much brighter, more telling register:

EXAMPLE 6.13

In Example 6.13(a) the melody is doubled an octave higher in the flutes, while the first oboe doubles the melody in unison with the first clarinet. In (b) the alto and tenor are both doubled an octave higher (in the clarinets); the melody is doubled an octave higher in the flutes. In (c) the melody, alto, and tenor are all doubled an octave higher, and the melody is doubled an octave lower in the bassoon. Remember that not all pieces of music lend themselves to a doubling of the melody an octave below the original pitch. In some cases the result would be too thick.

Notice that the clarinets frequently play above the oboes even though they are listed below them on the page. Actually, the strongest register of the oboe is roughly ♯ while the clarinet's brightest and most solid octave is ♯. Therefore, when brilliance and power are called for, it is often better to place the clarinets higher than the oboes.

SCORING FOR A LARGE WOODWIND SECTION

Following are three possible ways of scoring the same chorale excerpt for a woodwind section that includes piccolo, English horn, bass clarinet, and contrabassoon in addition to woodwinds in pairs.[2] Three different gradations of coloring have been aimed at: brilliant, medium, and dark. In Chapter 10, more will be said about color possibilities, woodwind doublings, and various ways of arranging the wind instruments in chords.

EXAMPLE 6.14

---

[2]The alto flute and the E♭ clarinet, less frequently used than the other auxiliary woodwinds, are not included here.

(c)

Picc.

S 2 Fl.

S 2 Ob.
A

T Eng.
   Hrn.

A 2 Clar.
S in B♭

B Bass
   Clar.

T 2 Bsns.
B

B Contra
   Bsn.

Notice that in Example 6.14(b) clarinets in A have been chosen in order to avoid a key signature of six sharps (or six flats) for the B♭ clarinet. Inasmuch as the only bass clarinet in current use is pitched in B♭, we are forced to write its part in either six sharps or the enharmonic equivalent of six flats. The latter key has been chosen here as being slightly preferable for a B♭ instrument.

In the dark version (c) the piccolo has been given rests. Obviously the brilliance of its upper register is not wanted here, and it is so weak and breathy in its bottom octave that in this case there is no point in writing for it there.

The examples that follow show passages for the woodwind section that involve musical situations different from that in the chorale excerpt used earlier in this chapter. Although the principles that govern the scoring of homophonic and contrapuntal music are not discussed until Chapters 12 and 16, respectively, much can be learned about those aspects from a study of these and succeeding examples.

EXAMPLE 6.15

(a)   Prelude to *Die Meistersinger*

*B stands for B♭ in German.

(b)   Fourth Symphony

(c) *Concerto for Orchestra*

Bartók

Note: *The score also includes soft string trills that are not shown here.*

(d) Variations

Stravinsky

Note: *This is a "C score"; that is, all instruments are written as they will actually sound. The use
of bass clef for the English horn is decidedly unusual.*

SUGGESTED ASSIGNMENTS

A. Know:

1. instruments involved in the woodwind section in a chamber orchestra and in a
   full orchestra.
2. arrangement of the woodwinds on the page—order and grouping.
3. indications for showing whether the first or second of each pair is to play or
   whether both are to play.
4. indications for slurring, tonguing, and phrasing.

5. principles of balance in the woodwind section.
6. ways of achieving brilliant or darker coloring in woodwind scoring.

B. The following are suitable as exercises in scoring for woodwinds:

1. Bach, any of the chorales. Select a short phrase from one of these and score it: (a) in three different ways for woodwinds in pairs, using no octave doublings; (b) in two different ways for full woodwind section, using octave doublings.
2. Beethoven, Sonata, Op. 2, No. 1, 3rd movt. Omit trio.
3. Beethoven, Sonata, Op. 2, No. 3, 3rd movt., meas. 1–36.
4. Beethoven, Sonata, Op. 7, 3rd movt., meas. 1–24.
5. Beethoven, Sonata, Op. 53, 1st movt., meas. 196–211.
6. Beethoven, Sonata, Op. 106, 2nd movt., meas. 1–46.
7. Schubert, Sonata, Op. 122, 1st movt., meas. 1–28.
8. Chopin, Prelude in A major, Op. 28, No. 7.
9. Mendelssohn, Song Without Words No. 41 (A major). Score for large woodwind section.
10. Schumann, "Burlesque" from *Album Leaves; Vogel als Prophet.*
11. Tchaikovsky, "A Winter Morning" from *Album for the Young.*
12. Mussorgsky, "Tuileries—Children Quarreling at Play" from *Pictures at an Exhibition.*
13. Debussy, "The Little Shepherd" from *The Children's Corner.*
14. MacDowell, "From Uncle Remus" from *Woodland Sketches.*
15. Hindemith, "Fuga Secunda in G" from *Ludus Tonalis.*
16. Křenek, *20 Miniatures,* No. 7.
17. Ginastera, *12 American Preludes,* Nos. 8, 9.

SUGGESTED LISTENING

Woodwinds

Mozart, Divertimentos and Serenades for woodwinds.
Beethoven, Violin Concerto, 1st 9 meas.
Mendelssohn, *Scherzo* from *Midsummer Night's Dream* music, beginning and other portions.
Tchaikovsky, Fourth Symphony, 3rd movt., *Meno mosso* section (middle).
Rimsky-Korsakoff, *Russian Easter* Overture, beginning (rare unison doubling of all woodwinds).
Wagner, Overture to *Die Meistersinger,* meas. 122–134 (E♭ major, *Im mässigen Hauptzeitmass*).
Strauss, *Don Quixote,* Variation I (imitation of rural band).
Mussorgsky-Ravel, *Pictures at an Exhibition, Promenade* preceding Part II ("The Old Castle"); Part III ("Tuileries"); *Promenade* preceding Part V; Part V ("Ballet of the Chicks in their Shells").
Stravinsky, *Symphony of Psalms,* Fugue, beginning; *The Rite of Spring,* beginning; *Petrouchka,* number 13 (page 22 in Kalmus edition) and following; Variations.
Bartók, *Concerto for Orchestra,* Part V (Finale), meas. 148–175 (*fughetta* beginning with bassoon solo).
Copland, Third Symphony, 3rd movt., end; 4th movt., beginning.
Lutoslawski, *Mi-parti,* figures 16 and 40.
Messiaen, *Chronochromie,* figure 30, many other passages.

7

The Horn

THE HORN

Italian: Corno   *French:* Cor   *German:* Horn
          Corni   Cors   Hörner

The term French horn is seldom used by musicians. The instrument is referred to simply as the horn, and that name is sufficient even in scores. Actually, it is difficult to understand why the adjective *French* was ever included in the name, since the development of the modern horn centers as much on Germany and Austria as on France.

In order to understand the workings of the horn, we must know something about the basic principles on which brass instruments operate. Whereas most of the woodwinds make use of a reed, brass instruments do not, but instead involve a mouthpiece and an air column vibrating sympathetically with the player's lips. Fractional vibrations of the air column produce overtones, and a certain number of these may be made to sound by proper use of the breath and lips. The fundamental or generating tone itself is either difficult or unobtainable on most brass instruments. If the length of tubing is altered by means of valves (or a slide, in the case of the trombone), a new set of overtones results. For purposes of initial tuning, each brass instrument is equipped with a "tuning slide" that enables the player to vary the basic tube length of the instrument somewhat.

Although in construction and technique of performance the horn is clearly a brass instrument, its tone is capable of blending almost equally well with either woodwind or brass, and it is very often used as if it were a member of the woodwind family. Its bore is substantially conical in shape, with the result that its sound is less sharp-edged and incisive than those of the trumpet and trombone, which have essentially cylindrical bores.

THE NATURAL HORN

Being basically hunting horns and valveless, the horns of Haydn's and Mozart's day could play only the notes of one harmonic series at a time, plus a few rather uncertain intermediary tones made possible by the insertion of the hand in the bell of the horn and/or by "lipping." Parts for the instrument were therefore extremely limited from a melodic standpoint; stepwise passages could be written only within a relatively small pitch area in the upper portion of the harmonic series, and chromatic passages were out of the question altogether. To cope with the problem of music in different keys, a system of "crooks" was in use, a crook being a piece of tubing which could be inserted into the tubing of the horn to alter the pitch of its fundamental tone and thus create a new harmonic series. The crook to be chosen was indicated by a direction at the beginning of the work or movement: "Horn in E♭" or "Horn in A," and so on, as the case might be, and the part was invariably written in the key of C. The written notes of the harmonic series usable on the horn were as follows (numbered on the basis of partials):

EXAMPLE 7.1

The fundamental, or first partial, was normally unplayable. Audibly "out-of-tune" notes (according to our system of tuning) are shown in black. The eleventh partial, for example, was really something between an F and an F♯ and could be humored so as to produce either note. Of course the actual sound of the horn's notes depended on the crook being used. Table 7.1 shows how the instrument sounded when crooked in various keys (and notated in treble clef).

Horns in other keys (E♭-alto, C-alto, B-alto, F♯, D♭, B-basso and A-basso) were called for only rarely. Horn in F♯ appears in Haydn's *Farewell* Symphony and horns in G♭ and D♭ (among numerous others) in *Carmen*.

Normally, parts for the natural horn were written in the treble clef. But in the rare cases where the bass clef was employed, a curious and illogical custom applied: the pitches were notated an octave lower than they would have been notated in the treble clef. That meant that they were *lower* than the concert pitches by the inversion of the interval that figured in the normal treble-clef transposition. For instance, in the bass clef, horn in D was notated a major 2nd lower than the sounds instead of a minor 7th higher, horn in F a perfect 4th lower instead of a perfect 5th higher, and so

TABLE 7.1

HORN IN	SOUNDING
B♭-alto*	a major 2nd lower than written
A	a minor 3rd lower than written
A♭	a major 3rd lower than written
G	a perfect 4th lower than written
F	a perfect 5th lower than written
E	a minor 6th lower than written
E♭	a major 6th lower than written
D	a minor 7th lower than written
C	an octave lower than written
B♭-basso*	a major 9th lower than written

*Alto and basso are used here to mean "high" and "low" respectively.

on. Example 7.2 shows the notation of a specific pitch for horn in E♭ in treble and bass clefs, respectively:

EXAMPLE 7.2

This system of notation in bass clef is no longer used, as will be explained shortly.

Here is an excerpt from a horn part of the Classical period:

EXAMPLE 7.3

Sixth Symphony

which will sound:

Another characteristic passage for natural horns is shown next:

EXAMPLE 7.4

Overture to *Der Freischütz*

C. M. Von Weber

During the Classical period the usual practice was to employ one pair of horns, pitched in the home key. However, if the music was in minor, a second pair pitched in the key of the relative major was occasionally added to supply certain important notes that were not available as members of the harmonic series in the home key. Also, the device of using two pairs of horns pitched in different keys was sometimes used even in major keys to provide richer possibilities in writing for the horns or to allow for modulations. In Example 7.4, for instance, the composer included a second pair of horns crooked in F. By alternating and combining the two pairs, he was able to employ the horn timbre throughout the *Adagio* at the beginning of the overture. With only one pair that would have been impossible.

We are told that in the day of the natural horn the player kept an assortment of crooks hanging on his arm in order to be prepared for necessary changes! Fortunately for player, composer, and audience, the introduction of valves revolutionized the technique of horn playing and the type of part that could be written for the instrument. Instead of having only one harmonic series at a time to work with, the horn boasted seven different series (the results of various combinations of the three valves), and a complete chromatic scale was available for the first time. As a result, the horn achieved the status of a real melodic instrument. Although the invention of valves occurred in 1813, the valve horn did not come into general use until about the middle of the nineteenth century, and even then the natural horn continued to be used with it for many years.

THE MODERN VALVE HORN IN F

EXAMPLE 7.5

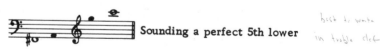

Sounding a perfect 5th lower

Of the many horns once employed, the horn in F seems to have proved the most satisfactory, and it has survived, with valves added, as the one horn in general use today. When parts written originally for the natural horn are played on it, players must transpose as they go—unless, of course, the original part happened to be for horn crooked in F.

Most players now use the so-called double horn (see Figure 7.1). That instrument has two sets of tubing, one in F and one in (high) B♭; a lever

FIGURE 7.1

Studio Gilmore, Austin, Texas

The Modern French Horn

enables the player to switch instantaneously from one to the other. Because of its shorter tubing, the B♭ horn (that is, the B♭ part of the double horn) allows for greater facility. But its use is entirely optional with the player, and the transposition problems involved in switching to B♭ horn are the player's concern; the part is always written as if for F horn—a perfect 5th higher than the sounds desired. Although the B♭ horn is capable of producing certain very low pedal tones not available on the F horn, these have seldom been exploited.

Other horns that have come into increasing use are the "triple horn" and the descant horn. The triple horn is in F, B♭, and F alto (an octave higher than the commonly used F tubing). Two valves operated by the left thumb enable players to choose which "horn" (i.e., set of tubing) they prefer to use for a given passage. The descant horn is in B♭ and F alto. The chief purpose of these two horns is to increase accuracy in the high register.

A professional hornist may choose one of these instruments to perform such works as Bach's *Brandenburg* Concerto No. 1 because of several florid high passages, or the second movement of Haydn's Symphony No. 51 in B♭, which contains a horn solo that extends to the twenty-first partial. Only a few professiona! horn players are likely to own either of these instruments, however.

Traditionally, horn parts have been written without key signatures, sharps and flats being written in wherever necessary. But it is possible nowadays to use a key signature, and that plan would seem to be a sensible one in scoring music of a diatonic nature. Enharmonic notation (for example, the key of D♭ instead of C♯ major) is not uncommon in horn parts.

Concerning notation in bass clef, the old custom of writing the F horn a 4th lower than the concert pitches was abandoned some years ago, and the current practice is to write the part a 5th higher in bass clef as well as in treble. Examples of the two systems of notation follow:

EXAMPLE 7.6

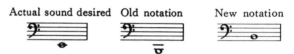

Because players have become used to the old system, it is wise to include a note in scores and parts whenever the new system is employed to the effect that notes in bass clef are intended to sound a 5th lower. However, the bass clef is little used since it is needed only for extremely low tones. Horn parts should be written in treble clef wherever possible, even if several ledger lines below the staff are involved.

In its bottom register, up to about the written note the horn is inclined to be a bit unsolid in quality, somewhat lacking in focus, and often doubtful in intonation. This register is useful chiefly for sustained tones; melodic passages at this level are generally awkward and ineffective. From up to about (written), the tone is considerably brighter. This is the middle and most characteristic register, in which the horn does the greatest part of its playing. From to the top , the notes become progressively more brilliant. Just as the high notes of a tenor voice sound much higher than they would if sung at the same pitch by a soprano, the top notes of the horn give the impression of being extremely high because the player must strain somewhat to get them. Notes above written are difficult to produce, and the player should not be asked to attack them without preparation. Because they are extremely difficult to play softly, it is better not to write for the horn in this register unless it is meant to be heard prominently.

Among the four horns commonly used in the orchestra today there is a certain "division of labor." In order to understand this point we must first become acquainted with the traditional arrangement of the horns in harmonic passages. Horns I and II are normally written on one staff and horns III and IV on the staff below. One might naturally suppose that in writing a four-note chord for horns, the two highest notes would be given to horns I and II and the two bottom notes to horns III and IV. But this is where tradition steps in and dictates a different procedure: The horns are written so as to interlock on paper; that is, horns I and III take the high notes, horns II and IV the low notes. For example, if we were to score an F major triad  for four F horns, it would look like this:

EXAMPLE 7.7

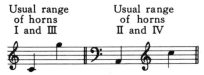

Even when only the first three horns are playing, horn III is generally placed between horns I and II (in a chord).

The basis for this practice may be traced to the use of two pairs of natural horns. Since each pair of horns was crooked in a different key, each first player was, naturally, a "high" player and each second player a "low" player. It was not at all uncommon for natural-horn players to travel about in pairs seeking employment in court orchestras.

Because the first-horn and third-horn players are accustomed to taking the higher notes, they have become specialists in this upper register; likewise, the second-horn and fourth-horn players are especially adept at taking lower pitches. Consequently we might divide the general written range given earlier in this chapter into two "usual" ranges, one for each pair of horns:

EXAMPLE 7.8

A tight, tense lip is required for high pitches, whereas lower notes call for a much looser embouchure. There is, therefore, a definite advantage in being able to concentrate on one general type of embouchure instead of having to switch constantly from one kind to another. Of course there is a middle ground (roughly from written) in which all the horns can play equally comfortably. And it must not be inferred from this talk of specialization that each pair of horns is never asked to exceed its own "usual" range. Particularly in passages where all four horns play in unison, the second and fourth are often taken quite high along with the first and third, and it is possible, though rare, for the first or third horn to play in the very low register.

The horn is not by nature a particularly agile instrument. Very fast running passages and quick leaps are simply not in its province except, with limitations, in virtuoso solo work. And because the player must "hear" each note in the mind's ear before playing it, the melodic lines written for the instrument should be as smooth as possible and should avoid awkward leaps. There should be sufficient rests. Since the horn is undoubtedly one of the most difficult of all orchestral instruments to play, scoring for it must be approached with special care and understanding.

Horns may be employed in various ways in the orchestra. The most important of these are:

1. *On harmony parts.* In its middle register, the horn tone is ideal for background because it can be made unobtrusive without losing warmth or body. Usually these harmony parts are sustained, although sometimes they consist of repeated notes or repeated short figures. Incidentally, repeated notes on the horn do not sound as sharply articulated as do repeated notes on some other instruments. The effect is more that of a pulsation on the pitch involved. Example 7.9 shows the horns in a typical harmonic role. (The melodic line in the violins has been included in order to show how the harmony parts fit into the general musical scheme; there are many other instruments playing.)

EXAMPLE 7.9

Symphony in D minor

Simply because the horns can handle this sort of part so successfully, there is a temptation to use them constantly in this way, with a resulting monotony of color and general effect. It is largely this frequent use of the horns on middle-register harmony parts that gives orchestral music of the Romantic period its characteristic plushy richness.

2. *In a solo capacity.* The horn is excellent as a solo instrument. It can be tender or heroic, as the music demands, and it possesses a wonderful nobility and breadth of tone all its own.

EXAMPLE 7.10

(a) Third Symphony

(b) Fifth Symphony

(c) *Siegfried*

(d) *Till Eulenspiegel*

3. *Two or more horns in unison on a melodic line.* Horns are frequently doubled on a part, sometimes for purposes of volume or balance, occasionally to give a greater degree of security in difficult passages. All four horns playing in unison, *f* or *ff*, give an especially robust, heroic sound.

EXAMPLE 7.11

(a) Ninth Symphony (*New World*)

(b) *Don Juan*

(c) *Arcana*

Note: *Horns in bass clef sounding a perfect 4th higher than written.*

In cases where horns I and III play one melodic line and horns II and IV another for a considerable length of time, it may be easier to write I and III on the upper staff and II and IV on the lower, with an "a 2" indication on each staff. In that way, only two melodic lines instead of four need be written for the horns.

The chamber orchestra usually includes one horn, the small orchestra one or two. Although four is the standard number employed today, it is possible, of course, to use only three if that number seems best fitted to the demands of the music in question. In most symphony orchestras there are five horn players on the stage. This does not mean that there are five separate horn parts. The extra performer is an "assistant first horn" player who sits beside the first horn player and doubles that part at times for added security or volume; or the fifth player may play some of the part for the first horn player when the latter has important solo passages to follow.

Certain works are actually scored for more than the standard four horns. For example, Stravinsky calls for eight horns in *The Rite of Spring,* where the proportions of all sections are unusually large; and the orchestra used by Wagner in the *Ring* includes eight horns, four of them alternating with Wagner tubas.

It might be well to include some comment on Wagner's horn notation, for it is likely to be confusing—and understandably so. The horn parts are intended to be played on valve horns, yet they are written as if for a succession of natural horns pitched in different keys. For example, we may have a passage for horn in E♭, then a few measures for horn in C, then a passage marked "Horn in F," and so on. Carse explains this seemingly contradictory situation as follows: "The valves acted, in fact, as a quick way of changing the crook, and players began to realise the advantage of playing on an instrument of one particular tube length. . . ."[1] As helpful as Carse's explanation is in understanding this transitional period in the horn's history, the presumed logic of the notational approach in question seems to be weakened by one feature: though nominally "in" a certain key,

---

[1]Adam Carse, *Musical Wind Instruments* (1939).

the horn player was often assigned as many notes outside the harmonic series of that key as notes within it. For example, a typical three-measure passage for horns in F from *Götterdämmerung* contains B♭, D♭, E♭, and G♭; it is difficult to understand how, in such a case, there was any advantage to the player in being told that the part was "in F"—or in any one key. Although this system may initially have appeared reasonable to hornists of that day (especially while natural horns were being used along with valve horns), from today's vantage point it seems peculiarly ill-suited to Wagner's music with its constantly shifting tonal centers and intense chromaticism. In view of the fact that horn players converted to the F horn as a chromatic instrument long before composers stopped using the old "various-keys" notation, one wonders why the conversion to writing for the F horn could not have occurred much sooner—to everyone's benefit.

In most of the preceding examples, the horn took the chief musical idea. But it can be equally effective on subordinate countermelodies. Several horns in unison may even be allotted to such a part if considerable volume and a broad, virile effect are in order.

SPECIAL EFFECTS

The tone quality of the horn is controlled chiefly by the position of the player's hand in the bell of the instrument. Normally, the hand is inserted only part-way into the bell and cupped. But there are special effects which demand a slightly different technique. Stopping, for example, may be achieved by inserting the hand farther into the bell, whereas muting is normally achieved by the use of an actual mute made of metal, wood, or cardboard. Orchestrators should be specific about which of these two effects they desire. As with the strings, at least a measure or two in moderate time should be allowed for putting in or taking out mutes. The muted effect is indicated in French by *sourdine* and in German by *mit Dämpfer* or *gedämpft*. When a return to the unmuted tone is wanted, the direction is *senza sordino* or "open" (*ouvert* in French, *offen* in German). Muting cuts down the volume of sound and veils the tone slightly. An excellent example of muted horns can be found in the closing measures of Debussy's *Prelude to The Afternoon of a Faun*.

Stopped notes on the horn are produced by inserting the hand (or a special mute) so far into the bell that the opening in it is almost completely blocked, the tones being forced out. The resulting sound is nasal and metallic, with a sharp edge to it. It is especially effective for single notes, played *fp*. A safe lower limit for stopped notes is the (written) G♭ below middle C, though lower pitches are possible with a stopping mute.

In both muting and stopping, the volume is reduced, and unless a nontransposing mute is used the pitch is raised a semitone. But the player will make the necessary adjustment; it need not concern the orchestrator. Stopped and muted tones are notated in the same way as open tones as far as pitch is concerned.

There are two methods for indicating the stopped effect, either or both of which may be used. In the first method, the French word *bouché* (or simply *stopped* in English) is written in. The German equivalent is *gestopft*, the Italian, *chiuso*. In the second method, a small cross is placed above each note to be played stopped. If a passage involving open tones follows, a small o is placed over each note to cancel the stopped effect. This method is most frequently employed when stopped and open tones occur in close juxtaposition. In the following example both methods are present.

EXAMPLE 7.12

Capriccio Espagnol

Another much-used direction in horn writing is the French word *cuivré*, meaning "brassy." The brassy quality is attained chiefly by increased tension of the lips and is possible in connection with open, muted, or stopped notes. *Bouché-cuivré*, a composite term often encountered, calls for a tone that is both stopped and brassy. Where only a suggestion of brassiness is wanted, Debussy marks the passage *cuivrez légèrement* (literally translated, "brass lightly").

Bells in the air (pavillons en l'air in French, *Schalltrichter auf* or *Schalltrichter hoch* in German) is a rarely used effect for which the horn is turned with the bell pointing either outward or upward so that the sound is projected toward the audience more directly than in the normal playing position. Inasmuch as the hand is not used in the bell here, the tone is completely open and lacking in any subtlety of coloring. *Bells in the air* is therefore appropriate only for loud, hearty passages in which refinement of tone is not called for.

The horn has an uncanny ability to sound as if it were being played a great distance away. When that effect is wanted, the part should be marked *pp* or even *ppp*, and the word *lontano* (Italian for "distant") may be added. To achieve this effect, some players employ a partly stopped tone; others stop completely; still others play open but extremely softly.

One of the most successful sounds available on the horn is the *fp* effect mentioned earlier. Used with a stopped tone, it has a biting, almost snarling quality; in open horn it is dramatic and arresting.

EXAMPLE 7.13

(a)   Fifth Symphony

(b)   Symphony in B minor (*Unfinished*)

Glissandos, which produce a loud, upward rush of sound, are sometimes seen in contemporary scores. They may be written so as to involve any portion of any harmonic series, provided they do not start lower than 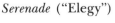 or end higher than . One example may help to give an idea of the usual notation:

EXAMPLE 7.14

The Rite of Spring

Sometimes a line between the two outer notes, plus the direction "gliss.," suffices.

In French scores one sometimes encounters the term *sons d'écho.* When this effect is called for, the horn player inserts the hand in the bell in such a manner as to extend the tube length, thereby *lowering* the pitches a semitone. To compensate for this, the composer directs the player to finger all pitches a half step higher than written. The resulting timbre is remote and haunting.

EXAMPLE 7.15

The Sorcerer's Apprentice

In the last two measures of Example 7.16 very slow semitone glissandos between the notes are achieved by moving the hand into the bell from the normal position to a point just short of the fully stopped position, and then withdrawing the hand to the normal position. These respective motions lower and raise the pitch a semitone. The hand glissando is very colorful here because while the cellos sustain the root and fifth, the horn wavers back and forth between the major and minor third. Incidentally, even professional horn players may have trouble producing the initial high C *pianissimo.*

EXAMPLE 7.16

Serenade ("Elegy")

By using alternative fingerings, the horn player is capable of producing quarter tones in some parts of the range. Thea Musgrave has used this device in her Horn Concerto.

SUGGESTED ASSIGNMENTS

A. Know:

1. the extreme possible range of the horn and the usual ranges of horns I and III and horns II and IV.
2. transpositions (including the old system of notation in the bass clef).
3. differences between the old natural horn and the modern valve horn, both as to their operation and the type of part written.
4. the color and weight of the horn in various registers.
5. the particular abilities and limitations of the horn.
6. special effects on the horn and foreign names for them.

B. Find five examples of parts for horns in keys other than F, and rewrite them for F horn (a few measures will suffice for each example). Write the original version above and the rewritten version on a staff below it.

SUGGESTED LISTENING

Horns[2]

Bach, Brandenburg Concerto No. 1, 1st movt., 3rd movt., Minuet II.
Haydn, Symphony No. 51, 2nd movt., finale.
Mozart, Symphony No. 40 (K. 550), 3rd movt., Trio.
Weber, Concertino for Horn and Orchestra, Op. 45, (cadenza includes an early example of one type of multiphonic).
Beethoven, Third Symphony, 3rd movt. (*Scherzo*), Trio.
Mendelssohn, Nocturne from *Midsummer Night's Dream* music, beginning.
Brahms, Second Piano Concerto, beginning; First Symphony, last movt., beginning of *Più Andante* section; Third Symphony, 3rd movt., meas. 40–52 and 98–110; Fourth Symphony, 2nd movt., beginning and many other passages.
Tchaikovsky, Fifth Symphony, 2nd movt., beginning.
Rimsky-Korsakoff, *Capriccio Espagnol,* section II ("Variazioni"), beginning.
Dvořák, Ninth Symphony (*New World*), 1st movt., beginning of *Allegro molto* following introduction; last movt., 11 bars after figure 6, also numerous other passages.
Strauss, *Don Juan,* measure 311; *Till Eulenspiegel,* meas. 6; Waltzes from *Der Rosenkavalier,* especially beginning.
Mahler, Third Symphony, beginning.
Debussy, *Prelude to The Afternoon of a Faun,* 5 bars after figure 5 to the end.
Ravel, *Pavane pour une Infante Défunte,* beginning.
Shostakovich, Fifth Symphony, 2nd movt., at figures 54, 56, 70, and 72.
Hanson, First Symphony, 2nd and 3rd movts. in particular.

---

[2]Examples of the horns in conjunction with the rest of the brass section are included in the Suggested Listening section at the end of Chapter 9.

Britten, *Serenade for Tenor, Horn and Strings,* Op. 31.
Stravinsky, *Requiem Canticles,* "Libera me."
Musgrave, Concerto for Horn and Orchestra, horn parts throughout (both solo and orchestral) *Night Music.*
Ligeti, *Melodien,* meas. 71–91.

8

The Trumpet,
Trombone,
and Tuba

THE TRUMPET

Italian: Tromba
Trombe

French: Trompette
Trompettes

German: Trompete
Trompeten

THE BAROQUE TRUMPET

In order to understand the trumpet parts in certain works of Bach and his contemporaries, it is necessary to know that at that time there existed the art of "clarino playing," which involved producing the very high partials of the instrument. Trumpet parts often extended to the sixteenth harmonic (four octaves above the fundamental) and occasionally even higher. Festive Baroque works for chorus and orchestra, such as Bach's *Ein' Feste Burg* and Handel's *Messiah,* almost always included two or three trumpets and two timpani. When trumpets were employed, Baroque composers usually preferred to write for three. The first and second trumpet parts were true "clarino" parts, florid and often contrapuntal in nature. Trumpet III, referred to as *principale* or *tromba principale,* played a line that often closely resembled (or duplicated) the timpani part in a higher octave. The following example suggests the flavor of such parts:

EXAMPLE 8.1

Mass in B Minor (II. "Gloria")

No. 4
Vivace

Bach

Tromba I in D

Tromba II in D

Tromba III in D

Timpani in D, A

This timpani part illustrates the now obsolete custom of employing tonic and dominant notes in the key of C to represent tonic and dominant notes in any key.

The trumpet was also frequently used as an *obbligato* instrument for vocal arias. "The Trumpet Shall Sound" from Handel's *Messiah* is a famous example. Bach's Cantata No. 51 (*Jauchzet Gott in allen Landen*) is scored for soprano, trumpet, strings, and continuo. The outer movements of this work feature extensive counterpoint between the soprano soloist and the trumpet.

The trumpet most often used for parts such as these was pitched in D (sounding a major 2nd higher than written). It was over seven feet in length (coiled or folded), twice the length of the modern trumpet in D; its harmonic series was therefore one octave lower than that of its modern counterpart. To illustrate this, Example 8.2 shows the same written pitches for both instruments along with their corresponding harmonic numbers. (For purposes of this comparison, only partials that occur in the harmonic series of both instruments are shown below. Several playable partials are omitted from the clarino trumpet's harmonic series.)

EXAMPLE 8.2

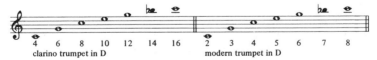

4   6   8   10   12   14   16   2   3   4   5   6   7   8
clarino trumpet in D   modern trumpet in D

Because the high notes are much lower in the modern D trumpet's harmonic series, they are somewhat easier to perform with accuracy. Modern trumpets in D and E♭ are frequent choices for performing the high trumpet parts of the eighteenth century. (Information about these trumpets is given in Chapter 18.) A recently developed piccolo trumpet in B♭, pitched one octave above the standard B♭ instrument, has also found favor among trumpet players for the performance of these parts. It should be noted that there is a considerable difference in timbre between the Baroque and the modern instruments. The latter is much more brilliant, assertive, and penetrating than the eighteenth-century instrument it has replaced.

The change in musical style that took place during the last half of the eighteenth century resulted in the disuse and eventual disappearance of the art of clarino playing. Classical trumpet parts are much more limited in range, function, and versatility than Baroque parts. It was not until the end of the nineteenth century that the trumpet regained anything approaching the prominence it enjoyed in the Baroque era.

THE CLASSICAL TRUMPET

Much of what was said in the preceding chapter about the natural horn applies to the natural trumpet as well. The latter's repertoire of written notes was also limited to certain members of the harmonic series on C, and crooks of different lengths were used to produce the desired pitches in various keys. As with the horn, the fundamental was unplayable on most trumpets; but in addition, the second partial was too doubtful in intonation to be usable, and after the mid-eighteenth century, the notes above the twelfth partial were seldom called for. Thus the written notes normally available on the trumpet during the Classical period were the following, numbered here on the basis of partials:

EXAMPLE 8.3

Unlike the natural horn, the natural trumpet could not fill in certain intermediate tones by the use of the hand in the bell, nor could it adjust the intonation of the seventh and eleventh partials by that method. Nevertheless, the latter notes were sometimes called for, and in such cases whatever correction of intonation was possible had to be accomplished with the lips. As a result of all these considerations, the natural trumpet was even more limited than the natural horn in the type of part it could play.

In the eighteenth century, crooks were used with trumpets of various sizes; by the early nineteenth century the trumpet in F had become more or less standard as the one to which crooks were added. When crooked in F, it sounded a perfect 4th higher than written. That possibility and those involving the crookings then available are shown in Table 8.1. Since there were not crooks for all keys, it was sometimes necessary to use a trumpet pitched in a key other than that of the music. For example, in the case of a composition in G, a trumpet in some other key (most often C) had to be employed if trumpets were to be included. Of course it was possible to omit them altogether if the key presented too many problems. Occasionally a composer elected to use a trumpet in a key other than that of the composition even when a trumpet in the proper key was available. For instance, Beethoven's Seventh Symphony in A major uses trumpets in D, presumably to avoid a combined crooking.

TABLE 8.1

	TRUMPET IN	SOUNDING
SOUNDING HIGHER THAN WRITTEN[1]	F	a perfect 4th higher than written
	E	a major 3rd higher than written
	E♭	a minor 3rd higher than written
	D	a major 2nd higher than written
	C	as written
SOUNDING LOWER THAN WRITTEN	B	a minor 2nd lower than written
	B♭	a major 2nd lower than written
	A	a minor 3rd lower than written

Example 8.4 shows a typical trumpet part of the Classical period:

EXAMPLE 8.4

Symphony No. 101

It can be seen that such parts necessarily tend to be repetitious and uninteresting melodically because of the limited number of notes available. Occasionally the natural trumpet was able to take portions of themes that happened to fit the harmonic series, as in the excerpt from the *Eroica* Symphony shown in Example 8.5.

EXAMPLE 8.5

Third Symphony

But the limitations of the instrument are all too apparent here. Beethoven apparently preferred not to risk taking the part up to a high written

---

[1]An easy way to remember which trumpets sound *higher* than written is to bear in mind that these are the ones pitched in keys that are closest to C when placed *above* it (e.g., the D a major second above C is closer to it than the D a minor seventh lower).

G in the third measure and had it descend to the lower octave of the theme instead. From the fifth measure on, the notes of the melody are not all available in the trumpet's harmonic series so that if the instrument is to continue playing, it must take other pitches that fit in. The most serious problem, however, is illustrated in the third measure from the end. There the second trumpet should logically go down a whole step from the E to the D and then to C in octaves with the first trumpet. However, a supertonic harmony is sounding at this point, and the closest available pitch in the harmonic series is the written D played by the first trumpet. The second trumpet leaps up a seventh to this note and then down a ninth in the following measure. The harmony in this bar is a secondary dominant of V, and once again, the only available note in the harmonic series below the first trumpet is that played by the second trumpet. (Note that the pitch played by the trumpets in this bar is the chord seventh and that it cannot resolve to the third of the dominant in the last measure of the example.) The alternative in such cases was, of course, simply to let the trumpet drop out for a beat or two at the points where it had trouble supplying an appropriate note, and that was sometimes done. But such an approach was likely to lead to a fragmentary and unsatisfactory part.

THE EARLY VALVE TRUMPET IN F

EXAMPLE 8.6

Sounding a perfect 4th higher

It was the F trumpet commonly used in Beethoven's day to which valves were added to produce the first valve trumpet that gained acceptance. This was apparently the only one of the "old family" (that is, the large type) to survive in valve form. Parts for it are found in many late nineteenth-century scores by such composers as Franck, d'Indy, Bruckner, Mahler, and Strauss.

At the same time, parts for trumpets in other keys of the crooks continued to appear. Presumably these parts were transposed and played on the valve trumpet in F, although there is uncertainty on this point (just as there is uncertainty as to whether all the parts labeled F trumpet were actually played on *that* instrument).

In any case, the much smaller trumpets in B♭ and C succeeded the valve trumpet in F and are standard today.

THE MODERN VALVE TRUMPET

EXAMPLE 8.7

In B♭, sounding a major 2nd lower.
In C, sounding as written.

142

FIGURE 8.1

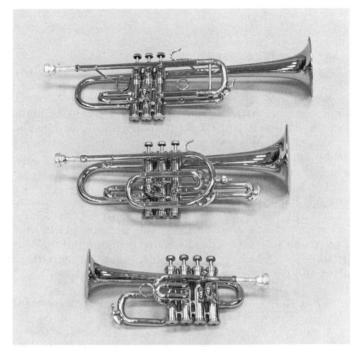

Dorf Photography, Austin, Texas

**Trumpet
Cornet
B♭-A Piccolo Trumpet**

The modern trumpet (see Figure 8.1) is far more flexible than its ancestor, and the tone is lighter. As Forsyth says, "It is not merely that the instrument has become chromatic. It has also become, except in name, a different instrument."

The modern trumpet in its open form has a written harmonic series an octave higher than that of the natural trumpet. The other series available by means of valve combinations have as their bottom notes the six semitones below middle C, respectively. In each series the seventh partial (not shown in Example 8.8) is flat and is normally avoided. The notes playable in the seven valve positions are shown in Example 8.8. The numbers below each series indicate the valve(s) depressed.

EXAMPLE 8.8

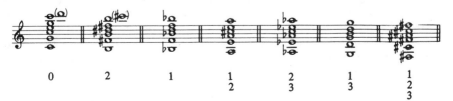

Passages written in the following register can be troublesome if very fast and prolonged.

EXAMPLE 8.9

The problem centers on the use of the third valve in combination with other valves. A half-step trill on written middle C, for instance, would require the alternation of a note that is "open" (no valves depressed) with a note played by depressing all three valves (see Example 8.8). Such a trill is very awkward to perform and produces a most unsatisfactory sound. Likewise, fast and technical passages that consistently require similar valve combinations are apt to sound clumsy. Such passages in this register are better avoided.

The C trumpet has now replaced the B♭ trumpet as the standard orchestral instrument. Its tone is a bit more brilliant and incisive than that of the B♭ trumpet. In *school* orchestras, however, trumpet parts continue to be written for the B♭ instrument.

From about [music example] is the trumpet's most used register. Notes below the C tend to be a little less penetrating, while those above the G are more difficult to produce softly and are best led up to. Although high D is given as the top note possible, symphonic trumpet parts rarely go higher than C, and it must be remembered that entrances above B♭ are extremely difficult.

At this point, readers who have had some experience with trumpet playing in jazz bands may object that the upper limit given here for the trumpet is too conservative. It is perfectly true that some jazz trumpeters go up to [music example] or even higher. But they usually achieve these very high notes only at the expense of tone quality; the shrillness that goes with this pitch level would normally be inappropriate in the symphony orchestra.

Obviously the trumpet is a much more agile and quick-speaking instrument than the horn. It can manage runs and arpeggios and skips as long as they are not extremely fast, but such passages should not be too extended or too frequent. Its use in fanfares is such a familiar and natural one as scarcely to require comment. (See the Beethoven and Strauss excerpts in Example 8.10.) Rapid repeated notes and double-tonguing and triple-tonguing are particularly well suited to the character of the instrument; even flutter-tonguing is possible. Along with the trombone, the trumpet is capable of tremendous volume and has extraordinary powers of crescendo. Although it lacks the noble warmth of the horn, it has a bright, incisive quality that is especially effective in crisply assertive passages. However, on occasion it may effectively take a lyrical melody.

The trumpet and the cornet must not be thought of as being one and the same instrument. Although the tube lengths of the two instruments are the same, the shape of the cornet is different (see Figure 8.1). The most important physical difference is the relative position of the conical and cylindrical portions of the tubing. The cornet is seldom employed in symphonic music today. Its tone is a bit mellower and more romantically colored than the trumpet tone, though it can be made to sound very much like the latter. Nineteenth-century French composers were particularly fond of the instrument, and their scores often called for two cornets (*pistons*) in addition to two trumpets. Cornets, like trumpets, may be pitched in B♭ or (rarely) C; the B♭ instrument is standard in band work. Everything possible on the trumpet is possible on the cornet, and the two instruments have the same range.

Muting is a frequent and effective device in orchestral trumpet writing—effective as long as it is not used too often or for too long a time. To the symphony player, *mute* means the straight mute unless another kind is indicated. The straight mute, made of wood, fiber, plastic, or metal, produces a cutting, nasal quality and reduces the volume of tone somewhat. So far, the many other types of mutes used in jazz or commercial music have been less used in serious symphonic music. Some of these are the harmon, the cup, the bucket, the solotone, and the whispa mutes, most of which are pictured in Figure 8.4. There is also the possibility, usable with either open or muted trumpet, of pointing the bell of the instrument into a hat or a music stand to achieve a more subdued tone. The direction is simply "hat" or "in stand." Still another device is the use of a "plunger," which may be used to cover the bell; the resulting sound alternating with the open sound

is used to produce a "doo-wah" effect, notated ♩ ♩ ♩ ♩ . The hand may be

used instead of a plunger for this effect. (Figure 8.4 on page 158 illustrates the various mutes used for brass instruments.)

EXAMPLES

EXAMPLE 8.10

(a) *Leonore* Overture No. 3

(b) *Scheherazade*

(c) *Ein Heldenleben*

(d) *An Outdoor Overture*

(e)   A Symphony of Three Orchestras

Carter

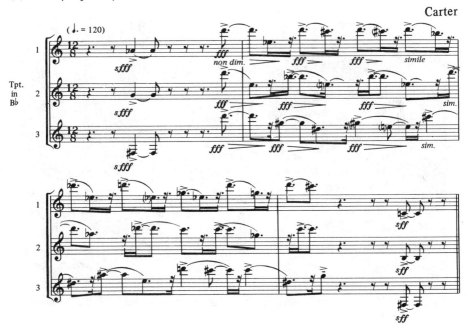

THE TENOR TROMBONE

Italian: Trombone   *French:* Trombone   *German:* Posaune
        Tromboni   Trombones   Posaunen

EXAMPLE 8.11

Pitches down to the low C are possible with an F attachment.

As a rule, instruments pitched in keys other than C are transposing instruments. Not so with the tenor trombone. Although built basically around the harmonic series of B♭, it sounds as written. It may be notated in either bass or tenor clef, the latter being commonly chosen for higher passages in order to avoid the use of too many ledger lines. (In music for school orchestras, however, trombones rarely use the tenor clef.) The alto clef, found in some older scores, is almost never employed for the trombone nowadays. It is a holdover from the period when the alto trombone was in common use. (That instrument is finding some use today in brass choirs.)

FIGURE 8.2

Studio Gilmore, Austin, Texas

Bass Trombone   Some have   F attachments   in
Tenor Trombone

wind   ensemble. trombone   sounds
as written

The mechanism of the trombone differs radically from those of the horn and the trumpet in that it includes no valves.[2] Instead, the length of tubing is varied by means of the slide. Seven different positions of the slide are possible, each one producing a different harmonic series. The seven fundamentals or generating tones of these series are shown in Example 8.12.

EXAMPLE 8.12

The first of these "pedal tones," the B♭, is easily playable and is seen frequently in commercial scoring, much less often in symphonic music. Below that, the notes become increasingly difficult to produce and insecure in quality; A♭ or G is the bottom limit for most tenor trombonists. In any case, pedal tones below the B♭ are called for only rarely.

---

[2]Valve trombones have had a considerable vogue abroad, notably in Italy. Although they are sometimes used by jazz musicians in the United States, they have never had any wide acceptance in American symphony orchestras.

The notes available in the series on E, known as seventh position, are as follows:

EXAMPLE 8.13

The seventh partial (sixth overtone) in each position is slightly flat. However, it can be brought into tune by an adjustment of the slide.

In sixth position the notes playable are

EXAMPLE 8.14

and so on, up to first position, where additional overtones may be used to stretch the upper range a bit higher:

EXAMPLE 8.15

By adding a B♮ and C♯ at the top of the second position, we get a complete chromatic scale up to the second F above middle C as a possible range. But notes above ⎯⎯⎯ are more difficult and are rarely used in orchestral parts.

Many tenor trombones are equipped with a so-called F attachment, a device that lowers the fundamental pitch of the instrument a perfect fourth from B♭ to F by adding extra tubing. When the F valve is depressed, entirely new sets of harmonic series are possible in the various slide positions. The pitches shown in Example 8.16 are the second harmonics of these sets. Of course higher partials are available in each slide position as demonstrated in Examples 8.13 through 8.15.

EXAMPLE 8.16

I II III IV V VI   with F slide extended to E
                         (or with E valve on Bass Trombone)

In addition to expanding the range of the instrument downward, the F attachment also simplifies technical problems by eliminating certain awkward changes of position. (See Example 8.18.)

In music for the trombone, it is not so much distance between pitches as distance between positions that determines the technical difficulty of the part. A little reflection will make it clear that certain notes can be taken in two or more different positions. For example, on a tenor trombone without

an F attachment the possibilities for playing 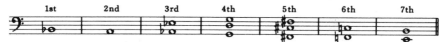 are first position (series on B♭); fourth position (series on G); or seventh position (series on E). The player can choose whichever position is easiest. With three choices, one of them is bound to be close to the position already in use, and such cases should cause no difficulty. But certain notes, such as those in Example 8.17, can be taken in only one position.

EXAMPLE 8.17

For the seventh position the slide is extended its full length; for first position it is drawn up as far as possible in the other direction. Therefore, very rapid or repeated changes from first position to seventh position (or vice versa) are awkward and are better avoided. Occasional changes of this sort, when not too fast, are acceptable. Less difficult are changes involving such other distant positions as the second and sixth, but frequent use of them in a rapid tempo naturally does not make for idiomatic trombone writing.

In order to illustrate what *not* to write for the trombone, we have devised the diabolically awkward passage shown in Example 8.18. (The numbers above the notes refer to the positions involved without the F attachment.) An actual performance of this by a trombonist will show very graphically why such changes as these are best avoided. The passage is much easier on a trombone with an F attachment. Slide positions for that instrument are shown *below* the example. The F valve is depressed for all positions except those circled.

EXAMPLE 8.18

Because the notes of the harmonic series lie closer together in the trombone's upper register, the whole problem of position becomes less acute there and the instrument therefore has a greater degree of agility in that register than it does in the lower positions of its compass.

The trombone's lowest register is dark and full, and the entire range up to the B♭ above middle C is solid and effective; the notes become progressively more brilliant toward the top.

A basic problem in trombone playing is the difficulty of achieving a completely legato effect when a change of slide is involved. If the air column were kept vibrating continuously, the result would be not only the intended notes but a glissando between each two of them as the slide moved from one position to another. Consequently, the player must stop the air column momentarily between notes. To give the effect of a legato connection under these circumstances would seem to be impossible, yet experienced trombonists succeed in doing it surprisingly well, especially at softer dynamic levels. The gap between notes is so slight as to be scarcely apparent to the ear. (Of course two notes in the same harmonic series, such

as 𝄢 o and 𝄢 ♭o , require no change in the position of the slide

and can therefore be played *legatissimo* by means of a lip slur.

In its most familiar role, the trombone is an instrument that excels at loud, heroic passages. But it can also play softly, either on the chief musical idea or as background; this side of its nature is too often forgotten. Rapid running passages and light, fanciful parts that skip around a great deal are obviously not well suited either to trombone technique or to trombone quality. However, the instrument can play rapid repeated notes, including double- or triple-tonguing, and *short* figures that move quickly. Flutter-tonguing is also effective.

Muting on the trombone works just as it does on the trumpet, and the effect is relatively the same. Even though the mute cuts down the volume somewhat (in addition to altering the quality), the muted trombone can still hold its own in a *tutti*.

The glissando effect mentioned earlier is normally avoided; but there are times when it is used purposely. The usual indication in the part is a line between the notes to be connected plus the abbreviation *gliss*. The largest interval that can be performed as a glissando is a tritone because this interval represents the full extent of the slide from first to seventh position. Glissandos must be carefully examined to ensure that they are playable without changing the direction of the slide.[3] As illustrated in Example 8.19, every pitch in the glissando must have the same harmonic number or the glissando will not work.

EXAMPLE 8.19

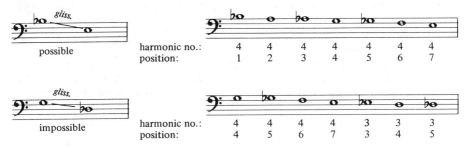

---

[3]Although it is possible to "fake" a glissando over a larger interval than the augmented fourth, the change in direction of the slide and the resulting break in the sound are almost always noticeable.

Glissandos need not cover a wide interval to be perceived.

Lip trills between adjacent harmonics that are a whole or a half step apart are possible and effective:

EXAMPLE 8.20

The Firebird (1910 version)

In Example 8.20, the second trombone plays a trill on the eighth and ninth harmonics in sixth position. Trombone I trills between the eighth and ninth harmonics in second position (or the ninth and tenth harmonics in fourth position). Although both parts are notated in alto clef here, this clef is found only in pre-twentieth-century scores and occasionally in modern Russian scores.

"Trigger trills" (valve trills) between some notes a whole or a half step apart are also possible. For these trills, the F valve is rapidly depressed and released while the slide remains stationary. To determine whether a trigger trill is possible, one must compare the two harmonic series available in one slide position with and without the F valve depressed. In Example 8.21, the first five harmonics on F and B♭ are shown.

EXAMPLE 8.21

first position (F valve)   first position

Notice that the fifth harmonic on F is a half step from the fourth harmonic on B♭. Because both of these pitches are played in the same position, a half-step trill on A is possible by using the F valve. These trills are similar in speed and quality to horn trills. Valve trills should not be employed in the extreme low register.

Although the trombone was employed as early as 1600 or so by Gabrieli and was later used by Mozart, Gluck, and others in opera, its first appearance in an actual symphony occurred in Beethoven's Fifth Symphony.

THE BASS TROMBONE

Italian: Trombone
basso

French: Trombone
basse

German: Bassposaune

EXAMPLE 8.22

Possible with an E attachment.

At one time there was a complete family of trombones: alto, tenor, bass, and contrabass. The alto and contrabass instruments are used infrequently, and the bass trombone in F (or G) has fallen into disuse, at least in the United States. For their bass trombone (see Figure 8.2), most orchestras now use a large-bore B♭ trombone equipped with an F valve and often one other valve that may be pitched in E, E♭, or recently G or G♭. These extensions are valuable because they make the low B-natural easily playable and thus provide a complete chromatic range above the first position B♭ fundamental (pedal tone). They are also useful because they can increase technical facility by providing even more alternate positions for pitches in the low register. Furthermore, they increase, quite dramatically in some instances, the low range of the bass trombone. The G♭ valve, for instance, is becoming increasingly popular with professional bass trombonists. When this valve is depressed, the harmonic series shown in Example 8.23 is available in first position:

EXAMPLE 8.23

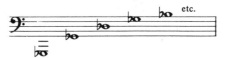

On this particular instrument, the F tubing and the G♭ tubing are "in line." That is, either valve may be depressed independently, putting the instrument in F or G♭, or the two valves may be depressed simultaneously, putting the instrument in D. When both valves are depressed, the tubing is lengthened considerably, and the harmonic series shown in Example 8.24 results:

EXAMPLE 8.24

When the slide is fully extended[4] with both the F and G♭ valves depressed, the pitch produced is

8va bassa

As of this writing, however, instruments with this extended low range are not in general use, and one had better limit bass trombone parts to the range given in Example 8.22. Moreover, the tuba is the brass instrument that would normally play orchestral brass parts in this extreme low register.

The bass trombone is usually made with a larger bell than the tenor trombone. Often it plays the bass, alone or in unison or octaves with the tuba. Although its upper range is theoretically the same as that of the tenor trombone, bass trombone parts involve a lower tessitura and seldom go above the F shown as the top practical note. Traditionally they use only the bass clef. Pedal tones are possible, as on the tenor trombone, and the bass trombone is, in fact, more often called upon to play them.

EXAMPLES

EXAMPLE 8.25

(a)   First Symphony

Note: *Here the complete scoring (except for timpani) is included to show how the bassoons, contrabassoons, and horns are combined with the trombones to complete the harmony.*

---

[4]Because of the increased length of tubing and the resulting longer distances between positions, only six slide positions are available to the trombonist when playing with the F, E, or E♭ valves depressed. Only five positions are possible when using the G♭ valve and the F valve simultaneously.

(b) Overture to *Tannhäuser*

(c) *Petrouchka*

(d) *Chemins IIb*

© Copyright 1973 by Universal Edition (London) Ltd., London. Used by permission of European American Music Distributors Corporation, sole U.S. agent for Universal Edition.

(e) Symphony: *Mathis der Maler*

Reproduced by permission of Schott & Co., Ltd., London.

THE TUBA

Italian: Tuba   *French:* Tuba   *German:* Tuba (*or* Basstuba)

EXAMPLE 8.26

155

FIGURE 8.3

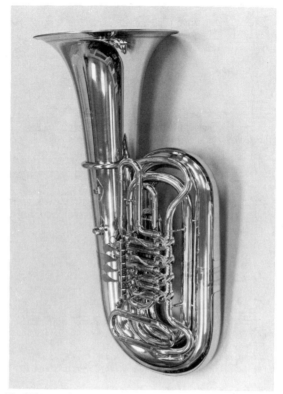

Dorf Photography, Austin, Texas

Tuba

Tubas in various keys are employed in the orchestra, those in C, F, and BB♭ being the ones most favored today.[5] The choice of instrument rests with the player and is determined by the range of the part, fingering problems, and personal preference, among other things. All the tubas are non-transposing (i.e., sound as written) and virtually all tubas used in the orchestra have four or more valves. Although they differ slightly as to range, it seems unnecessary to catalog the individual ranges here since in writing a tuba part we can be governed by the composite range just given and since all tubas are capable of playing within the practical range shown.

The tuba seldom has occasion to go very high inasmuch as the notes in the upper part of its register are as a rule better given to trombone or horn.[6] The extremely low notes, those below the low F, tend to be weaker

---

[5]The double letters (presumably derived from the usual designation for notes in the "contra" octave) are commonly used to indicate the lower of two instruments pitched in a given key. Thus "BB♭" avoids possible confusion with a B♭ tuba pitched an octave higher. Although tuba players often speak of the "CC tuba" as well, technically the single C is correct.

[6]An exception is the amusing passage from Stravinsky's *Petrouchka,* quoted at the end

and less solid in quality and are better avoided. The fundamental is obtainable on each of the tubas but is practical only for brief sustained tones.

For such a large instrument the tuba is perhaps more agile than might be expected. Though there are definite limits to the speed and complexity of the parts it can play, double- and triple-tonguing are entirely feasible. Even flutter-tonguing has been used on occasion, as in Schönberg's *Erwartung.* Orchestral scores rarely call for these techniques, however.

The most important thing to consider when writing for the tuba is that it requires the expenditure of a great deal of breath in performance. In the lower register at *forte,* a single note can be sustained for only about four seconds. The performer who is faced with a situation such as the one that occurs in the finale of Tchaikovsky's Symphony No. 6, a *fortissimo* pedal E that extends over nine $\frac{3}{4}$ measures at *Moderato assai,* must break the sustained tone at several points in order to breathe. Parts for the instrument, then, should not be too continuous and should include sufficient rests.

The tone quality of the instrument has been both praised and maligned in orchestration books. Our experience is that with a good instrument and a good player, the tuba tone can be unusually velvety and pleasant in soft passages, robust and exciting in a *forte* or a *fortissimo.* It differs from those of the trumpet and trombone in being rounder and less cutting. This difference results partly from the fact that the tuba is essentially conical in bore. Also, the tuba bore is relatively larger than that of the other brass instruments (the horn included).

Muting of the tuba is a device that is employed only rarely. An example occurs in the introduction of Strauss's *Don Quixote.* (Brass mutes are shown in Figure 8.4.)

The most frequent use of the tuba in the orchestra is as a bass for the brass section, but it can also be used to strengthen the double basses or lower woodwinds. On rare occasions it can take the bass alone or play a solo part.

Because it has so often been combined in unison with the double bass and the contrabassoon, both of which sound an octave lower than written, students sometimes insist that the tuba should use the same transposition. But its part should be written at its actual pitch.

EXAMPLES

EXAMPLE 8.27

(a) Prelude to *Die Meistersinger*

of this section, where the tuba in its extreme upper register gives exactly the right "lumbering" effect for a dance by a trained bear.

FIGURE 8.4

Dorf Photography, Austin, Texas

BRASS MUTES

Back row (from left):	**Tuba:** mute; *Trombone:* straight, cup, solotone, harmon (no stem), bucket
Middle row (from left):	**Trumpet:** straight (piccolo trumpet), straight, cup, solotone, harmon (stem part-way out), bucket; *Horn:* transposing mute, mute
Front row (from left):	**Trumpet:** plunger mute (may be used with or without plunger), plunger

(b) *Siegfried*

Wagner

Tuba

f dim. *p* *p*

Note: *The tuba is used here to personify Fafner, the dragon.*

(c) *Don Juan*

Strauss

Tuba

f espress. *ffp*

158

(d) *Petrouchka*

Stravinsky

(e) *St. Thomas Wake*

Peter Maxwell Davies

Example 8.27(e) is unusual because of the wide range involved and the use of the tenor clef beginning in measure 8. The passage is exceptionally difficult, and only professional players should be expected to perform it.

THE OPHICLEIDE

Certain nineteenth-century scores, including some by Wagner, Berlioz, Mendelssohn, Verdi, and Schumann, contain parts for the bass ophicleide. This was "the bass of the Keyed-Bugle," as Forsyth puts it, a metal instrument with a broadly conical upright bell and of "coarse, powerful tone." It customarily played bass parts in the orchestra until about the middle of the nineteenth century, when the tuba began to supplant it. Since it is now obsolete, parts written for it are played by the tuba.

SUGGESTED ASSIGNMENT

Know:

1. harmonic series through the sixteenth partial beginning on any pitch.
2. characteristics of the clarino trumpet.
3. ranges of the trumpet, trombone, and tuba.
4. transpositions where involved.
5. principles involved in the positions on the trombone and in the various harmonic series available on the other brass instruments by means of different valve combinations.
6. colors and relative weights in different registers.
7. abilities and limitations.
8. possibilities for muting and special effects.

SUGGESTED LISTENING

Trumpet (Clarino Parts)

Bach, *Lobet Gott in seinen Reichen,*[7] first and last choruses.
Bach, *Mass in B Minor,* "Gloria in excelsis Deo."
Bach, *Jauchzet Gott in allen Landen,* first aria, chorale.
Handel, *Samson,* "Let the Bright Seraphim."
Handel, *Dettingen Te Deum,* "We Praise Thee, O God," "Thou Art the King of Glory."

Trumpet

Beethoven, *Leonore* Overture No. 3, meas. 272.
Wagner, Prelude to *Parsifal,* meas. 9; *Siegfried,* scenes of Mime; *Die Meistersinger,* scenes of Beckmesser (latter two are examples of *muted* trumpet).
Scriabin, *The Poem of Ecstasy,* 4 bars after figure 32; many other passages.
Mussorgsky-Ravel, *Pictures at an Exhibition,* opening "Promenade"; also Part 6 ("Samuel Goldenberg and Schmuyle"), figure 58 (muted trumpet).
Strauss, *Ein Heldenleben,* fanfare section, figure 42; *Don Quixote,* figure 3 (muted trumpets).
Debussy, *Nocturnes:* II. "Fêtes," 9 bars after figure 10 (3 muted trumpets).
Ravel, *Daphnis and Chloe* Suite No. 2, 2 bars before figure 204.
Respighi, *Pines of Rome,* 2nd movt., last movt.
Stravinsky, *The Rite of Spring,* 4 bars before figure 84 (muted).
Stravinsky, *Pulcinella,* VIII (a) Minuetto, VIII (b) Finale.
Stravinsky, *Agon,* meas. 1–60, 124–131, 278–285.
Bartók, Piano Concerto No. 2, 1st movt.
Bartók, *Concerto for Orchestra,* 2nd movt. at meas. 90, Finale at meas. 234.
Bloch, *Schelomo,* figure 5.
Copland, *An Outdoor Overture,* meas. 16.
Copland, Third Symphony, fanfare section near beginning of 4th movt. (figure 85).
Carter, *A Symphony of Three Orchestras,* figure 9 to figure 34, figure 329, many other passages.
Henze, Sixth Symphony, many passages (score includes piccolo trumpet).
Ligeti, *Melodien,* meas. 84–99.

Cornet

Berlioz, *Harold in Italy,* 2 bars after figure 4. Compare cornet and trumpet parts 19 bars before figure 7.
Stravinsky, *Petrouchka,* scene 1, "The crowds," 4 bars after figure 69.

Trombone

Mozart, *Requiem,* "Tuba Mirum."
Berlioz, *Roman Carnival Overture.*
Wagner, Overture to *Tannhäuser,* letter A; *Die Walküre,* "The Ride of the Valkyries."
Rimsky-Korsakoff, *Russian Easter Overture,* letter M.

---

[7]This cantata appears in Volume 3 of the Telefunken series of recordings of the Bach cantatas using original instruments or reconstructions of original instruments. It is highly recommended listening, for the trumpets employed in the recording closely approximate in timbre and "weight" those used in Bach's time.

Tchaikovsky, Fourth Symphony, last movt., meas. 84; Sixth Symphony, last movt., letter L.

Strauss, *Salome*, closing scene (muted trombone).

Mahler, Third Symphony, 1st movt., figure 33.

Sibelius, Seventh Symphony, 1st movt., letter L.

Stravinsky, *Pulcinella*, VII Vivo, VIII (a) Minuetto; *Petrouchka*, figure 112.

Stravinsky, Variations, meas. 74.

Schönberg, *Five Pieces for Orchestra*, Op. 16, 1st movt.

Bartók, Violin Concerto, meas. 593 (2nd "Fine").

Berio, *Chemins IIb*, 2 bars before letter A.

Penderecki, *De natura sonoris No. 2*, meas. 34–55.

Tuba

Wagner, *Siegfried*, beginning of Act II.

Mahler, First Symphony, beginning of 3rd movt.

Mussorgsky-Ravel, *Pictures at an Exhibition*, beginning of Part 4 ("Bydlo").

Strauss, *Don Quixote*, figure 3 (muted tubas), figure 9, etc. (This work illustrates the use of both tenor and bass tubas.)

Stravinsky, *Petrouchka*, 2 bars after figure 100.

Prokofieff, Fifth Symphony, 1st movt. at figure 3 and throughout.

Gershwin, *An American in Paris*, after figure 67.

Revueltas, *Sensemaya*, figure 2.

Shostakovich, First Symphony, 3rd movt., before figures 7 and 20.

Davies, *St. Thomas Wake*, meas. 136–150.

9

The Brass Section

Trumpets are the "melody" instrument of the brass section

1 and 3 horns (SA)   2 and 4 (TB)

The brass section to be used here for purposes of illustration is the average one: four horns, two or three trumpets, three trombones, and tuba.

An accepted axiom in scoring for brass is this: if the dynamic marking is *mf* or louder, two horns are needed to balance one trumpet or one trombone; below that dynamic level, one horn will give satisfactory balance. Consequently we must know just how loud a passage is to be before we can score it properly for brass. In the examples that follow, various dynamic markings have been assumed.

The horns have been written in some cases without key signature (the traditional way) and in others with key signature (which seems the more sensible way here). As in the examples for woodwinds, different possibilities in slurring are shown.

Once again we have elected to use the chorale excerpt that has served for illustration in earlier chapters:

EXAMPLE 9.1

Jesu, meine Freude

Bach

Example 9.2 illustrates some of the many ways in which the passage can be scored for brass instruments.

EXAMPLE 9.2

Version (c) shows how the instruments are usually arranged in scoring for a brass quartet.

Although the arrangement of the horns in (f) may appear to be a natural and workable one, it is actually not too satisfactory. The range in most four-voice music is such that the first horn is apt to be taken uncomfortably high, while the fourth horn is so low that it may become weaker and unsolid. With good players, this sort of arrangement is possible in certain pieces; with school groups or less experienced performers, it had better be avoided.

Unlike the versions in Example 9.2, those in 9.3 use keys other than the original, and all but (a) include octave doublings.

EXAMPLE 9.3

In Example 9.3(c) the upper octave of the chorale melody has been given to two trumpets in order to bring it out more strongly than the other voices; in (d) the bottom octave of the melody has been weighted a great deal more heavily than normal balance would require (four horns in unison plus a trombone).

In (d) and (e) three trumpets rather than two are included. Since third trumpet parts are apt to get down into the lower, less penetrating register, it is often a wise idea to reinforce them with a trombone or a horn.

* 3 trombone Tuba often share the same staff.

That has been done in (d) with a trombone, in (e) with a horn. Of course, if the third trumpet part lies fairly high, no such reinforcement is necessary.

In general, trumpets and horns sound better in close spacing (close position) than they do in open. Trombones may also be arranged in close spacing in their middle and upper registers. (If placed quite high, they give an effect of great brilliance.) But since they must often play the lower notes of the harmony, where close spacing would be too muddy, they are seen

about as frequently in open spacing. Such arrangements as  in

three trombones give a fine solid resonance.

Beginning orchestrators often make the mistake of expecting the brass instruments to enter on an extremely high note. Such entrances are risky. Even when successful, they are likely to sound unpleasantly strained and tense. The following written pitches in Example 9.4 might be set as safe upward limits for entrances in horn, trumpet, and trombone, respectively:

EXAMPLE 9.4

Horn   Trumpet   Trombone

Of course higher pitches are practical when the player has a chance to lead up to them instead of having to attack them without preparation.

The excerpt in Example 9.5 shows effective scoring for brass choir alone. The scoring is complete except for two chords for full orchestra, which occur at the two holds.

EXAMPLE 9.5

Symphony: *Mathis der Maler*

Reproduced by permission of Schott & Co., Ltd., London.

In Example 9.6(a) note the careful attention to dynamics and to attacks and releases. Practically every note is provided with a specific articulative or dynamic marking. In Example 9.6(b) Rochberg achieves a very distinctive sound. Compare the register in which each instrument plays relative to the others, and examine the texture and the distribution of instruments on each melodic line throughout the example.

EXAMPLE 9.6

(a) *Zodiac*

Note: *All instruments are written here as they will actually sound.*

(b)

© Copyright 1974 Theodore Presser Company. Used By Permission Of The Publisher,
Letter Dated 7/9/81.

Note: *All instruments are written here as they will actually sound.*

Example 9.7 features the brass in a contrapuntal, imitative texture.

EXAMPLE 9.7

Concerto for Orchestra

Bartók

SPECIAL EFFECTS

Many new methods of producing sounds on brass instruments have been explored in recent music. Descriptions of some of these effects follow.

Some scores have called for performers to remove the mouthpiece and play on it alone, thereby producing a windy, buzzing sound. Most performers can cover an extremely wide range using this technique, and of course a complete pitch continuum from the lowest to the highest sound is possible. Exact pitches can be played, but these may be difficult for performers without absolute pitch. A more resonant mouthpiece "buzz" can be obtained by cupping the hands and blowing through the mouthpiece into them.

By slapping the mouthpiece while it is in the instrument with the palm of the hand, one can create a resonant "pop" that has a definite pitch. However, this cannot be done too forcefully or it may cause the mouthpiece to stick in the leadpipe. Since the number of available pitches produced by this method is limited, the orchestrator should consult with a performer before employing this technique.

Occasionally brass players are instructed to sing, whisper, shout, and blow (without producing a normal tone) into their instruments. These devices seem to produce better results on the larger brass instruments. Multiphonics of one type are produced on brass instruments by playing one note and humming another. Carl Maria von Weber's Concertino for Horn and Orchestra, Op. 45, contains a cadenza that ends with four-part chords for the solo horn—and with good voice leading! (The other two parts of the texture are the result of summation and difference tones.) Although this is one of the earliest instances of notated multiphonics, evidence indicates that performers were aware of the technique and using it long before Weber's time.

By rapidly depressing and releasing the valves (without blowing) in an exaggerated manner, a rattling percussive sound can be obtained. This sound can be made much more pronounced on the trumpet (and tuba, if it has piston valves) by slightly unscrewing the valve caps. The effect is not as striking on rotary-valved instruments. If one or more valves are depressed only half-way and the instrument is blown in the normal fashion, a peculiar, unfocused sound results. It is possible to play a very wide glissando when half-valving.

A very useful timbral resource is playing a single pitch using different fingerings. In Example 9.8, each E has a slightly different color.

Example 9.8

Alternate fingerings do not exist for every pitch on the trumpet (see Example 8 in Chapter 8); so the use of this technique is somewhat limited. Instruments with more than three valves have more fingerings available for more single pitches.

Although it is true that if only one player performs some of these special effects in isolated circumstances the part may seem eccentric or even ridiculous, when eleven or more brass players participate the sound produced can achieve real musical substance. The success of these devices depends, as always, on composers' inventiveness and the power of their ideas—as well as the good will of the performers. Some of the special devices discussed above can be heard in Donald Erb's *The Seventh Trumpet*.

SUGGESTED ASSIGNMENTS

A. Know:

1. makeup of the average brass section.
2. arrangement of instruments on page—order and grouping.
3. principles of balance as applied to the brass section.
4. commonly used "voicings" (in brass scoring).

B. The following are suitable as exercises in scoring for brass:

1. Morley, *My Bonny Lass.*
2. Weelkes, *Hark, All Ye Lovely Saints.*
3. Bach, a short excerpt from any of the chorale harmonizations, to be scored for (a) two B♭ trumpets and two trombones; (b) two C trumpets, one F horn, and one trombone; (c) full brass section, including three trumpets if desired. In this last version, use octave doublings.
4. Bach, *Wachet Auf* (chorale harmonization).
5. Bach, Fugue in G minor, from *Eight Little Preludes and Fugues for the Organ.*
6. Bach, *The Art of Fugue,* Fugue I, Contrapunctus IX, many other portions.
7. Schumann, "Norse Song" from *Album for the Young.*
8. Schumann, "War Song" from *Album for the Young.*
9. Grieg, *Sailor's Song.*
10. Chopin, Prelude in C minor.
11. Franck, *Prelude* from *Prelude, Aria, and Finale,* meas. 1–12, transposed to E♭ major or F major.
12. Mussorgsky, "Promenade," beginning of *Pictures at an Exhibition.*
13. Bartók, Folk Song No. 8, from *Ten Easy Pieces for Piano.*
14. Kabalevsky, Prelude 24 from 24 Preludes, meas. 46–55 (suggests inclusion of piano and percussion as well).
15. Sessions, *From My Diary,* 3rd movt.
16. William Schuman, *Three Score Set,* 2nd movt.

SUGGESTED LISTENING

Brass

Berlioz, *Fantastic Symphony, Roman Carnival Overture.*
Dvorák, Ninth Symphony (*New World*), last movt.
Brahms, First Symphony, last movt., "chorale" section.
Franck, Symphony in D minor, last movt., "chorale" section.
Wagner, Prelude to *Parsifal;* Funeral Music from *Götterdämmerung;* Overture to *Tannhäuser.*
Tchaikovsky, Fourth Symphony, 3rd movt., Tempo I following the *Meno mosso* section; last movt., many passages.
Rimsky-Korsakoff, *Capriccio Espagnol,* beginning of section IV ("Scena e Canto Gitano").
Mussorksgy-Ravel, *Pictures at an Exhibition,* opening "Promenade"; Part 8 ("Catacombs"); Part 10 ("The Great Gate of Kiev").
Janáček, *Sinfonietta,* first and last movements.
Kodály, *Háry János* Suite, Part IV ("The Battle and Defeat of Napoleon").
Bartók, *Concerto for Orchestra,* Part I ("Introduzione"), meas. 342 (about the middle); Part II ("Giuoco delle Coppie"), meas. 123 (middle portion); Part V ("Finale"), meas. 556.

Hindemith, Symphony: *Mathis der Maler,* "Alleluia" at end (brass parts shown in Example 9.5); also many other portions, especially 1st movt.

Stravinsky, *Firebird* Suite, Finale.

Respighi, *Pines of Rome,* last section ("Pines of the Appian Way"); *Roman Festivals.*

Copland, Third Symphony, 2nd movt., beginning; 4th movt., figure 85 to figure 88, figure 126.

Schuman, (William), Third Symphony, Sixth Symphony.

Rochberg, *Zodiac,* sections I, V, VI, IX.

Schuller, *Seven Studies on Themes of Paul Klee,* first and third movts.

Argento, *In Praise of Music,* first, second, and fifth movts.

Erb, *The Seventh Trumpet.*

Shapey, *Praise* (for baritone, chorus, and orchestra).

10

Scoring Chords
for Each Section
and for Orchestra

WOODWIND CHORDS

There are four ways in which instruments of different kinds can be combined in a chord. These are demonstrated here, using woodwinds in pairs. (All notes shown are actual sounds.)

EXAMPLE 10.1

| Juxtaposition* | Interlocking* | Enclosure | Overlapping |

*In Rimsky-Korsakoff's Principles of Orchestration the translator has used the term overlaying rather than juxtaposition and crossing rather than interlocking. Certain other orchestration books refer to interlocking as dovetailing. The terms chosen here are those which seem to offer the least chance for ambiguity or confusion.

Juxtaposition is used very frequently. Pairs of instruments are simply put one above the other, usually in the normal order of register.

Interlocking has the slight advantage of mixing the colors in such a way that a more homogeneous blend results. However, there are cases in which interlocking does not work well. For instance, in the following chord the second flute would be relatively weak:

EXAMPLE 10.2

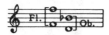

A similar lack of balance would result if interlocking forced the oboe, for example, to play in an abnormally high register where it would be too thin.

Enclosure is likely to be less successful than the first two methods in arranging woodwinds, at least when one *pair* encloses another. The difficulty is that when two instruments of a kind are spread an octave or more apart, they are likely to be playing in different registers and therefore to differ considerably from each other in strength and color; consequently, balance and blend may suffer. Consider the difference in sound between the first and second flutes in Example 10.3 for instance.

EXAMPLE 10.3

The second flute is obviously too weak.

The overlapping method, though much in vogue during the Classical period, is seen less often today. Its weakness is the fact that the outer notes (especially the bottom one) are not as strong as the others.

Whereas overlapping involves only a partial duplication of notes, there is another more complete and balanced form of duplication that is much used, as in Example 10.4.

EXAMPLE 10.4

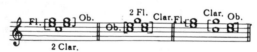

The obvious question at this point is, How does the arranger decide on the best method to use? No general answer can be given to that question; range, voice-leading, instruments involved, the coloring desired, and other factors will all enter into the choice. Juxtaposition and interlocking are chosen much more frequently than the other methods, however. Two or more methods are often used in the same chord—when the chord consists of more than four notes. In any case, the difference in sound between a chord that uses juxtaposition, let us say, and one that uses interlocking is not very pronounced.

Except in small orchestras that include only one of each woodwind, chords are rarely arranged with a different color on each note (Example 10.5).

EXAMPLE 10.5

Because of the several different timbres involved in such an arrangement, a good blend is difficult to achieve. If the chord were a widely spaced one in a higher register, the resulting sound would be somewhat better (Example 10.6).

EXAMPLE 10.6

However, this sort of spacing is almost never used today in writing for wind instruments in the orchestra. Although at one time woodwind chords were often arranged with gaps between the upper chord members, the current practice (which is usually preferable) is to write the upper woodwinds in close spacing. The occasional gaps that occur as a result of special voice-leading or doubling are not objectionable (Examples 10.7[a] and [b]) nor is the octave gap that is caused by a doubling of the top voice an octave higher (Example 10.7[c]).

EXAMPLE 10.7

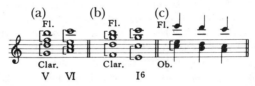

Before going on to the examples of chords scored for woodwinds, review the hints on spacing and doubling given near the end of Chapter 3. One small point should be added here, even though it does not figure in the scoring of isolated chords: when a progression involves both stationary and moving voices, it is better to give the stationary voices to one color, the moving voices to another.

EXAMPLE 10.8

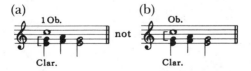

In the examples that follow, some of the chords are scored for woodwinds in pairs plus two horns (the latter included because they are so often combined with woodwinds). Another section of the illustrations makes use of a large woodwind section: piccolo, two flutes, two oboes, English horn, two clarinets, bass clarinet, two bassoons, and contrabassoon. And there are a few examples for woodwinds in threes, a less frequently used combination. With both the large woodwind section and woodwinds in threes, juxtaposition works far better than any of the other systems.

Complete duplication, with three of each woodwind, allows for a uniformly mixed color in three-note chords. (See Example 10.9.)

EXAMPLE 10.9

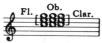

In scoring for a large woodwind section, the piccolo may double the flute an octave higher or may take the top chord tone immediately above the flutes. The English horn may be placed just below the oboes to form a three-note chord in close spacing or it may play lower down, with other instruments between it and the oboes. The bass clarinet, on the other hand, is much less often placed immediately below the clarinets to form a three-note chord; it is far more apt to take the bass because it is most effective in its lower and middle registers. It is, in fact, better than the bassoon for the bass of a woodwind chord; it has enough body to give a solid foundation to the chord, whereas two bassoons would often be required to achieve the equivalent sense of solidity. The role of contrabassoon as the bottom of the chord is obvious. It normally doubles the bass an octave lower.

Most of the chords in the following examples are scored in such a way as to be fairly brilliant in coloring, but in two of them, (g) and (m), the instruments have been placed relatively low in their respective registers to produce a darker coloring. The clarinets in their bottom octave are particularly good at adding a somber tinge. Obviously, there is no point in including the piccolo in such cases, and even the flutes have been omitted in (m). In actual practice, any instrument may be allowed to rest for reasons of color or volume or possibly to keep it fresh for an entrance that is to follow.

EXAMPLE 10.10

(For woodwinds in pairs and two horns)

176

(For large woodwind section)

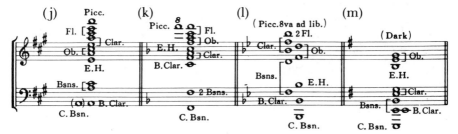

(For woodwinds in threes)

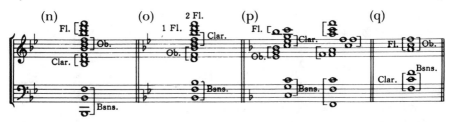

In general, the same dynamic marking can be given to all the instruments in each one of the arrangements just shown. One possible exception concerns the horns. Since they are capable of a more robust *forte* than any of the woodwinds, it would be safer to mark them *mf* when the woodwinds are marked *f* and *f* when the woodwinds are marked *ff*.

BRASS CHORDS

Juxtaposition, interlocking, and enclosure are all used frequently in scoring chords for brass. Overlapping as a method is rarely seen, though a low trumpet note is sometimes overlapped by the top trombone or by a horn for the sake of better balance.

If our brass section consists of four horns, two trumpets, three trombones, and tuba, we have ten instruments. As long as the dynamic marking is softer than *mf*, these instruments can actually play ten notes. But in a *mezzo-forte* or louder, the horns will normally be used two to a note, and the section can then cover only eight notes at the most. When chords of more then eight notes are to be scored *forte* or louder for the brass section we have just described, the two-horns-to-a-note principle must obviously be abandoned; the horns are given four different pitches and (when possible) marked one degree louder than the rest of the brass. This type of arrangement is shown in Example 10.11(i). Of course if the chord to be scored has fewer than eight notes, instruments may simply be omitted, or certain ones may be doubled on a pitch to bring out a particular voice if that is appropriate.

Some of the following examples have been scored for two trumpets, some for three, since brass sections vary in that respect. Three would seem to be the more satisfactory number because it allows for a complete three-note harmony in the trumpet color.

As before, the chords have merely been sketched on two staves at concert pitch. The examples here and elsewhere in this chapter make no pretense of exhausting all the possibilities; they simply show some of the more usual arrangements.

CHORDS FOR BRASS

EXAMPLE 10.11

(With two trumpets)

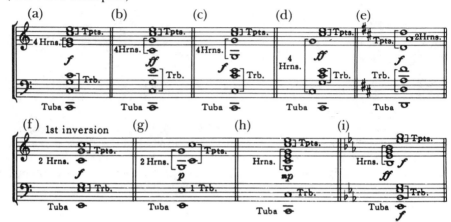

(With three trumpets)

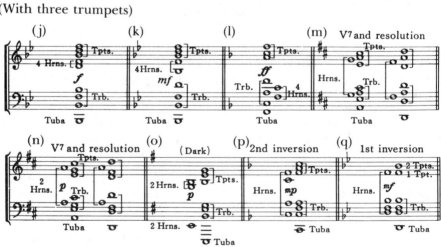

STRING CHORDS

Scoring chords for strings is a bit less involved than scoring woodwind and brass chords. In the first place, the difference in color between one string group and another is not nearly so decided as the difference in color between, say, a flute and an oboe. Consequently the strings present fewer problems of blend. And they do not vary in strength from register to register as much as the woodwinds do. This means that balance is more easily calculated.

Furthermore, strings involve two possibilities that wind instruments do not: (1) double, triple, and quadruple stops and (2) the use of an entire section that can be divided into any number of parts. As pointed out earlier, double stops may be used even in sustained chords, whereas triple and quadruple stops are valuable principally for short, sharply punctuated chords. In this latter type of chord, the main objectives are usually maximum resonance, fullness, and volume, and it is unnecessary to worry much about exact balance or correct voice-leading because the chord is not heard long enough for these features to be very apparent to the ear. The open strings so often involved in chords of this sort not only give added resonance but simplify the technical problem for the player.

As for *divisi* writing, remember that the fewer the players the riskier it is to divide a section. This is particularly true of division into more than two parts. Ideally, of course, we are scoring for an orchestra of full professional proportions, in which case a division of the violas into four separate parts is quite practical. But the sad reality is that we are much more likely to be working with a civic or a school orchestra that is perhaps able to muster only three viola players. Under such circumstances, division into four or more parts is obviously an impossibility; division into three parts, though possible, is hardly advisable if the parts involve any technical difficulties, for each player is left alone and unsupported on a part. Furthermore, when such small string groups are divided, the result is a solo quality rather than a group quality on each voice. (It takes at least three violins or violas on a part to give the effect of a group of strings.) While the other string groups tend to be somewhat better staffed than the viola section, they can still suffer from overdivision if the orchestra is not full-sized or if the players are inexperienced.

Juxtaposition (illustrated in the first three of the chords in Example 10.12) is the method used most often in arranging strings. Sometimes, interlocking is employed to achieve a more complete blend (d). Overlapping of one string group with another (also rare) produces a richer, composite quality (e). Enclosure seldom figures in string scoring. As mentioned earlier, open spacing is more successful in strings than in woodwinds or brass. Examples (f) through (j), which are shown in actual score form, are string chords taken from orchestral literature. Each illustrates a particular effect or device. Notice the interlocking of the notes in the triple stops in (f), a frequent arrangement in multiple-stop chords. Interlocking also figures in (g) and (h).

EXAMPLE 10.12

(Condensed at actual pitch)

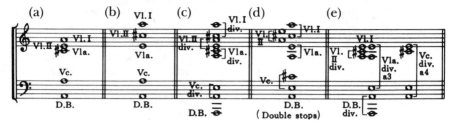

(In score form)

(f) Beethoven, Seventh Symphony (last movt., letter A)

(g) Hindemith, Symphony: *Mathis der Maler* (second measure)

(h) Strauss, *Don Juan* (eight measures after G)

(i) Bartók, Concerto for Orchestra (fifth measure of Finale)

(j) Wagner, *Lohengrin,* Prelude to Act I (beginning)

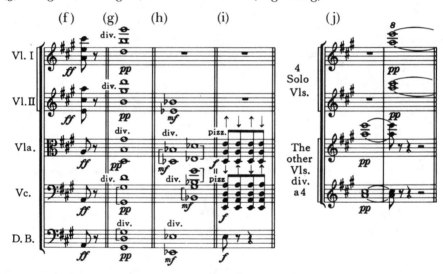

Example 10.12(g) reproduced by permission of Schott & Co., Ltd., London; Example 10.12(i) copyright, 1946, by Hawkes & Son (London) Ltd. By permission of the copyright owner, Boosey & Hawkes, Inc.

CHORDS FOR ORCHESTRA

In considering the scoring of chords for orchestra, we must remember that there is a vast difference in the weight of the three sections (woodwinds, brass, and strings). That is, if each section is marked *ff*, the brass will be louder than the woodwinds or strings. Though still present in a *forte* marking, this imbalance in terms of decibels diminishes as the dynamic level gets softer. Example 8.25(a) illustrates the successful use of woodwinds to fill in certain notes not taken by the brass in a passage marked *p*, *dolce*. But at higher dynamic levels that approach will seldom work; there the brass must generally be balanced as a unit.

If we carry this process over into the woodwinds and strings and arrange the chord in such a way that each section would sound complete and balanced if played by itself, the composite sound of the three sections playing at the same time is bound to be good. This is, in fact, a foolproof method and one that is often used. It is demonstrated in Example 10.13(a), (e), and others that follow. But it is not the only way, nor is it necessarily the most effective, because it sometimes involves putting the upper woodwinds in the same register as the trumpets, in which case the woodwinds are all but drowned out and actually add little. If the flutes and clarinets, especially, are placed well above the trumpets, they will be better able to make themselves heard, first because they are not covered by the trumpets in the same octave and second because they are much more powerful and brilliant in the higher register. (We are assuming here that a loud, brilliant effect is wanted.) With this sort of arrangement, there is often a gap in the middle of the woodwind chord, but that is not objectionable. Although the woodwind section would not sound entirely satisfactory if playing by itself, it will be effective when combined with the brass and strings.

The same general principle applies to the role of the strings in a chord for orchestra; that is, they may either play the complete chord or merely reinforce certain notes of it. But unlike the woodwind section, they are frequently arranged in open spacing. Sometimes, in fact, they are spread out even more widely, with gaps of an octave or more between certain notes. At other times they are simply arranged in straightforward four-part fashion, using close spacing. Octave doublings may be added or not, depending on whether a full, rich effect is wanted. As with the upper woodwinds, placement of the violins (and possibly even the violas) *above* the brass section produces a stronger and more brilliant string presence. Some of the more likely possibilities can be seen in the examples that follow, all of which are condensed at actual pitch.

Chords (a), (b), (c), and (d) in Example 10.13 use woodwinds in pairs, (e) and (f) a large woodwind section. In (d) a dark coloring has been aimed at. In (e) and (f) are shown two different scorings of the same chord, the first very brilliant, the second about medium color. Chords taken from well-known scores are given in (g) to (m). The last chord (m) differs from the others in being a bitingly dissonant one.

EXAMPLE 10.13

(Condensed at actual pitch)

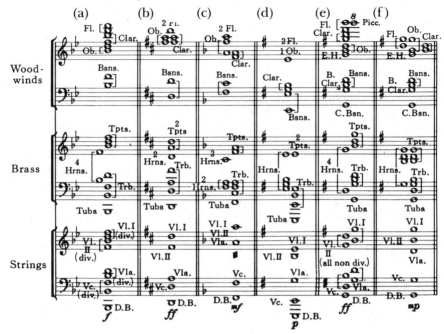

Note: *The dynamic marking below each chord applies to all the instruments.*

(From actual scores)

(g) Beethoven, Fifth Symphony (measure 316)

(h) Franck, Symphony in D minor (last chord)

(i) Strauss, *Till Eulenspiegel* (five measures before 37)

(j) Wagner, *Götterdämmerung* (*Trauermusik*, measure 16)

(k) Wagner, *Tristan und Isolde* (last chord)

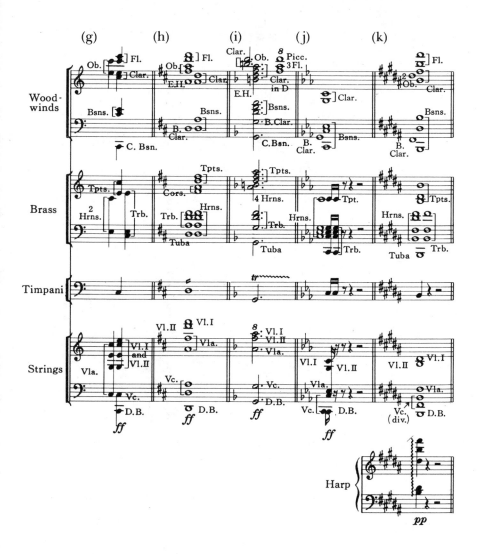

(l) Prokofieff, Fifth Symphony (last chord in first movt.)

(m) Copland, Third Symphony (figure 117)

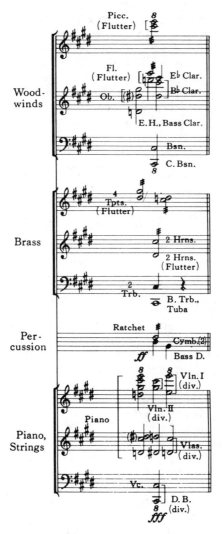

Example 10.13(m) Copyright 1947 by Aaron Copland. Copyright renewed. Reprinted by permission of Aaron Copland, Copyright Owner, and Boosey & Hawkes, Inc., Sole Licensee and Publisher.

It should not be inferred from the comments and examples given here that in a chord for orchestra all the sections must have the same dynamic marking. There is no law, for instance, against marking the strings and woodwinds *ff*, the brass *f* or *mp* or even *pp*, if that will produce the particular sound that is wanted.[1] (It is important, by the way, to re-

---

[1]See pages 323–26 for a more detailed commentary on this point and for an example that illustrates it.

member that the brass, particularly the trombones and horns, can provide an extremely quiet but rich background for the other instruments if need be.) Similarly, it would be possible to mark the strings louder than the woodwinds or vice versa in order to bring out a certain timbre or register. However, there would seldom be any point in marking the brass much *louder* than the strings or woodwinds, since the latter tend to be overshadowed by the brass even when the dynamic markings are equal. Certain scores, particularly pre-twentieth-century scores, use "block" dynamics— all the instruments invariably marked the same in a *tutti;* but in such cases the conductor is expected to adjust the dynamic proportions wherever that becomes necessary.

Dissonances are more prominent and acute when given to instruments of the same kind, milder when allotted to different instruments.

For instance, [musical notation: 1 Tpt. / 2 Tpts.] accentuates the dissonance much more than [musical notation: Vl.I]. This principle has been used in intensifying the dissonance in chord 10.13(m).

It would be impractical to attempt to catalog all the doublings possible between woodwinds, brass, and strings. Some of the possibilities in woodwind and string doubling are discussed in Chapter 12, and a few of the combinations involving woodwinds and brass will now be mentioned. In general, the doubling of woodwinds in unison with brass makes the brass tone somewhat less transparent and brilliant in timbre; clarinets and flutes "soften the edges" of the trumpet tone, whereas oboes tend to accentuate the nasal quality of it. Clarinets in their *chalumeau* register add a rich, dark touch to the brass. Bassoons doubled in unison with horns or trombones make those instruments a little grayer and more opaque in quality; the bassoon color is largely absorbed by the brass color.

Leaving the matter of actual doublings, it might be helpful to pass on a small point that Rimsky-Korsakoff and others have mentioned: there is a certain resemblance between the tone of the oboe (or English horn) and that of stopped horn or muted trumpet. Consequently these instruments can be combined in a chord (on different notes) with surprisingly good results. Even the unmuted trumpet tone is close enough to the oboe tone for the two instruments to give a fairly unified sound when combined in a chord. One hears chiefly the trumpet quality; in fact, such combinations may even give the illusion of being played entirely by trumpets. A similar affinity of tone quality exists (surprisingly) between the low notes of the flute and soft trumpet tones in that register.

SUGGESTED ASSIGNMENTS

Score the following chords as directed. The chords are to have the root in the bass unless an inversion is indicated. Either they may be written with a key signature (assuming that each is the tonic chord), or the key signature may be omitted and accidentals inserted where necessary. Include dynamics in every case. (Supply your own where none are given.) Use the principles discussed in the text to produce the type of coloring called for. You will achieve better results and save time in the long run if you sketch the layout of each chord at actual pitch before writing out the scored version.

A. For two flutes, two oboes, two clarinets, two bassoons, and two horns:

1. F major, F in the soprano, brilliant.
2. C major, G in the soprano, medium color.
3. E♭ major, 1st inversion, E♭ in the soprano, brilliant.

B. For piccolo, two flutes, two oboes, English horn, two clarinets, bass clarinet, two bassoons, and contrabassoon:

1. E major, G♯ in the soprano, very brilliant.
2. B major, B in the soprano, medium color.
3. D minor, A in the soprano, dark (omit piccolo).

C. For four horns, two or three trumpets (B♭ or C), three trombones, and tuba:

1. D♭ major, F in the soprano, brilliant, *forte*.
2. F minor, C in the soprano, medium color, *mezzo piano*.
3. F major, F in the soprano, rather dark, *pianissimo*.

D. For string orchestra:

The chord of G major, G in the soprano, arranged in four different ways to illustrate (1) close spacing; (2) open spacing; (3) octave doublings (use either *divisi* writing or double stops or both here); (4) triple and quadruple stops (this chord is to be the short, vigorous type).

E. For orchestra consisting of two flutes, two oboes, two clarinets, two bassoons, four horns, two trumpets, three trombones, tuba, and strings:

1. B minor, F♯ in the soprano, brilliant, *fortissimo*.
2. F major, A in the soprano, medium color, *pianissimo*.

F. For orchestra consisting of piccolo, two flutes, two oboes, English horn, two clarinets, bass clarinet, two bassoons, contrabassoon, four horns, three trumpets, three trombones, tuba and strings:

1. A♭ major, 2nd inversion, A♭ in the soprano, very brilliant, *fortissimo*.
2. C minor, G in the soprano, medium color, *piano*.
3. E minor, G in the soprano, very dark, *mezzo forte*.

11

Problems
in Transcribing
Piano Music

In scoring piano music for orchestra the arranger often comes across certain features that are essentially pianistic rather than orchestral. In such cases a literal transcription of the notes is likely to be awkward technically or ineffective or both. A better solution is to translate the *effect* wanted into orchestral terms.

In order to save space and to illustrate the points in question as simply as possible, the problem has been limited in the body of this chapter to arrangements for string orchestra. However, except for devices and patterns peculiar to string writing, the material can be applied just as well to scoring for other instruments. At the close of the chapter are some excerpts from transcriptions of piano pieces for an orchestra that includes woodwinds, brass, and percussion in addition to strings.

First, if the original music is in a remote key—say, for example, more than four sharps or flats—it is sometimes wise to choose a more comfortable and resonant key for the orchestral version (probably a half step higher if the piece is brilliant, a half step lower if it is not). This is particularly true in the case of school orchestras. Readers with pitch recognition may protest at this point, for they will be painfully aware of a transposition from the original key in music they know. And one does not have to have absolute pitch to object that altering the key of a work can destroy its characteristic color and flavor. Admittedly, the business of tampering with the composer's choice of key is questionable from an esthetic standpoint. But the advantages to be gained from playing in a more grateful key are often impressive enough to justify transposition. In choosing a key, remember that sharp keys are better than flat keys for the strings. Because of the tuning of stringed instruments, the resonance is much greater in sharp keys, and the fingering is easier. This is only a general principle and does not mean that in string writing flat keys must be avoided altogether.

Then there is the matter of the damper pedal, which figures almost constantly in piano music (this is the pedal on the right, which, when depressed, allows the tone to ring). Obviously it must be changed (raised and lowered again) at each new harmony if a blur is not to result. In some piano music these changes are indicated by a small "*Ped.*" beneath the staff, with an asterisk for a release. But in a great deal of music no directions for pedaling are shown; in such cases the arranger must consider whether pedal would be used, and if so, what the effect would be. (Usually when no pedal is to be used in a given passage, *senza pedale* is written in.)

Here is the beginning of a Chopin Nocturne:

EXAMPLE 11.1

Nocturne, Op. 9, No. 1

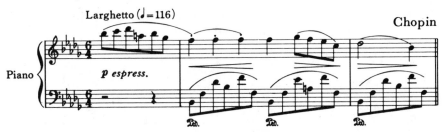

Because of the sustaining effect of the pedal, the music will actually sound more or less like this:

EXAMPLE 11.2

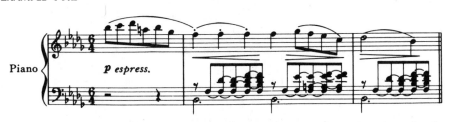

Therefore, certain notes must be written with longer values in the orchestral arrangement than in the original piano version. Not all notes sustained in the piano version need be sustained in the arrangement; it is simply a matter of aiming at the general effect of the original. Very often it is possible to divide up the figuration among the various string groups. That has been done in Example 11.3, which has also been transposed to a better key for the strings.

EXAMPLE 11.3

Or it may be possible to have some instruments taking the harmony in block-chord fashion while others take the figuration:

EXAMPLE 11.4

In both versions, the background has been marked a degree softer than the melody so that the latter will be sure to stand out.

It is impossible to transfer music from one medium to another intelligently without understanding its harmonic structure. For instance, if unaware that the second harmony in this Chopin excerpt involves a tonic pedal point beneath the dominant seventh, one might make the mistake of using the tonic note among the upper harmonies as if it were an actual chord tone (with very bad results) or of putting some other note in the bass, thereby destroying the pedal-point effect. If the harmonic skeleton of the original piece is not perfectly clear at the outset, analysis should precede the scoring.

In transcribing, it is sometimes best to change the pattern of the pianistic figuration altogether (not the harmony, of course, and usually not the *rhythm* of the figuration). Let us suppose that this excerpt from the last movement of the Beethoven *Moonlight* Sonata is to be scored for strings:

EXAMPLE 11.5

Sonata, Op. 27, No. 2

Although the Alberti-bass figure in the left hand is *possible* for the cellos, it is not well suited to string technique, and the effect would be thin and a little ludicrous that way. Also, the spacing is poor for orchestral purposes; the third of the chord is too low, the small intervals are at the bottom, and there is a wide gap between the left-hand part and the melody in the right. It would be better to rearrange the chord and distribute the notes among the string groups, possibly like this:

EXAMPLE 11.6

Example 11.7 shows another pianistic figure that is better rearranged.

EXAMPLE 11.7

Here, again, the solution is to lift and respace. Of course there are other patterns of figuration that might profit from the same treatment.

Widely spread-out arpeggio passages, such as the left-hand part in the next example, offer several problems in scoring.

EXAMPLE 11.8

The White Peacock

Griffes

Piano

In the first place, they cover so much ground that they can seldom be handled comfortably by any one orchestral instrument except the harp. Because of this fact and because the harp is so eminently suited to arpeggios, it is often the best choice for such passages (usually with sustained harmony elsewhere in the orchestra). But not all orchestras include a harp, and the instrument would not be appropriate in all types of music. Nor does it have enough volume to supply the requisite sense of motion on its own in some heavily scored passages. Therefore, another solution may be required. In some cases it is possible to reduce the spread of the arpeggios to a point where they can be taken by one instrument (by one group in the case of the strings). Actual rearrangement of the figures will also be necessary as a rule. Sometimes it is best to divide the figuration between two or more instruments, again with whatever rearrangement will make for idiomatic parts and effective sonorities. Example 11.9 shows one way in which the left-hand part of Example 11.8 could be transcribed for strings. (We are assuming here that the violins are engaged in playing the upper parts of the original version and therefore cannot be called on to help out with the figurated background.)

EXAMPLE 11.9

Vla. (div.)

Vc.

D. B.

Occasionally passages of the sort we have just been discussing can be carried over almost literally into the orchestral version by simply dividing them among the strings. In such cases it is wise to let each string group end its figure *on* a beat instead of just before a beat and to overlap the last note played by each group with the first note of the group that follows it. These points are illustrated in Example 11.10, which shows first the left-hand part of a piano piece and then a possible arrangement of it for strings.

EXAMPLE **11.10**

Sustained harmony in other instruments usually accompanies this sort of arrangement.

In piano music, melody and accompaniment are often assigned to the same hand, and it is important to distinguish one from the other in scoring. Example 11.11 illustrates this point.

EXAMPLE **11.11**

Here it is obvious that the right-hand part actually includes two distinct musical ideas: a melody on top (the first, third, and fifth eighth-notes in each measure) and a repeated-note figure below, in spite of the fact that the notation gives the appearance of a single melodic line. In scoring the example, then, we would break up this line into its component parts and allot these to separate instruments. One possible version is given in Example 11.12.

EXAMPLE 11.12

Chords such as the one in Example 11.13 can be dramatic and effective on the piano.

EXAMPLE 11.13

The same thing in the orchestra would sound poor; the bottom notes are much too thickly spaced for that low register, and the gap in the middle needs to be filled in. Something like Example 11.14 might be a satisfactory solution in the strings.

EXAMPLE 11.14

Triple and quadruple stops are used here for greater fullness and volume. Notice the use of open strings and of the interlocking principle.

It sometimes happens that piano music contains three-note chords that must be divided, in the orchestral arrangement, between second violins and violas. The best solution in that case is to give two notes to the second violins and one to the violas (which are fewer in number). The two notes in the second violins can be taken *divisi* or, if convenient, as a double stop; but this latter method should not be called for with inexperienced players or in a quick succession of chords where double stops would be awkward. Four-note chords can be taken by double stops in both second violins and violas or by *divisi* parts in each.

Broken octaves are especially characteristic of piano music of the Beethoven period (see Example 11.15).

EXAMPLE 11.15

Sonata, Op. 22

These are best rendered, in the strings, by the sort of arrangement found in Example 11.16.

EXAMPLE 11.16

The same applies to broken 6ths and other intervals (although broken 3rds are practical on most orchestral instruments).

In piano music of the Romantic period (especially in song accompaniments) this sort of tremolo sometimes appears:

EXAMPLE 11.17

The obvious solution in the orchestra is a string tremolo (see Example 11.18).

EXAMPLE **11.18**

Although a bowed tremolo has been used here and is ordinarily preferable for such passages, a fingered tremolo might be employed if a softer, more placid effect were called for.

When scoring piano music one occasionally encounters passages with a pronounced soloistic or even cadenzalike character. Sometimes such a wide range is covered that it would be impossible for any orchestral instrument to play a literal transcription of the passage convincingly. In these situations it is usually best to retain the solo quality and alter the music to preserve the general overall effect of the original. Example 11.19, for instance, shows an excerpt from Mozart's Variations on *Unser dummer Pöbel meint* that covers nearly four octaves. Tchaikovsky, in scoring this work as part of his Suite No. 4 (*Mozartiana*), gives the passage to a solo violin (see Example 11.20) and alters the run so that it lies within the violin's range. Later in this work a similar passage is altered so that it can be played by a solo clarinet.

EXAMPLE **11.19**

Variations on *Unser dummer Pöbel meint*

EXAMPLE **11.20**

Suite No. 4 for Orchestra

In piano music, chords are sometimes written with a wavy line at the left to indicate that they are to be arpeggiated or broken slightly, or the arpeggiation may be written out in small notes. At other times the chord is broken into two parts, the lower part being played as a "grace note" to the upper. Such devices may be introduced for the sake of artistic effect or out of sheer pianistic necessity if the chords involve stretches that are too wide to be played at once. In any case, the arpeggiated or broken effect is often omitted altogether in transcribing such passages for orchestra. In case it is felt to be such an integral part of the music that it should not be changed, it may be given to the harp if that is stylistically appropriate or to strings playing either bowed broken chords (for a vigorous passage) or pizzicato chords in arpeggiated fashion. (Much use is made of the latter effect in Examples 11.21 and 11.22.)

Staccato notes in the piano version may be given to strings playing pizzicato or spiccato or slurred staccato, depending on the degree of shortness required and on the dynamics and tempo. Remember, however, that pizzicato is not practical in very fast passages.

The Italian phrase *una corda,* meaning literally "one string," is the standard direction in piano music for using the soft pedal (the one at the left). In the orchestra, muted strings are often an effective parallel for the *una corda* sound on the piano. But there are other times when the muted effect would seem out of place, and in such cases very soft dynamic markings in the orchestral parts must suffice.

Not every piece of piano music can be successfully transcribed for strings—or for orchestra. A good many works are so purely pianistic in conception that it would be absurd to attempt an orchestral version of them. Nevertheless the problems discussed here are likely to come up from time to time if only because at least part of the work in orchestration courses normally consists of arranging piano music.

In order to demonstrate the application of some of the principles just discussed to scoring that involves other instruments in addition to strings, some excerpts from music written originally for the piano and later transcribed for orchestra by the composer are shown next. Points to observe include the following: ways of rendering rolled chords; ways of rendering left-hand arpeggios; the treatment of staccato notes; the use of sustained notes (where none are included in the original) to approximate the effect of the pedal; the introduction of octave doublings; the addition of voices for greater fullness. The excerpts from the Ravel *Pavane* consist of three different versions of the same theme that occur in the course of the piece. The *cors simples en sol* are two natural horns in G, sounding a 4th lower than written. Ravel presumably wanted their quality as opposed to the "modern" sound of the valve horn. The principle behind the enharmonic notion in the harp part (C♭ for B♮) is explained in Chapter 15. The original piano versions are included here for purposes of comparison and are not meant to be played in the orchestral versions. These last examples give a preview of some possibilities in scoring for woodwinds, horns, and strings—the subject of Chapter 12. Here and in some later examples, the names of instruments are listed as they appear in the published score—in the original language.

Example 11.21

Pavane pour une Infante Défunte

(c)

EXAMPLE 11.22

Le Tombeau de Couperin

(a) *Forlane*

(b) *Menuet*

Ravel

EXAMPLE 11.23

Orchestral Variations (1957)

(a)   Theme   (b)   Variation XIV

Copland

Piano Variations: © Copyright 1932 by Aaron Copland. Copyright renewed. Reprinted by permission of Aaron Copland, Copyright Owner, and Boosey & Hawkes, Inc., Sole Licensee and Publisher. Orchestral Variations: Copyright 1960 by Aaron Copland. Reprinted by permission of Aaron Copland, Copyright Owner, and Boosey & Hawkes, Inc., Sole Licensees and Publisher.

(c)   Variation XX

EXAMPLE 11.24

(a) *Zodiac*, VIII

George Rochberg

Note: *All instruments are written here as they will actually sound.*

(b) Bagatelle 8, from *Twelve Bagatelles*

Example 11.24(a): © 1974 Theodore Presser Company. Used By Permission Of The Publisher, Letter Dated 7/9/81. Example 11.24(b): © 1955 Theodore Presser Company. Used By Permission Of The Publisher, Letter Dated 7/9/81.

SUGGESTED ASSIGNMENTS

The following are suitable as exercises in transcribing pianistic music for strings (or for other combinations). Bowing should be included in all cases. Respacing, filling of gaps, rearrangement of figuration, and so on are to be introduced where necessary.

1. Beethoven, Sonata, Op. 2, No. 3, 1st movt., meas. 1–16.
2. Beethoven, Sonata, Op. 10, No. 3, 1st movt., meas. 1–30.
3. Beethoven, Sonata, Op. 22, 1st movt., meas. 1–20.
4. Mozart, Sonata in B♭ major, K. 333 (excerpts).
5. Chopin, Nocturne, Op. 9, No. 2 (E♭ major), meas. 1–4.
6. Chopin, Nocturne, Op. 27, No. 2 (D♭ major), meas. 1–5.
7. Grieg, Sonata in E minor (excerpts).
8. Brahms, Intermezzo, Op. 117, No. 2, beginning.
9. Liszt, Etude in D♭ major (*Un Sospiro*), beginning.
10. Any of the works in the "Suggested Listening" list that follows. Much can be learned by making an orchestral arrangement of one of these from the piano score and comparing it with the published orchestral arrangement. In that case the student should, of course, not listen to a recording of the published arrangement until the scoring has been completed. Because most of these works suggest the use of the complete orchestra, projects in scoring them should ordinarily be delayed until Chapters 12 through 16 have been covered.

SUGGESTED LISTENING

The following are works written originally for piano and later arranged for orchestra either by their composers or by other skilled orchestrators:

Bach, many works transcribed by Sir Edward Elgar, Sir Henry Wood, Leopold Stokowski, Alexandre Tansman, Schönberg, and others.
Liszt, *Mephisto Waltz.*
Brahms, *Variations on a Theme by Haydn* (issued first in a version for two pianos).
Grieg, *Aus Holbergs Zeit.*
Dvořák, *Slavonic Dances* (originally for piano duet).
Tchaikovsky, Suite No. 4 for Orchestra (the fourth movement is an orchestration of Mozart's Variations on *Unser dummer Pöbel meint*).
Mussorgsky, *Pictures at an Exhibition* (orchestrated by Ravel and Sir Henry Wood, among others).
Debussy, *Petite Suite.* (Busser) (originally for piano duet).
Ravel, *Pavane pour une Infante Défunte; Alborado del Gracioso; Mother Goose* Suite (originally for piano duet); *Le Tombeau de Couperin; Valses Nobles et Sentimentales.*
Albéniz, *Iberia; Catalonia.*
Griffes, *The White Peacock;* Scherzo (retitled *Bacchanale*).
Bartók, *Fifteen Hungarian Peasant Songs; Roumanian Folk Dances.*
Copland, Piano Variations (1930), scored by the composer and published as Orchestral Variations, 1957.
Rochberg, George, *Twelve Bagatelles* (piano), published 1955, scored by the composer and published as *Zodiac*, 1974.

12

Scoring
for Woodwinds,
Horns, and Strings

In an earlier chapter we took up the scoring of chords for the various sections and for orchestra. There we made a practice of using all the instruments of a section in each chord in order to learn how to calculate balance and blend in a complete group. In this chapter a different problem is involved, one requiring much more taste and imagination and one that represents the usual situation in practical orchestration: we are given some music to score for an orchestra of a particular size, and we must choose the instruments that seem appropriate to the musical ideas. When an instrument is not actually needed in the scoring, it will simply be given a rest; even whole sections will rest from time to time. (In full-orchestra scores of the common-practice period, the brass section is apt to rest a good deal of the time; woodwinds, both individually and as a section, normally rest a bit more than strings.)

As we look over the music to be scored with an eye to the possible ways in which it could be orchestrated, certain questions naturally suggest themselves:

What is the character of the passage in question—lyric and *espressivo*, or airy and fanciful, or sharply rhythmic, or dirgelike, or any one of the many other possibilities?

Does the passage suggest a relatively light or heavy scoring? Does it call for a simple texture or should it be expanded by means of octave doublings?

What coloring seems appropriate—brilliant or somber, warm or cool?

How does the passage relate to what has gone before and what is to come after it? (In other words, we must consider the form of the piece as a whole.)

What instruments are best fitted to play the respective parts from the standpoint of (1) range and (2) technical abilities?

What *style* of scoring is appropriate, considering the period and composer involved?

Is the music chordal, or homophonic, or polyphonic, or a combination?

As for the last question, we have already had some experience in scoring a chordal texture, and the arranging of polyphonic music for full orchestra is discussed in Chapter 16. But this is a good point at which to consider the orchestration of homophonic music, that is, music that consists of a prominent melodic line against a subordinate harmonic background.

Suppose, for instance, that we wished to transcribe this excerpt from a Brahms piano piece for strings, woodwinds in pairs, and four horns:

EXAMPLE 12.1

Intermezzo, Op. 119, No. 2 (middle section)

Inasmuch as we cannot score this or any other music well without understanding its structure, we had better take time for harmonic analysis before going on to the orchestration. The harmony in the first measure proves to be tonic (E major) with a nonharmonic C♯ on the first beat in the right hand. (The important thing here is that the C♯ must not be included in the harmony parts; the "added 6th" effect would hardly be appropriate in Brahms!) Because of the sustaining effect of the pedal, the notes in the left hand that are written as eighths actually sound through the measure. The second measure involves a V^7 sound above a tonic pedal point. (The E in the bass has the effect of a pedal point because it is held through the bar by the pedal.) We are not going to pursue the harmonic analysis any further here since the examples that follow involve only the first two bars and bars 9 and 10, which have the same harmonic pattern as the first two. Looking at the music from the standpoint of form, we discover that the eight-measure melody is repeated in octaves beginning with the upbeat to the ninth bar. (Not all this repetition is shown here.)

To make use of some of these observations in planning our scoring, we must first find some way of approximating the sustained effect of the piano version in the orchestra. A good solution is to add a B and G♯ on the first beat of the first measure (below the E in the treble staff) that will hold through the measure and then continue on harmony notes in the measures that follow. This has the added advantage of filling in the large gap that occurs at the beginning of each measure. Also, we shall want to hold the E in the bass, and it would even be possible to hold the B above it as well. The eighth-note arpeggios could be given entirely to cellos or divided between cellos and violas as in Example 12.2(b), or even given to bassoons as in Example 12.3(d), although that plan seems a little less desirable. If a harp were included, it might take these arpeggio figures.

In music of this sort it seems appropriate to let the melody stand out clearly from the background, and we can best achieve that effect by giving the melody to one color, the background to another. In this case the simplicity and delicacy of the first eight bars suggest a relatively light scoring, possibly a solo woodwind against soft strings. Flute, though weak in this register, would come through if the background were kept light, and it would have a certain quiet charm. Oboe in its most characteristic register would be more pungent and penetrating. Clarinet would also be possible— a bit more warm and romantic in quality than the other woodwinds. Incidentally, clarinet in A is preferable to B♭ clarinet here since the latter would have to be written with a key signature of six sharps (or enharmonically, six flats), whereas clarinet in A involves a signature of one sharp. Violins on the melody would be expressive and effective; the harmonic background in that case might be given to horns rather than strings in order to let the melody stand out more sharply, or it could still be allotted to strings. (Muting of the string background would produce a slightly different color from the melody.) By taking the melody down an octave we could give it to the cellos or to one solo cello in a particularly expressive register of the instrument. If that is done, some rearrangement of the harmony parts is necessary. This last scoring is used in version 12.2(d).

The second eight measures seem to demand a fresh color on the melody as well as a little more weight. If a solo woodwind has been used in the first version, the melody might well be given to strings in octaves here or to strings and woodwinds doubled in octaves. If strings took the melody in the first eight bars, an octave doubling of woodwinds would give the greatest contrast in the second eight, or the combination of strings and woodwinds in octaves would be effective. Even two-octave doublings could be used, as in versions (b), (c), and (d) of Example 12.3. There are additional harmony parts in the second eight bars.

Examples 12.2 and 12.3 show some of the possibilities in scoring the first eight bars and the second eight bars, respectively. For reasons of space, only the first measure or two of each version is given here.

EXAMPLE 12.2

EXAMPLE 12.3

*Horn in bass clef to sound a 5th lower.

DOUBLINGS IN THE WOODWINDS

It is very common in scoring to give a melodic line to two or more different woodwinds in unison. We did not make use of that device in the first eight measures of the Brahms example, but some woodwind doublings (both unison and octave) were involved in the scoring of the second eight measures. Table 12.1 shows some of the more usual combinations.

Three-octave doublings are possible with the addition of piccolo at the top or bass clarinet or contrabassoon at the bottom; even four-octave doublings are occasionally seen.

TABLE 12.1

UNISON DOUBLINGS IN THE WOODWINDS	COMMENTS
Flute and Oboe	Oboe predominates but is "softened" (in quality) by flute.
Flute and Clarinet	Warm, round tone; not strong in the octave above middle C.
Oboe and Clarinet	Mixes oboe's tang with clarinet's mellowness.
Clarinet and Bassoon	Rich; somber if clarinet is low.
Flute, Oboe, Clarinet	Thoroughly mixed color.

OCTAVE DOUBLINGS IN THE WOODWINDS	COMMENTS
{ Flute (upper 8ve) / Oboe (lower 8ve)	Good; frequent.
{ Flute / Clarinet	Good; frequent
{ Oboe / Clarinet	Good; frequent.
{ Clarinet / Oboe (or English Horn)	Infrequent with oboe; English horn usually better because its range extends lower.
{ Clarinet / Bassoon	Very dark if instruments are in their lower register.
{ Flute and Oboe / Clarinet and Bassoon	May take bassoon uncomfortably high; English horn may substitute for bassoon.
{ 2 Fl., 2 Ob., 1 Clar. / 1 Clar., 2 Bns. (and/or Eng. Horn)	Strong; good composite color; better balance with English horn included.

TWO-OCTAVE DOUBLINGS IN THE WOODWINDS	COMMENTS
{ Flute / Oboe / Clarinet	Effective.
{ Flute / Oboe / Bassoon	Fairly frequent in scores of the Classical period (also with violins in the middle).
{ Flute / Clarinet / Bassoon	Effective.
{ Flute / ..... (2 8ves apart) / Bassoon	Good. Omission of the middle octave makes for a particular effect.
{ Flute / ..... (2 8ves apart) / Clarinet	Rare; unusual coloring; uses bright register of flute with dark register of clarinet.

There is not room here for detailed comment on the more rarely used doublings, such as flute and bassoon in unison, flutes an octave below oboes, low flutes with piccolo two octaves higher, clarinets two octaves apart, and so on. These combinations produce unusual and intriguing colors, but one must have a very intimate knowledge of the orchestra to use them successfully.

DOUBLINGS BETWEEN WOODWINDS AND STRINGS

In unison doublings of woodwinds and strings, the woodwind tone tends to be overshadowed by that of the strings. Flute chiefly adds body, although not much. Oboe makes the string tone a bit more nasal and may even give it a pinched quality if the number of strings is small. English horn, on the other hand, can be combined with violas to produce an unusually poignant and attractive tone. (Remember, for example, the "love theme" in Tchaikovsky's *Romeo and Juliet*.) Clarinet lends a certain warmth and roundness to string timbre, plus a dark richness in its lower register. Bassoons are constantly associated with cellos or violas for the sake of added body. The unison combination of horn and cello in the tenor register gives an expressive, noble sound that is well suited to slower, *cantabile* melodies.

Certain doublings in which a woodwind (or pair of woodwinds) plays one octave and strings another are effective and allow the woodwind tone to be heard more clearly than it is in unison doublings. Flute above violins is good, clarinet or oboe above violins less satisfactory. But clarinets or bassoons can play an octave *below* violins with good effect. The combination of woodwinds in octaves plus strings in octaves is a powerful and useful one.

In closing these remarks on doubling, it seems appropriate to issue a small word of warning: remember that a constant use of mixed or composite colors becomes uninteresting and tends to make a score sound opaque and nondescript. Pure colors are needed for sparkle and transparency.

THE USE OF CONTRASTING SECTIONS

In order to deal with another aspect of scoring, let us turn to a small excerpt from the second movement of Beethoven's *Moonlight* Sonata:

EXAMPLE 12.4

Sonata, Op. 27, No. 2 (second movement)

(a)	Woodwinds	Strings	Woodwinds (same as before or different)	Strings
(b)	Strings	Woodwinds	Strings	Woodwinds (same or different)
(c)	Strings (*arco*)	Strings (*pizz.* or *arco,* short)	Woodwinds	Woodwinds
(d)	Strings & Woodwinds (doubled)	Strings	Strings & Woodwinds (doubled)	Strings

Beneath the music are four possible layouts, the sections being listed below the measures they would play. This passage involves two four-measure phrases, each one consisting of two segments. We can accentuate the strong antiphonal feeling between the segments of each phrase by using contrasting colors every two measures, as in (a), (b), and (d); or we can use one color on the first four measures, another on the second four, stressing the antiphonal feeling between the two *phrases,* as in (c). Of course this excerpt is an extreme case; few pieces of music would lend themselves to so many contrasts of color within a few measures. It is quite possible to overuse the device of contrasted sections, with a resulting "patchy" quality in the scoring. In fact, beginning orchestrators often tend to think in terms of separate sections and fail to make use of the possibilities for combining instruments of different sections.

In light of what was said earlier about avoiding remote keys, transposition to D major or C major may seem to be in order in the Beethoven excerpt. However, the original key has been retained here for several reasons: the music demands no great resonance and presents no technical problems; most important, transposition to another key would completely destroy the striking parallel relationship between the somber C♯ minor of the famous first movement and the bright D♭ major of the second (it is assumed that both movements are being scored and that the original key is being retained in the first).

Of course the layouts shown beneath the excerpt do not exhaust the ways in which it could be scored. They are merely a few possibilities that demonstrate the technique of contrasted sections.

This is the way version 12.4(a) might look written out in actual score:

EXAMPLE 12.5

The examples that follow illustrate scoring for woodwinds, horns, and strings in music of several different periods, styles, and textures. (The instrumentation of the works quoted in Examples 12.6, 12.8, and 12.10 includes two trumpets as well, but these do not play during the passages shown here.) The examples should be studied for doublings, balance, the distribution of the various musical ideas, the use of pure color versus composite color, and stylistic characteristics, among other things. Of course they represent only a few of the endless possibilities in scoring for this combination of instruments. Clarinets are among the woodwinds used in the works quoted in Examples 12.6 and 12.8, although they do not figure in the excerpts shown. They are not included in the instrumentation of Example 12.7, however.

EXAMPLE 12.6

Overture to *The Marriage of Figaro*

Mozart

EXAMPLE 12.7

Fifth Symphony (B♭ major, D. 485)

EXAMPLE 12.8

Variations on a Theme of Haydn. Var. III

Note: *This score departs from the usual practice in using slurs to indicate phrasing rather than bowing in the string parts.*

EXAMPLE 12.9

Prelude to The Afternoon of a Faun

(a)

(b)

EXAMPLE 12.10

Classical Symphony, III. Gavotta

*The clarinets are written here at actual pitch.

Example 12.11

Sinfonietta, III. Tarantella

CHECKLIST FOR SCORING ASSIGNMENTS

Before handing in scoring assignments, students should check to make sure they have included the following:

1. A tempo indication, shown above the top staff and just above the strings. (It is advisable to leave a blank staff above the first violins to allow space for the initial tempo marking and for other tempo indications that may follow—accelerando, rallentando, etc.) Such directions are not written above each part in the score but are transferred to individual players' parts by the copyist.

2. Dynamics, including crescendos and diminuendos, beneath each part.

3. Bowing indications in the strings (including down-bow and up-bow signs and "pizz." and "arco" where necessary) and articulation (slurring or phrasing) in the winds.

4. The number of each woodwind or brass instrument included in the instrumentation (e.g., "2 Oboes," not simply "Oboes"); also the key of transposing instruments (e.g., "Clarinets in B♭").

5. Indications to show whether the first of a pair of winds is playing ("1."), the second of the pair ("2."), or both ("a2"). After a rest of more than eight measures or after a page turn, it is safest to repeat the indication in parentheses—assuming the same arrangement continues.

6. Rehearsal numbers or letters if the score is to be played.

SUGGESTED ASSIGNMENTS

A. Be able to comment on:
1. considerations in scoring music that involves a prominent melodic line against a subordinate background.
2. possibilities in contrasting one section of the orchestra with another.
3. the effect of doubling various woodwinds with each other or with strings, either in unison or at the octave.

B. The following are suitable as exercises in scoring for woodwinds, horns, and strings:
1. Beethoven, Sonata, Op. 10, No. 2, 1st movt.
2. Beethoven, Sonata, Op. 10, No. 3, 2nd movt.
3. Beethoven, Sonata, Op. 14, No. 1, 2nd movt., meas. 1–32.
4. Beethoven, Sonata, Op. 90, 1st movt., meas. 1–24.
5. Schumann, "Little Romance" from *Album for the Young*.
6. Schumann, "Echoes from the Theater" from *Album for the Young*.
7. Schubert, Sonata, Op. 143, 1st movt.
8. Schubert, Sonata, Op. 147, 3rd movt.
9. Chopin, Prelude in A major, Op. 28, No. 7.
10. Chopin, Nocturne in F minor, Op. 55, No. 1. Score the first two measures in five different ways. Make some use of octave doublings.
11. Tchaikovsky, "Polka" from *Album for the Young*. Score for one flute, one oboe, one clarinet, one bassoon, one horn if desired, and strings.
12. Tchaikovsky, "At Church" from *Album for the Young*.
13. Tchaikovsky, "Morning Prayer" from *Album for the Young*.

14. Brahms, "Es ist ein Ros' Entsprungen" from *Eleven Chorale Preludes for the Organ,* Op. 122.
15. Brahms, *Variations and Fugue on a Theme by Handel,* Var. X.
16. Grieg, Nocturne in C major.
17. Scriabin, Etude in C# minor, Op. 2, No. 1.
18. Debussy, *The Girl with the Flaxen Hair* (No. 8 in first book of Preludes).
19. MacDowell, "A Deserted Farm" from *Woodland Sketches.*
20. Bartók, No. 12 from *Fifteen Hungarian Peasant Songs.*
21. Kabalevsky, Sonatina, Op. 13, No. 1, 1st movt.
22. Kennan, Prelude I from Three Preludes.
23. Rochberg, Bagatelle VIII from *Twelve Bagatelles.*

C. The following suggest the use of harp in addition to woodwinds, horns, and strings. It is therefore suggested that they not be assigned until after Chapter 15 has been studied.

1. Fauré, *Pavane.*
2. Debussy, "Clair de Lune" from *Suite Bergamasque.*
3. Palmgren, *May Night.*
4. Ravel, Minuet from Sonatine.
5. Ravel, *Pavane pour une Infante Défunte.* (The completed scoring should be compared with Ravel's.)
6. Ravel, *Le Tombeau de Couperin,* any of the movements. (The completed scoring should be compared with Ravel's.)

SUGGESTED LISTENING

Scoring for Woodwinds, Horns, and Strings[1]

Haydn, Symphonies.
Mozart Symphonies; Divertimenti; Overture to *The Marriage of Figaro.*
Beethoven, Symphonies (the Fifth, Sixth, and Ninth also include trombones).
Mendelssohn, *Midsummer Night's Dream* music (particularly the *Intermezzo* and *Nocturne*); Symphonies No. 3 and 4; *Fingal's Cave Overture.*
Schumann, Second Symphony, 3rd movt. (good example of different scorings of the same theme).
Brahms, Serenades; *Variations on a Theme of Haydn.*
Schubert, Fifth Symphony.
Wagner, *Siegfried Idyll.*
Debussy, *Prelude to The Afternoon of a Faun; Nocturnes:* I. "Nuages"; *Rondes de Printemps.*
Ravel, *Mother Goose* Suite; *Pavane pour une Infante Défunte; Le Tombeau de Couperin.*
Prokofieff, *Classical* Symphony.
Delius, *On Hearing the First Cuckoo in Spring; Summer Night on the River.*
Britten, Sinfonietta.
Thea Musgrave, *Night Music,* for chamber orchestra (see Example 17.11).

---

[1]These scores (or some of them) also include parts for trumpets. However, since in these cases the trumpets play only a small portion of the time, the works serve for the most part as examples of scoring for strings, woodwinds, and horns. The same is true to a lesser extent even of works scored for a larger instrumentation; that is, even when a full brass section is included, it will not play constantly by any means, and there will therefore be abundant instances of scoring that involves only woodwinds, horns, and strings.

13

The Percussion:
Instruments
of Definite Pitch

With a few notable exceptions, percussion parts in orchestral works written prior to the twentieth century tended to be of minimal importance. It is uncommon to find an eighteenth- or nineteenth-century orchestral composition in which a percussion instrument other than the timpani is an essential element of the musical fabric. The percussion parts that do occur are most often decorative and incidental in nature and could even be omitted without serious damage to the overall effect.

In this century and especially since 1960 the importance of the percussion section has increased enormously, along with the sophistication and complexity of music written for it. Percussion instruments provide the "characteristic sound" of a good deal of recent music, and composers consider that section equal in importance to the other sections of the orchestra.

It is impossible to provide an exhaustive treatment of the percussion here. Instead, the most common and frequently encountered instruments, as well as some of the most recent performing techniques and special effects, are described. These descriptions may suggest something of the inventiveness composers have brought to bear upon contemporary percussion parts.

BEATERS[1]

Most of the instruments discussed in this and the following chapter produce their sound when struck by a "beater" of some sort. (Various kinds of

---

[1]The term *beater* is used to refer to any object (mallet, stick, brush, hammer, etc.) used to strike a percussion instrument.

FIGURE 13.1

Back row (from left): **Crotales (mounted on a stand), two Almglocken, Tubular Bells, four Roto-toms**

Front row: **Four Timpani**

beaters can be seen in Figure 14.1.) Many instruments can be played with several different kinds of beaters, and the sound will vary considerably depending on which one is chosen. This variety of sound is due in large part to the characteristics of the beater head (the part that actually comes into contact with the instrument), including its size, weight, shape, and degree of hardness or softness. Other factors that influence an instrument's sound are the angle at which it is struck and the beating spot.

In the past, composers seldom troubled themselves about such matters, leaving the choice of an appropriate beater to the performer. The fact that many composers now specify, at least in general terms, what kind of beater they want is a good indicator of the increasing awareness on their part of the wide variety of percussion sounds possible—even on a single instrument.

Although the only way to gain an accurate aural impression of the many nuances of percussion timbre is through an actual demonstration, some general observations will be offered that may prove helpful to the beginning orchestrator.

The two factors that influence a percussion instrument's sound most crucially are the size and the degree of hardness of the beater's head. These heads range in size from those found on a bass drum stick or gong mallet (about the size of a grapefruit) to those found on a brass-headed glockenspiel mallet (about the size of a dime) to no head at all—as on the triangle beater. Soft beaters are made of felt, yarn, or lamb's wool; wood, brass, or plastic constitute the hardest mallets. Most soft beaters have relatively large heads; hard beaters usually have small heads.

Hard beaters are especially useful in passages where a crisp, well-defined rhythmic effect is desired. Contact sounds (i.e., sounds produced when one object strikes another) are more pronounced with hard sticks, and this kind of sound contributes to rhythmic definition. Soft beaters minimize or eliminate contact sounds; therefore, instruments played with these beaters produce sounds that are "rounder" and more subdued.

The size of the beater head has an important effect on pitch definition. For instance, a large-headed mallet used on a timpano tends to emphasize the fundamental pitch because the large contact area of the head stifles higher overtones before they have a chance to sound. Small heads, on the other hand, produce higher partials because they do not impede the free vibration of the drumhead at the moment of contact.

Since an appreciation of the subtleties of percussion sounds is critical if one is to write for these instruments with understanding, it is strongly urged that demonstrations of all the instruments discussed in the ensuing pages of this chapter be arranged.

THE TIMPANI (OR KETTLEDRUMS)

Italian: Timpani   *French:* Timbales   *German:* Pauken

EXAMPLE 13.1

The spelling *tympani* (the plural of the Latin *tympanum*) is sometimes seen, but *timpani* (the plural of the Italian *timpano*) is preferred inasmuch as Italian rather than Latin forms are used for most of the other instruments.

The most characteristic timpani sound occurs in the middle of the range of each timpano. Notes that are high in an instrument's register tend to sound strained and tight; very low notes sound flabby. If a timpani solo juxtaposes high-tuned and low-tuned drums, the difference in sound can be quite pronounced. Timpanists will always place a given pitch in the middle of an instrument's range if they have a choice.

At one time timpani were hand-tuned; changes in pitch were made by tightening or relaxing screws around the edge of the drumhead. Considerable time (a minimum of about eight measures in a moderate 4/4) was required for each change. During the Classical period, the two timpani normally used were tuned in advance to the tonic and dominant notes of the home key and not altered in the course of the work or movement, although changes between movements of symphonies were sometimes called for. Later on, composers began to require changes in the midst of a composition or movement and to use three timpani instead of two.

Today the standard number is four, and pedal timpani have completely replaced the hand-tuned kind. Changes in pitch are made by means of a foot pedal that controls the degree of tension in the head, which is now often made of plastic rather than calfskin. The motion of the foot can be made quickly, and many players are able to arrive at the new pitch with considerable accuracy simply by estimating the proper angle of the pedal. Nevertheless it is safer to allow a few measures (at least four in a moderate 4/4) for each change in order that there will be time to test the new pitch softly.

Tuning gauges, which are included on some timpani, give the player a mechanical means of arriving at pitches quickly with a high degree of accuracy. They are of particular value in such passages as the one shown in Example 13.13(g). It should be pointed out, though, that that passage is an exceptional one in its demands for rapid changes; such parts are rare and should be written only with professional timpanists in mind.

Normally there is one player for all the timpani, no matter what their number. If, as happens very infrequently, the part is designed to be performed by more than one player, that must be specially indicated. (See, for example, the *Fantastic Symphony* of Berlioz or Stravinsky's *The Rite of Spring.*)

Timpani are notated in bass clef at actual pitch. The tuning is shown at the beginning of the composition in either of the two ways illustrated in Example 13.2.

EXAMPLE 13.2

Ordinarily the part is written without key signature, accidentals being added wherever necessary. In older scores even the accidentals were sometimes omitted once the tuning of each drum had been shown. Another obsolete custom occasionally found in older scores is that of using the notes C and G to indicate the tonic and dominant notes, respectively, in keys other than C. In that case the actual tuning of the drums was shown at the beginning of the part. (See Example 8.1.)

As a general rule, timpani should be used only on notes that fit in as members of the harmony. The chord member most frequently allotted to them is the bass, but they can also take any other harmony note with good effect. For example, let us suppose that we have started a piece with three timpani tuned to G, C, and F, as in Example 13.2. At a certain point in the music we have a C major triad and want to include a timpani note or roll. C would be the most natural choice, but G would also fit in. In an F major triad, either F or C could be used with the tuning at hand, whereas in a G major triad, G would be the only possibility. If a diminished seventh sound on G♯ (G♯, B, D, F) were involved, we would probably use the F already "set" on the top drum rather than tune the bottom drum up to G♯.

Let us imagine now that we have come to a G♭ major triad at a point where timpani are needed. With the present tunings, no one of the three drums is capable of supplying a tone that fits into the harmony. Assuming that there is time for a change before this passage, any one of five different retunings would give us a chord tone: (1) G down to G♭; (2) C up to D♭; (3) C down to B♭; (4) F down to D♭; or (5) F up to G♭. Any such change must be indicated in the part, preferably at the first rest where the player could make the change in order to have as much time as possible for the retuning operation. If the first of the five possible changes were chosen, we would write in the part "Change G to G♭."[2] Scores using Italian terms throughout would indicate "G muta in G♭," the French version would be "Changez Sol en Sol♭," and in German the same direction would be "G nach Ges umstimmen." More than one change may be called for, provided there is sufficient time. It should now be obvious that in writing for timpani one cannot simply put down any notes desired and let the player worry about how to get them. It is necessary to score with a specific number of timpani in mind and to plan each note for a particular timpano; problems of retuning must be kept in mind constantly.

Occasionally it is possible to "get by" with timpani notes foreign to the harmony. These cases usually involve a chord of such short duration that the ear scarcely has time to be aware of the foreign timpani note before the next chord is heard. In a passage where the harmony is sustained, any deviation from a chord tone would be apparent. In cases where it is impossible to prepare the required note on the timpani in time and a foreign note is unacceptable, one solution is to use the bass drum instead since its pitch is indeterminate. The effect, of course, is not the same.

Single notes, rhythmic figures, and rolls are all effective on timpani. The roll may be written in either of these ways:

EXAMPLE 13.3

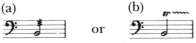

(As with bowed tremolos in string writing, three lines through a stem ordinarily signify an unmeasured roll, two mean measured sixteenths, and one means eighths.) The trill sign would seem preferable for an unmeasured roll because the other type of notation may be confused with an actual measured thirty-second note roll (particularly in slow tempos). In music since 1950, however, most composers seem to prefer the first notation. Where several measures of the roll are involved, it is safest to connect the notes with a tie to avoid any possibility that the player may think a fresh attack is wanted on each note:

EXAMPLE 13.4

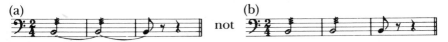

Or if the trill sign is used, write as in Example 13.5(a).

---

[2]A simpler way of expressing the same direction and one often seen today is "G–G♭."

EXAMPLE 13.5

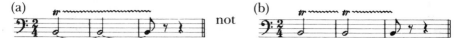

(a)   not   (b)

With the last notation shown, the player would make a new attack on each note. Notice that in these illustrations the roll is carried over so as to end on the beat. This is a frequent practice in percussion writing, the reason being that it is difficult to end a roll neatly on the last fraction of a beat. However, there are cases in which it would be inappropriate to carry the roll over into the next beat, and skilled players are able to cope with such spots. If a separately articulated stroke is wanted at the end of a roll, then the tie into the last note is omitted and the wavy line is stopped short of the last note:

EXAMPLE 13.6

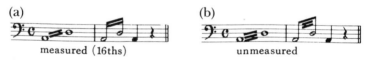

Rolls (measured or unmeasured) on two different timpani are also a possibility:

EXAMPLE 13.7

(a)   (b)

measured (16ths)   unmeasured

The importance of careful and detailed dynamic markings in percussion writing cannot be overstressed. It is not enough to write:

EXAMPLE 13.8

The intended height of the crescendo here might be anything from *p* to *fff* as far as the player can tell from the part. To give complete directions we would have to write:

EXAMPLE 13.9

In long rolls it is not too much to indicate dynamics along the way:

EXAMPLE 13.10

Adagio

Probably the most frequent and obvious use of the timpani is that of backing up the rest of the orchestra in rhythmic figures. (It was conventional in the Classical period to give the timpani and the trumpets the same rhythmic figure.) At other times they may play a separate rhythm of their own. They are also excellent for reinforcing crescendos and for providing excitement or support in climaxes by means of rolls. Extended solos are seldom given to them, though isolated notes and groups of two or three notes played solo are frequent and highly effective. (See certain of the excerpts in Example 13.13; see also Example 14.4[k].) Other works containing notable timpani solos are Hanson, Third Symphony; Harris, Third Symphony (in the fugue); William Schuman, Sixth Symphony; Shostakovich, First Symphony (last movement). It is a mistake to think of the timpani as being valuable only for loud passages. Although they can supply a tremendous volume of sound, they are equally telling and dramatic in soft passages; in fact their tone can be reduced to a barely audible pulsation. One word of warning should be added: because their tone quality is very different from that of other instruments, they must not be expected to fill in a chord tone by themselves—except that they can effectively play pedal points that are not doubled elsewhere in the orchestra.

Several special effects are possible on the timpani. One involves the use of wooden sticks in place of the usual soft felt-headed sticks (Italian: *bacchette di legno;* French: *baguettes en bois;* German: *mit Holzschlegeln*).[3] Usually the object is to produce a harder, more sharply percussive quality, though soft effects are also possible, as, for example, the soft roll with snare drum sticks in Elgar's *Enigma Variations.* The indication for soft sticks is not normally included unless the player has been using hard sticks (Italian: *bacchette molli,* or *bacchette morbide;* French: *baguettes molles;* German: *mit weichen Schlegeln*). Still different types of tone result from using sticks with felt heads or sticks with large or small heads. Another device calls for the use of both sticks at once on a drum; it is indicated by double stems. The result is thicker and weightier than the normal sound (see Example 13.11).

EXAMPLE 13.11

Fourth Symphony

Mahler

Timp.

---

[3]In scores of the Strauss-Mahler period, "stick" in German was spelled *Schlägel.* Today the preferred spelling is *Schlegel.*

It is also possible to play on two different timpani at the same time, as in Example 13.12:

EXAMPLE 13.12

Till Eulenspiegel

Strauss

Berlioz even wrote three-note and four-note chords for timpani in the *Fantastic Symphony*, but of course these require two players. A particular tone quality can be achieved by striking the drum in the center instead of near the edge. (See Gershwin's *An American in Paris*.) Timpani may be muffled (or muted) by placing a cloth about two inches square on the head of the drum near the edge. The Italian direction is *timpani coperti*. A special effect, achieved by changing the pedal while the drum is sounding, is the glissando. As in string writing, the indication is a line between the notes (both of which must be within the range of one timpano, of course). Example 13.13(f) involves repeated use of the glissando device. Example 13.13(h) is unusual in its demands for pitches outside the normal range; the high B would presumably be played on a 20-inch timpano.

Some recent scores have called for various objects to be placed on the head of a timpano and then struck. A cymbal, for instance, is placed upside down on the head and struck lightly. The cymbal and the timpano head vibrate, and the hollow cavity of the timpano amplifies the resulting sound.

EXAMPLES

EXAMPLE 13.13

(a) Ninth Symphony

(b) Ninth Symphony (*New World*)

(c) *Don Juan*

(d)   First Symphony

(e)   Third Symphony

(f) *Music for String Instruments, Percussion and Celesta*

(g)   Concerto for Orchestra

(h)   A Symphony of Three Orchestras

THE ROTO-TOM

Italian: Roto-tom-tom   *French:* Roto-tom   *German:* Tom-Tom-Spiel

EXAMPLE 13.14

This instrument, introduced in 1968, is a small tom-tom that can be tuned to specific pitches by rotating the drum on a base to which it is attached, thereby tightening or relaxing the tension of the drumhead. It is made in several sizes (see Figure 13.1), the respective ranges of which are shown in Example 13.14. Normally, a mechanical device prevents each drum from rotating beyond the point at which the top note shown for each range will be produced. If that device is removed, each drum is capable of extending its upward range, but these higher tones are of a different quality—extremely dry and lacking in resonance. There is, as a matter of fact, a great difference in timbre between high and low notes within the range given for each drum. For this reason, a roto-tom passage that involves several different drums seldom presents a unified or homogeneous sound. The roto-tom may be played with yarn-covered xylophone mallets, with felt timpani mallets, with the hands, or with wire brushes.

Recently a pedal mechanism such as the one found on the timpani has been introduced. Pedal roto-toms are not in common use, however.

THE XYLOPHONE

Italian: Silofono   *French:* Xylophone   *German:* Xylophon
(*or* Xilofono)

EXAMPLE 13.15

Sounding an 8ve higher.

234

The xylophone consists of a set of wooden or synthetic bars of varying lengths arranged in the same pattern as the notes on the piano and with a tuned resonator beneath each bar (see Figure 13.2). It is played with hard mallets, normally two, although three or four may be used to play chords. Forsyth gives a good idea of the tone of the instrument when he speaks of its "hard dry clatter." The notes are necessarily short and crisp, for there is no way to sustain them except by means of a roll. The xylophone is therefore generally unsuited to music of a lyric or *espressivo* nature, but it can perform rapid scales, arpeggios, repeated notes, glissandos, and many other figures with surprising ease. (Incidentally, passages entirely on the "white" keys are more difficult than those involving both black and white keys.) In certain music it manages to give a saucy, mocking quality; at other times it may simply add a brittle edge to a melodic line or point up certain notes. (See Debussy's *Ibéria*, the section entitled *Les parfums de la nuit*, for an example of this last use. An excerpt from that section is given in Example 16.20.)

Xylophones are built in various sizes; consequently, it is impossible to give one range that will apply to all of them. A few do not include the notes below middle C. Notation is on a single staff, in treble clef, one octave lower than the sounds desired. The authors of some books on orchestration recommend writing the xylophone part at actual pitch, and that system has been much used. But it was based on the belief that the instrument's range

FIGURE 13.2

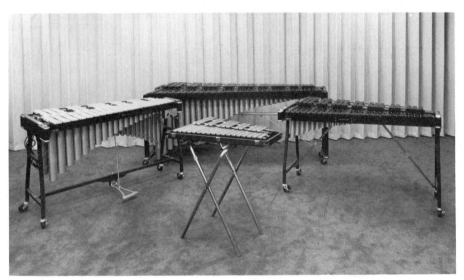

Dorf Photography, Austin, Texas

Vibraphone **Marimba** **Xylophone**

Glockenspiel
(Orchestra Bells)

extended only up to $\underset{\circ}{\overset{8}{}}$, whereas the top sound on all xylophones is
actually c⁵, an octave higher than the pitch just shown. In view of this fact,
the system of notation recommended here is a much more sensible one
since it avoids the use of an unreasonable number of ledger lines in high
passages.

Xylophone parts should be written with a key signature where that is
appropriate.

Mallets of different degrees of hardness will produce correspon-
dingly different gradations of intensity in attack; the range of materials is
from medium-hard rubber to hard rubber to plastic.

EXAMPLES

EXAMPLE 13.16

(a) *Petrouchka*

(b) *The Young Person's Guide to the Orchestra*

(c) *Chronochromie*

THE MARIMBA

Note: *The "Symphonic Grand" marimba extends to low F.*
The "Concert" marimba extends to low A.

The marimba resembles the xylophone in appearance (see Figure 13.2), but its bars are larger and of a different shape. Each bar has a tuned resonator beneath it. The marimba is played with relatively soft sticks because its bars, unlike those of the xylophone, would be easily damaged by the use of hard sticks. The tone of the marimba is much more mellow and subdued than that of the xylophone. Its timbre is easily absorbed or covered, and it must be given a somewhat exposed part if it is to come through.

In Example 13.16(c), both xylophone and marimba are used to imitate the call of a bird (the Attila, of Mexico). In measure 2, both instruments perform a glissando over the white keys. (Because of the keyboard layout, white key glissandos are the only kind possible on each of these instruments.) The *d* and *g* markings beginning at the end of the first measure are French abbreviations for right- and left-hand (mallets), respectively. The use of four mallets to perform rolled chords is illustrated in Example 13.18. This approach is practical as long as the interval in each hand is no larger than an octave. Although marimba parts are usually written on one staff, two may be employed if necessary.

EXAMPLE 13.18

Two Sonnets by Michelangelo

Karel Husa

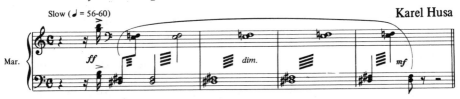

THE GLOCKENSPIEL OR ORCHESTRA BELLS[4]

Italian: Campanelli   *French:* Jeu de Timbres   *German:* Glockenspiel
                               (*or* Carillon)

EXAMPLE 13.19

The glockenspiel generally used in orchestras today consists of a set of metal bars attached to a portable case which is opened up and placed on a table in performance (see Figure 13.2). Another type, now rarely seen, includes a supporting frame and resonators beneath the bars.

The bright, ringing tone of the glockenspiel is normally produced by striking the metal bars with plastic or brass mallets. A somewhat more subdued quality can be achieved by using rubber mallets, but these should be called for specifically in the part when desired. Although it is possible for the player to hold two mallets in each hand and therefore to play three-note and four-note chords, parts for the instrument usually consist of a single melodic line. Their most frequent function is to add a bright tang to melodies taken by other instruments, but solos are practical and effective. The part is normally written two octaves lower than it is intended to sound. However, in Wagner scores and in certain others, it is notated only *one* octave below the concert sounds. Glockenspiels, like xylophones, are built in various sizes; not all of them have the complete range shown here.

A small portable glockenspiel is now made for use in marching bands. That has replaced the "bell lyre," a vertical and abbreviated version of the instrument that suffered from inferior intonation and harsh tone quality.

There is also a keyed glockenspiel which is commonly used in Europe but is rarely seen in this country. This is the instrument for which the formidable looking glockenspiel part in Dukas' *The Sorcerer's Apprentice* was designed.

The glockenspiel's tone decays much more slowly than that of the xylophone. Rapid passages on the glockenspiel if very extended will be blurred. This produces a shimmering effect that can be quite attractive in the proper context but inappropriate if maximum clarity is desired. It is possible for the performer to damp a pitch with a finger if given enough time. The indication for this effect is a small "x" placed after the note to be damped.

---

[4]Not to be confused with tubular bells, or chimes, which are discussed later.

Example 13.20

Finger (or mallet) damping can also be used with other instruments whose sounds have a slow rate of decay (vibraphone, crotales, etc.).

EXAMPLES

Example 13.21

(a) Symphony: *Mathis der Maler*

(b) *Formel*

(c) *A Mirror of Whitening Light*

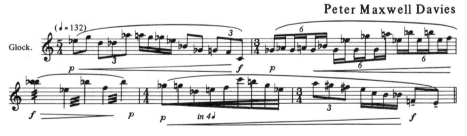

(d) *Green*

Toru Takemitsu

THE VIBRAPHONE

Italian: Vibrafono   *French:* Vibraphone   *German:* Vibraphon

EXAMPLE 13.22

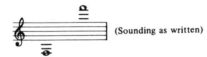

(Sounding as written)

The vibraphone (Figure 13.2) is a relative newcomer to the instrumental scene. Although for a time it was associated chiefly with jazz and commercial music, it has since found great favor with many serious composers. It resembles the xylophone in general pattern. Metal bars arranged in "keyboard" fashion on a stand are resonated by tuned tubes below. But the instrument is distinguished by an ingenious feature: small metal discs, one at the top of each resonating tube, are made to revolve by means of an electric motor, producing a kind of pulse or vibrato in the tone (a quantitative rather than a pitch vibrato, however). The speed with which the discs revolve can be regulated, with a corresponding variation in the speed of the vibrato. It is possible to cut out the vibrato effect entirely by turning off the motor (direction: "motor off"). There is a damper pedal which may be used to sustain or damp the sound. The same pedal indications used for the piano's damper pedal are used for the vibraphone.

Parts for the vibraphone may be either melodic or harmonic in character. Chords (up to four notes) that are allowed to ring show off the peculiar floating, undulating tone to good advantage in the orchestra. It is possible to play isolated notes by bowing the edge of the bars with a double bass bow. This device is sometimes used by composers in very delicate textures because it completely eliminates contact sounds. The tone seems to appear out of nowhere. If this technique is called for, the performer must be given a good deal of time to prepare for each note. "Black and white" keys must be bowed on opposite sides of the instrument. (It is possible to bow other percussion instruments, the crotales and tam-tam being the most frequent choices.)

Another excellent effect is to turn the motor on shortly after a single pitch or chord has been played. The change from the "cool, white" timbre to the pulsating vibrato is quite perceptible and very effective.

The instrument may be played with either hard or soft sticks, most often the latter. The part is written on a single staff, in the treble clef, at actual pitch.

EXAMPLE 13.23

(a)   Third Symphony

Roy Harris

(b)   *Echoes from an Invisible World*

Leslie Bassett

(c)   *Nr. 6 Gruppen für drei Orchester*

Karlheinz Stockhausen

TUBULAR BELLS (OR CHIMES)

Italian: Campane   *French:* Cloches   *German:* Glocken
       (Tubolari)   (*or* Tubes de Cloches)   (*or* Röhrenglocken)

EXAMPLE 13.24

(Sounding as written)

Of the various kinds of bells that have been tried in the orchestra over the years, the tubular bells, or chimes, are the only type now in standard use. They are hung from a rack and, when used as a complete set, are arranged like the white and black keys of the piano (see Figure 13.1); that is, the tubes that correspond to the black keys are hung behind the others and slightly higher so that there will be space to strike them. But since bell parts often consist of only a few notes, it is usually easier to hang up only those tubes actually needed for a given work. Most sets of chimes include a pedal by means of which the sound may be damped or allowed to ring. Because of the varying sizes of different makes of bells, the range given here is not an invariable one but may be considered more or less standard, at least in the United States.

There has long been disagreement regarding the octave in which the tubular bells sound. Some persons hear the notes as being in the octave shown in Example 13.24, whereas others claim that the actual sounds are an octave lower. (Recent research supports the first view.) Such disagreement stems from the special acoustical processes associated with vibrating tubes: One strange feature is that the *apparent* pitch of each tube is not actually present; what the ear perceives is instead a product of the complex set of vibrations involved. In any case, bell parts should be notated within the range given here.

A colorful white-key glissando can be played on the instrument. This is performed with two hammers, one for the glissando and the other for the terminating pitch (which may be either a white or black key). Very high overtones can be elicited from a chime by lightly striking it from above at the center point with a brass mallet. The resulting sound is soft and delicate.

The three excerpts in Example 13.25(b) are from a work that makes extensive use of the tubular bells. Three percussionists are required, each of whom plays a set of chimes. The composer directs that the percussionists be widely separated on the stage. The chimes begin the piece alone, as shown in the first excerpt. In the second excerpt, percussionist I uses two hammers to perform the tremolo. The third excerpt shows the beginning of a three-part canon up to the point where the second voice enters. Only the chimes participate in the canon, and they continue unaccompanied for seventeen measures in a highly contrapuntal texture.

EXAMPLES

EXAMPLE 13.25

(a) *Ibéria*

(b) *A Ring of Time*

later

later

THE CROTALES AND ANTIQUE CYMBALS

Italian: Crotali   *French:* Cymbales antiques   *German:* (Antike) Zimbeln
(*or* Crotales)

EXAMPLE 13.26

Antique
Cymbals   Sounding an 8ve higher (see text).

There exists some confusion today as to precisely what instrument may be desired when a composer specifies crotales or antique cymbals. Reginald Smith Brindle, in his splendid book *Contemporary Percussion*, describes several different instruments that may be referred to as "crotales."[5] He also notes that there is no consensus as to whether crotales should be played singly or in pairs or even if they are definite- or indefinite-pitched instruments.

In the past when composers specified "antique cymbals," they had in mind very small cymbals played in pairs that sounded a definite pitch. These cymbals are held one in each hand and struck together lightly at the rims, the small bell-like sound being allowed to ring. Obviously the method of performing upon this instrument limits the number of notes and the complexity of parts that can be played. Among the composers who have used antique cymbals are Berlioz (*Romeo and Juliet*), Debussy (*Prelude to The Afternoon of a Faun*), Stravinsky (*Les Noces, The Rite of Spring*), and Ravel (*Daphnis and Chloe* Suite No. 1). The first four works call for two pairs, the last for six pairs.

When contemporary composers desire instruments of this type, they usually specify antique cymbals "in pairs" to distinguish them from crotales that are played singly with a beater.

The antique cymbals have been written both at actual pitch and an

---

[5]The term *crotales* appears to be replacing the term *antique cymbals* in English.

octave below the sounds desired. Therefore, parts for them should state which method of notation is used.

Today's crotales are circular in shape and made of heavy metal. They vary in diameter from about 5½ inches to 3 inches and are about a quarter of an inch thick (see Figure 13.1). Parts for antique cymbals are often played by this instrument. The range is

EXAMPLE 13.27

These crotales may either be mounted on a stand in keyboard fashion or suspended from a frame. They are played with a variety of beaters, including plastic or brass mallets, or triangle beaters, and as demonstrated in Example 13.28, complex technical passages are possible on crotales when they are played in this fashion. The timbre is crystalline and pure and is most effective at soft dynamic levels. Pitch definition tends to diminish at louder dynamic levels. The glockenspiel and the crotales share approximately the same range, and loud passages in this register that require a definite-pitched metal percussion instrument would be more suited to the glockenspiel than to the crotales.

The composers of a number of recent works (George Crumb in *Echoes of Time and the River,* for instance) have instructed that crotales be distributed to and played by members of the orchestra other than the percussionists. This is feasible because the instruments are small and easy to play. Sidney Hodkinson's *November Voices* requires a number of crotales players to be dispersed in the audience. They play only at the end of the work and with magical effect.

EXAMPLE 13.28

Symphony

Peter Maxwell Davies

© *Copyright 1978 by Boosey & Hawkes Music Publishers Ltd. Reprinted by permission of Boosey & Hawkes, Inc.*

THE MUSICAL SAW

Italian: Sega cantante   *French:* Scie musicale   *German:* Spielsäge

EXAMPLE 13.29

Though rarely used, the musical saw has a colorful timbre that could well be exploited more often in the orchestra. It consists of a steel blade fastened to a wooden handle. (There is also a larger version that attaches to a base that rests on the floor.) The handle is placed between the knees while the performer holds the blade in the left hand and either bows the edge or strikes the blade with a soft stick. When bowed, the instrument produces a singing tone well suited to sustained lines that do not move too quickly. Intonation is difficult, and a pronounced glissando is audible between each two notes. Most percussionists will not be able to play an involved and demanding part without a great deal of practice.

ALMGLOCKEN

Italian: Campane da   *French:* Sonnailles de   *German:* Almglocken
pastore   troupeau

EXAMPLE 13.30

These oval Swiss cowbells (Figure 13.1) may be played with hard or soft mallets. The sound is hollow and rather somber, especially at soft dynamic levels. Stockhausen's *Nr. 6 Gruppen für drei Orchester* requires thirteen almglocken.

THE ANVIL

Italian: Incudine   *French:* Enclume   *German:* Amboss

The anvil is a small, solid steel bar played with a metal hammer or a steel beater. When writing for the instrument, one specifies the pitch but not the octave in which it will occur. The anvil appears in scores by Verdi, Berlioz, Wagner, Mahler, Copland, and others.

BRAKE DRUMS

As the name implies, brake drums are actually automobile parts—circular metal discs. When struck with a mallet they produce a sound similar to that of the anvil, though not so high, and they are sometimes substituted for anvil parts. Mallets made of brass, yarn, or rubber are particularly effective. Brake drums of various sizes are available, and a number of composers have called for three or more in their scores. Although brake drums produce specific pitches, it is impossible to count on the availability of a brake drum with the specific pitch one may need. It is wiser to write for the instrument as if it were of indefinite pitch, or to specify only relative pitches when more than one brake drum is required.

THE FLEXATONE

Italian: Flexatone　　　　*French:* Flexatone　　　　*German:* Flexaton

EXAMPLE 13.31

This instrument consists of a band of metal bent somewhat in the shape of an inverted U, to one side of which are attached two small pieces of metal topped by wooden knobs, which strike the metal band when the instrument is shaken. The player holds it by a cylindrical handle at the bottom and uses the thumb to control the angle (and therefore the pitch) of the metal portion that is vibrating. The resulting sound is a bit like that of a musical saw, although more percussive. In the Khachaturian Piano Concerto, a footnote to the flexatone part at measure 49 of the second movement says, "Whistling sound required." Other instances of the instrument's use can be seen in the Schönberg *Variations for Orchestra,* Op. 31 (Variation 3) and in Penderecki's *De natura sonoris,* No. 2.

PICTOGRAMS

Some composers identify beaters and percussion instruments in their scores by using symbols called pictograms. The pictograms for the beaters and instruments discussed in this chapter are shown in Figures 14.2 and 14.3.

SUGGESTED ASSIGNMENTS[6]

A. Know:

1. ranges of timpani of various sizes.
2. which timpani are in common use.
3. how tuning operation works.
4. special effects possible on timpani.
5. ranges, transpositions, and special abilities of other instruments discussed in this chapter.

B. Write a part for four timpani for "The Star-Spangled Banner." The timpani need not play continuously.

C. Write a part for three timpani (one 28-inch, one 25-inch, and either a 23-inch or a 30-inch) for "America" or for another short, vigorous composition.

D. Write a timpani part (the number of timpani to be specified by the instructor) for "Important Event" (from *Scenes from Childhood*) by Schumann.

---

[6]Material for suggested listening is given at the end of Chapter 14.

14

The Percussion: Instruments of Indefinite Pitch

THE SNARE DRUM (OR SIDE DRUM)

Italian: Tamburo
(Militare)

French: Tambour
(Militaire)
(*or* Caisse Claire)[1]

German: Kleine Trommel

Along with other instruments of indeterminate pitch, many of which are shown in Figure 14.1, the snare drum may be notated, in the score, either on a staff or on a single line:

EXAMPLE 14.1

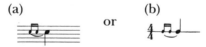

For a long time it was common in scores using the staff notation to include a treble clef to distinguish the snare drum part from the bass drum and cymbal part, which often used bass clef. That system is no longer recommended. Today percussion instruments of indefinite pitch are written either with no clef at all or with a "neutral" clef:

---

[1]Strictly speaking, the *caisse claire* is a very small drum; but the name is often used in contemporary French scores to mean snare drum.

FIGURE 14.1

Dorf Photography, Austin, Texas

Back row (from left):	**Tam-tam, Gong, Triangle, Bamboo Wind Chimes, Bass Drum with beater**
Table (back row from left):	**Four Temple Blocks, Cowbell, Tambourine, Bell Tree**
Table (foreground from left):	**Two Antique Cymbals in front of two Wood Blocks, Claves, Maracas, mounted Castanets, Flexatone, Guiro, Slapstick, five kinds of beaters in front of Tambourine, Cymbals**
Stand-mounted drums (from left):	**Tom-toms, Bongos, Timbales**
Front row on floor (from left):	**Snare Drum, Tenor Drum, Conga Drum**

The snare drum part may be written in the third space or anywhere else on the staff that is convenient. (More will be said about this later.) When two percussion parts are written on the same staff in order to save space, separate stems—one up, one down—are used.

The snare drum is at its best in crisp, sharply rhythmic passages. It is usually played with wooden sticks, although softer sticks (such as hard timpani sticks) or wire brushes may occasionally be called for.

In order to write well for the snare drum—and most of the other drums discussed in this chapter—it is necessary to be familiar with at least the following rudimental strokes:

The *flam* ♪ . In the closed flam, which is the usual orchestral

form, the first note is played unaccented before the beat and joined quickly with the second. This stroke is used to strengthen or lengthen a note. The open flam, in which the first note is articulated separately with more of an accent, is rare in orchestral playing. It is used primarily in music of martial character or on drums with slow response, such as the tenor drum. Composers are not consistent in their notation of closed and open strokes. The authors recommend using a slur when the stroke is to be closed and omitting it when the open effect is desired.

Another type of flam sometimes encountered is the French flam. As the following notation implies, both sticks strike the drumhead at almost the same time and with the same force: ⊥ .

The *drag*, usually ⎮, consists of two very rapid notes preceding an accented note. These preparatory notes are generally not heard separately but merge into a brief roll effect that is performed so quickly as to seem almost like a part of the note it precedes.

The *four-stroke ruff*, ⎮, consists of three notes preceding an accented note. This stroke is played open (with the preparatory notes articulated).

The *roll* ⎮ or ⎮.

Comments on the notation of the roll made in connection with the timpani apply here as well. This is one of the snare drum's most effective devices. As anyone who has ever seen a tightrope act will remember, an extended roll on the snare drum has an uncanny way of creating a sense of tension and expectancy. Shorter rolls are used constantly in march rhythms and in other orchestral parts played by the snare drum.

All these strokes should be freely employed by the orchestrator because they provide performers with idiomatic parts they can play with relish.

A special effect that originated in the dance band and occasionally finds its way into the concert hall is the "rim shot." It may be performed in either of two ways. In the first, one stick is placed with the tip on the drumhead and the butt on the rim and is then struck with the other stick. The result is a sharp, dry sound. The performer needs to be given a brief moment to prepare this effect. The other type, which Reginald Smith Brindle refers to as the "hoop crack," is performed by striking the head and the rim at the same instant with one stick. The hoop crack needs no preparation and may be employed within an active passage involving other strokes. However, it is more difficult to perform and the resulting sound is less uniform than the previously described rim shot. The two effects may be notated as follows:

EXAMPLE 14.2

(a)   Rim shot   (b)   Hoop crack

Rhythmic patterns of all kinds and complexities are possible on the snare drum. But it must not be kept going steadily, for if overused it becomes either ineffective or downright tiresome. Forsyth comments, "Like almost all the other Percussion Instruments, its principal effect is its entry." Apropos of this point, an axiom to keep in mind is that instruments of highly individual color are generally effective in inverse proportion to the amount they are used.

The snare drum's timbre can be varied by loosening the snares, in which case the instrument sounds rather like a tom-tom. The clearest direction for this effect is "snares off." Another special effect can be achieved by covering the drumhead with a handkerchief (direction: "cover head"). This is, by the way, the crispest sound obtainable on the snare drum. The term *muffled snare drum* has unfortunately been used to describe both these effects; consequently it has become ambiguous and is better avoided altogether.

Certain modern composers, Bartók among them, occasionally specify whether the snare drum is to be played at the edge or at the middle of the head. The sound rings more at the rim, while at the middle it has a duller sound. All drums are normally played between the center and the rim.

(Examples of passages for snare drum and for other instruments discussed here are given in Example 14.4.)

THE FIELD DRUM

Italian: Tamburo (Militare)	*French:* Tambour	*German:* Rührtrommel

As can be seen, there is a good deal of ambiguity in connection with the foreign names for the field drum since some of them are used for other, slightly different instruments.

The field drum is longer than the snare drum, and its tone is somewhat deeper and less brittle. It is usually equipped with gut snares. This drum is regularly used in bands, and parts for it in orchestral literature are not uncommon. (One example occurs in Hindemith's *Symphonic Metamorphosis of Themes by C. M. von Weber*.)

THE TENOR DRUM

Italian: Tamburo Rullante	*French:* Caisse Roulante	*German:* Rührtrommel

Also longer and larger than the snare drum but not nearly so large as the bass drum, the tenor drum is used much less frequently than either of these two. It has no snares, and its tone is more somber than that of the snare drum. It is normally played with wooden sticks.

THE TABOR

Italian: Tamburo   *French:* Tambour de Provence   *German:* Tambourin
                         (*or* Tambourin)

This is a very long drum, equipped with a single snare in most cases. It is rarely seen in the United States. The part for it in Bizet's second *L'Arlésienne* Suite is labeled "tambourin," and even eminent conductors have been known to make the mistake of having it played on the tambourine. Examples of the use of the tabor in contemporary music can be found in Aaron Copland's *Appalachian Spring* and *El Salón México*.

THE TOM-TOMS

Italian, French, and German: Tom-toms

When writing for tom-toms, composers usually call for at least two drums, but it is not uncommon to see parts for five or even more. The drums are of different sizes, each with its own relative pitch. They are generally arranged so that the lowest drum is at the performer's left, with the medium instruments in the middle and the high instruments at the right, but other arrangements are possible and may be requested in order to facilitate the performance of a difficult part. Tom-toms have a relatively pure sound that is uniform from the lowest drum to the highest. For this reason they are extremely valuable in a musical texture where several different indefinite-pitched drum sounds with a unified timbre are required. Percussionists can perform rapid passages over five or more drums with brilliant effect and dazzling virtuosity, provided the part avoids such difficulties as awkward hand crossovers.

   Tom-toms have no snares. They usually have two heads, each adjusted to a different degree of tension. It is possible to tune the drums, although the closely related roto-toms would be a better choice for passages requiring definite pitches. A wide variety of beaters—from snare drum sticks to soft sticks, as well as the fingers and hands—may be used.

THE BASS DRUM

Italian: Gran Cassa   *French:* Grosse Caisse   *German:* Grosse
   (*or simply*   Trommel
   Cassa)

The bass drum is a more versatile instrument than one might suspect. Obviously it is well equipped to add volume or percussive accent to the orchestral *tutti*. However, its effectiveness in soft passages is too often ignored; at lower dynamic levels, it is "felt" rather than heard, and the lay listener may even be unaware that it is playing. Soft rolls, which give a faintly threatening sound not unlike distant thunder, are especially useful for color effects. Also, the instrument can be played with snare drum sticks. Since these have much smaller and harder heads than the usual bass drum beater, more active and involved rhythmic figurations are possible. As one might expect, the listener senses a "surfacy" kind of sound accompanied by a faint echo from the large cavity of the instrument.

Occasionally the bass drum can give the impression of producing a definite pitch. For instance, if a bass drum roll were combined with a low pedal point in double basses and cellos, the bass drum could sound like a very low timpano playing a definite pitch (the pedal note). In Example 14.4(n), the composer calls for the bass drum to be tuned to a specific pitch.

Unlike the snare drum, the bass drum has a slow rate of decay, and it is wise to specify the exact duration of isolated or separated notes. Despite this, it is possible to play staccato passages, the tone being damped with the hand. These passages should be marked "secco."

As with other percussion instruments of indefinite pitch, the bass drum may be written on a single line or on a staff.

THE CYMBALS

Italian: Piatti   *French:* Cymbales   *German:* Becken

Among the various ways of producing sound on the cymbals, the crash or "two-plate stroke" is by far the most frequently used. The word *crash* must not be construed in this case as meaning only a loud sound, for this stroke can be performed at any dynamic level, from *ppp* to *fff*. One of the most ingenious and effective spots in orchestral literature occurs at the end of the *Fêtes* section in Debussy's *Nocturnes,* where the cymbals are merely brushed together softly to produce a single note. Loud cymbal crashes are much more frequent and are apt to be used for moments of excitement or for climax points. Since there is considerable ring to a cymbal crash, it is wise to indicate in actual note values just how long the sound is to last before being damped. (Damping is achieved by touching the cymbals to a player's clothing.) If the sound is to be allowed to ring indefinitely, an easy

indication is a small tie that simply ends in the air: ⚬⌐. Sometimes *l.v.,*

the abbreviation for the French expression *laissez vibrer* ("let vibrate"), is used. If, on the other hand, the note is to be "choked" (made very short), it

should be written like this: ♪ ⅞ ⅜⌐. Instead of *secco, choke* may be writ-
secco

ten in.

In the "two-plate roll" the cymbals are rubbed together with a circular motion. The effect is much inferior to a roll on the suspended cymbal and is little used today.

THE SUSPENDED CYMBAL

Italian: Piatto sospeso   *French:* Cymbale   *German:* Hängendes
                                        suspendue   Becken
                                                                  (*or* Becken frei)

A single cymbal can be mounted on a stand and struck with a stick, or two sticks can be used to produce a roll. Single notes (which may be either damped or allowed to ring) are usable not only in *forte* for purposes of percussive accent but also in a *piano* for a particular color effect. Widely contrasting timbres may be obtained by using different kinds of sticks and by striking at different places on the cymbal. For example, striking near the rim with a soft beater produces a low, warm, undulating kind of sound, while striking near the raised center of the cymbal with a triangle beater produces a high, percussive sound without much body. Rolls can produce anything from an almost imperceptible shimmer to a deafening volume of sound. They are especially useful for accenting a crescendo played by the rest of the orchestra. Normally, yarn-covered marimba mallets are used, but for special effects snare drum sticks, triangle beaters, wire brushes, darning needles, and so on may be substituted. Soft timpani sticks, though frequently specified by composers, are relatively ineffective and are not recommended.

Orchestral scores sometimes call for a "sizzle cymbal." This is an instrument similar to the suspended cymbal but with holes drilled near the rim and loosely fitted rivets placed in them. When the cymbal is struck, the rivets vibrate along with the cymbal, producing the characteristic sizzling sound. Sometimes a light chain is fastened to the center of the cymbal and laid over its surface to create the sizzle effect. Single strokes on the instrument are more highly colored and of longer duration than those on the ordinary suspended cymbal.

Occasionally one sees several cymbals of different sizes suspended from a frame by a single chord. Single strokes and rolls can be played on any of the cymbals, and the different relative pitches are an added timbral resource.

Cymbal parts are occasionally printed in diamond-shaped notes, and commercial arrangements commonly use an X in place of a real note. Although these systems make the cymbal part easy to spot in the score, they have certain disadvantages: the diamond-shaped notes are difficult to make in writing music by hand, and the X's do not show the actual value of each tone. Ordinary notes appear to be the best solution.

THE FINGER CYMBALS

Italian: Cimbalini   *French:* Cymbales   *German:* Fingerzimbeln
                                     digitales

Similar to antique cymbals in appearance, finger cymbals are normally played in pairs. They are struck together at the rims to produce a high, thin, bell-like sound. They are often tuned approximately a semitone apart. When both cymbals are allowed to ring, however, the resulting sound seems to be of indefinite pitch. It is also possible to hang one finger cymbal from a frame and strike it. If this is done, the ear is much more likely to perceive a definite pitch than when two cymbals are used.

THE TRIANGLE

Italian: Triangolo   *French:* Triangle   *German:* Triangel

Single notes, tremolos (rolls), and not-too-complicated rhythms are all effective on the triangle, and the *flam* and *drag* figures mentioned in connection with the snare drum are common. Normally the instrument is suspended from one of the player's hands and struck with a single steel beater held in the other hand; more complex rhythms may be executed by suspending the triangle from a rack and using two beaters, one in each hand.

The silvery, ringing tone of the triangle is valuable for adding brilliance in either a *forte* or a *piano,* and a triangle roll at climax points can give an extra degree of excitement and intensity. The instrument should not be used too long at a time, however, for its distinctive tone tends to pall quickly.

Solos for the triangle are rare, though Liszt's E♭ major Piano Concerto includes a well-known one. Notation is either on a staff or on a single line.

Triangles and triangle beaters are made in different sizes, and the tone quality varies accordingly. The smaller the triangle and the beater, the higher and more delicate the sound.

THE TAMBOURINE

Italian: Tamburino   *French:* Tambour de   *German:* Schellentrommel
(*or* Tamburo Basco)   Basque   (*or* Tambourin)

The tambourine consists of a small wooden hoop with a plastic or calfskin head stretched across one side of it and pairs of small metal plates called jingles attached in openings cut in the hoop. The instrument can be played in various ways.

1. It may be struck with the fist. This method is suitable for isolated notes and for fairly simple rhythms. It produces the percussive sound of the knuckles striking the head, along with the sound of the jingles. The word *fist* is sometimes written in. Some players prefer to strike the tambourine on the knee to produce the same effect, and in rapid passages alternate fist and knee strokes are sometimes used.

2. It may be shaken, in which case a roll on the jingles results. This is a brilliant sound, useful as an added touch of excitement and color and especially good

    in dynamics of *forte* or louder. The notation is either _♩_ or _♩_

    (preferably the first).

3. The thumb may be rubbed over the head to produce a roll on the jingles. This

effect is especially appropriate for softer dynamic levels, though it can also be played *forte*. Each note played as a thumb roll must be of short duration (no more than two or three seconds), since the player has only a small surface on which to move the thumb. Ravel uses ⬩ for this thumb method and ⬩ when the tambourine is to be shaken, a simple and efficient way of distinguishing between the two effects.

4. The tambourine may be laid on a table or flat surface and played with sticks. The result is a combination of struck sound and jingle sound. When this method is to be used, some such direction as "played with soft sticks" or "played with snare drum sticks" must be included. For soft passages the tambourine may be placed head downward on a cloth and the rim played with the fingers.

Of course no one method of playing need be used consistently. It is quite possible to have, for example, a "fist" note on the first beat of a measure and a roll on the succeeding beats. Obviously the fourth method takes a moment to set up and cannot be intermingled quickly with the others (except by using two tambourines). The tambourine is frequently used to back up vivid rhythms, or it may simply add color or accent at certain points. Characteristic parts for the instrument can be seen in Rimsky-Korsakoff's *Capriccio Espagnol* and Wagner's *Tannhäuser* Overture, among other works. Another effective part appears in Example 11.24.

THE TAM-TAM

Italian: Tamtam   *French:* Tam-tam   *German:* Tamtam

The tam-tam is a circular piece of hammered or spun metal that is struck with a heavy soft-headed beater. Its tone is most effective when the instrument is allowed to vibrate a moment; therefore, when successive strokes are used, they should be spaced far enough apart to allow for ample vibration on each. However, rolls are possible. Although the tam-tam is not ordinarily damped, *secco* (short) notes are occasionally used. In *The Rite of Spring*, Stravinsky requires the player to describe an arc on the surface of the tam-tam with a triangle beater.

The instrument need have neither oriental connotations (as it so often does in commercial music) nor the sinister and macabre character it assumes in the context of such works as Strauss's *Death and Transfiguration* or Tchaikovsky's Sixth Symphony. Sometimes it is used simply to add an unexpected and exotic touch of color, as in Example 14.4(h); or it may supply loud notes which have much the same function as cymbal crashes, as in Example 14.4(i). Tam-tams are made in various sizes, and some composers specify "large tam-tam" or "small tam-tam" in their scores.

In much recent music, composers have successfully experimented with the tam-tam in efforts to achieve novel and arresting timbres. Bowing the rim of the instrument with a double bass bow and playing it with beaters not used for it in the past are just two of many recent performing techniques.

A few scores call for a "water gong." This is a tam-tam (usually small), which is struck and then lowered into a tub of water. That process lowers the pitch of the instrument and produces a glissando effect.

THE GONG

Italian, French, and German: Gong

The gong is often confused with the tam-tam, but composers should be aware of differences between the two. The tam-tam is flat or slightly convex in shape, whereas the center of the gong normally features some kind of dome-shaped protuberance. And unlike the tam tam, the gong usually produces a definite pitch.

Although the gong can contribute a deep, majestic, somber timbre to the orchestra, there is neither a standard range nor a standardized number of instruments that composers can rely on. It is therefore risky to count on the availability of a specific instrument in all performance situations. Definite-pitched gong parts are often played by almglocken when the required gongs are unavailable.

When writing for the gong, it is customary to specify the pitch but not the octave.

CASTANETS

Italian: Castagnette   *French:* Castagnettes   *German:* Kastagnetten

The sound of castanets is familiar to everyone through Spanish music. But for the sake of those who have never seen them close at hand, they can be described as resembling oversized hickory nuts, chopped in half and partially hollowed out. The name itself means "chestnuts" and was presumably derived from the type of wood used. Today castanets are most often made of ebonite. They were designed originally to be clicked in the hand, but the current practice in orchestras is to use a mechanically mounted set that is played with the fingers.

Granted that castanets are most often heard in music with a Spanish flavor, they can sometimes be included effectively in non-Spanish music when a crisp rhythmic background is in order. Stravinsky, Walton, and Varèse have all used them in that fashion.

THE WOOD BLOCK

Italian: Cassettina   *French:* Wood block   *German:* Holzblock
(*or* Blocco di   (*or* Bloc de bois)
legno)

The wood block, as its name implies, is a small rectangular piece of wood (or plastic), solid except for slits cut into it on two sides to give a resonating space. Wooden drumsticks or hard rubber mallets are used in playing it, and rhythms of all kinds are possible. The tone is dry and brittle—a little reminiscent of horses' hooves, especially in certain rhythms. Single notes on the wood block have an impudent, unexpected quality that may verge on the comic. Wood blocks are made in several sizes, and it is feasible to write for two, three, or even more. (See Example 14.4[l].) Notes on different lines or spaces indicate the various sizes.

TEMPLE BLOCKS

Italian: Blocchi di legno coreani (*or* Blocchi cinesi) *French:* Temple blocks *German:* Tempelblöcke

Temple blocks are a series of hollow wooden blocks, roughly circular in shape and often painted in fantastic dragonhead patterns. Medium to hard rubber mallets are normally used in playing them. However, yarn mallets and snare drum sticks are also effective. They come in any number from two to five (five is the standard number) and are graduated in size so that the pitch varies from one to the other. The tone is similar to that of the wood block but is a little rounder and hollower. Although temple blocks are tuned to a penatonic scale, no attempt is made to notate their real pitches; a note is arbitrarily assigned to each block. Probably the best solution is to use the five lines of the staff to indicate the five blocks, respectively.

WIND CHIMES

	Italian:	*French:*	*German:*
Bamboo:	Tubi di bambu	Bambou suspendu	Bambusrohre
Wood:	Bacchette di legno sospese	Baguettes de bois suspendues	Holz-Windglocken
Glass:	Bacchette di vetro sospese	Baguettes de verre suspendues	Glas-Windglocken
Metal:	Bacchette di metallo sospese	Baguettes métalliques suspendues	Metall-Windglocken
Shell:	Bacchette di conchiglia sospese	Baguettes de coquille suspendues	Muschel-Windglocken

In its most familiar form, this instrument consists of several hollowed-out wooden or bamboo cylinders suspended from a frame. When set in motion by the hand, the cylinders strike each other in random fashion and produce a dry, rattling sound. Wind chimes are also made of metal, glass, or shells. A wonderfully delicate, tinkling sound can be achieved with small metal or glass instruments by blowing on the chimes to set them in motion. Wind chimes are particularly effective in soft, light-textured passages.

An instrument similar in appearance to the wind chimes but much larger is the "Mark tree." Some larger models of the instrument have metal cylinders that are suspended from a frame and controlled by a damper pedal, much like the tubular bells. The Mark tree's sound is a hybrid of the metal wind chimes (the random striking of the cylinders against one another) and the bell tree (the high, metallic, bell-like sound).

In notating parts for these instruments, the exact duration of the sound should be shown. The performer will keep the cylinders in motion for the full value indicated. Usually, the cylinders are set in motion by a single stroke of the hand, and the sound dies away as the motion decreases.

THE BELL TREE

The bell tree is comprised of two dozen or so cup-shaped bells mounted on a single rod. The bells become smaller from top to bottom, giving the instrument the appearance of an inverted cone. Although the bells do have definite pitches, they are not tuned precisely, nor are they precisely arranged in terms of relative pitch. A metal beater is used to stroke them. The bell tree is most frequently employed to provide a bright, ringing glissando, either ascending or descending, at loud or soft dynamic levels. The following notations have been used in parts for it:

EXAMPLE 14.3

LATIN-AMERICAN PERCUSSION INSTRUMENTS

Some of the instruments frequently used in Latin-American music are the following:

The *claves*, two short cylindrical sticks that are struck together. One is held in such a way that the cup of the hand resonates the sound.

The *maracas*, two hollow gourds with handles attached and dried seed or buckshot inside. They are shaken to produce the characteristic sound.

The *guiro*, a serrated gourd that is scraped with a stick.

Bongos, single-headed drums open at the bottom and played with the fingers. They are made in pairs, one slightly smaller than the other.

Timbales, like the bongos but larger, and played with small sticks. For a special effect, the drum may be muffled with one hand and struck with a stick held in the other. It is also possible to play with one stick on the shell (side) of the drum and the other on the head.

Congas, single headed like the bongos but much larger, are played with the hands. Skilled performers elicit an amazing variety of sounds from the instruments by playing with different parts of the hand and varying the beating spot.

OTHER PERCUSSION INSTRUMENTS

There are, in addition to the instruments already mentioned, others that are less frequently used. In this category can be listed the ratchet or rattle, the wind machine, and the thunder machine, all found in the Strauss tone poems; the slapstick or whip (see Copland, Third Symphony, and Mussorgsky-Ravel, *Pictures at an Exhibition:* "Gnomus"); cowbells, used by Milhaud in his *La Création du Monde* and by Copland in his Orchestral Variations; and sleighbells, which figure in the Mahler Fourth Symphony (see Example 17.3) and in Respighi's *Roman Festivals,* for example. The list could be extended by the addition of sandpaper blocks, switches, chains, the siren, and the jawbone of an ass. The foreign names of most of these instruments are included in Appendix A.

THE PERCUSSION SECTION AS A WHOLE

Percussion parts fall into two broad categories:

1. Those that point up the actual thematic or structural aspects of the music (timpani parts, for example, are most often of this sort).
2. Those that are included chiefly for purposes of color.

But since the possibilities in both categories are almost infinite, an attempt to catalog them would be futile. Furthermore, each composition to be scored is an individual case with its own peculiar demands and possibilities. The best solution is to fix the sounds of the various percussion instruments in one's aural memory and draw on them as imagination and taste dictate.

The dynamic range of the percussion section is greater (at both loud and soft extremes) than the dynamic range of the rest of the orchestra. This relationship can be illustrated on paper in the following manner:

Dynamic range of the percussion: —————————————————

Dynamic range of the rest of the orchestra: ——————————

EXAMPLES

EXAMPLE 14.4

(a) *Scheherazade*

Rimsky-Korsakoff

(b) *Boléro*

Ravel

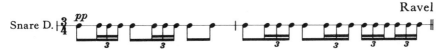

(c) *American Festival* Overture

William Schuman

(d) *Firebird* Suite

Stravinsky

(e) *El Salón México*

Copland

(f) *Capriccio Espagnol*

Rimsky-Korsakoff

Vivo e strepitoso

Tamb-
ourine

Vl. I

261

(g) *Carmen*

Cast.

Carmen, dancing with Cast.

La ———— la— la———— la ———— La ————

Bizet

(h) *The White Peacock*

Fl.

Harp

Tam-tam

Largamente
1.Solo

Griffes

Copyright renewal assigned, 1945, to G. Schirmer, Inc.

(i) *Boléro*

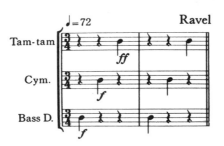

Tam-tam

Cym.

Bass D.

Ravel

(j) *Capriccio Espagnol*

Rimsky-Korsakoff

(k) *Symphonic Metamorphosis of Themes by C. M. von Weber*

Hindemith

Reproduced by permission of Schott & Co., Ltd., London.

Note: *This passage is for percussion alone and continues for eight more measures.*

(l) *Metamorphoses* (Second Symphony)

Roberto Gerhard

largest Korean block
(with semisoft rubber-headed stick)

largest wood block
(with hard stick)

submedium wood block

smallest Korean block
(with semisoft rubber-headed stick) Perc.
medium Korean block

3 smallest wood blocks

medium wood block
(with hard stick)
submed. Korean block
(with semisoft rubber-headed stick)

second largest wood block
(with hard stick)
second largest Korean block
(with semisoft rubber-headed stick)

(m) *Tableau III*

Roman Haubenstock-Ramati

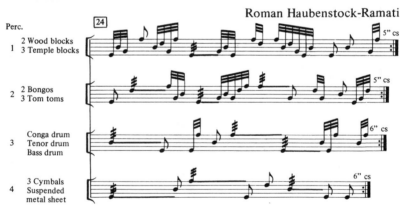

Perc.

1 2 Wood blocks
   3 Temple blocks

2 2 Bongos
   3 Tom toms

3 Conga drum
   Tenor drum
   Bass drum

4 3 Cymbals
   Suspended
   metal sheet

Seven Studies on Themes of Paul Klee

Gunther Schuller

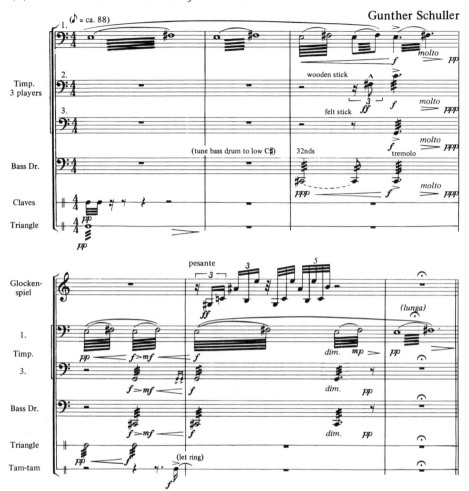

(o) *Heliogabalus Imperator*

Hans Werner Henze

THE ARRANGEMENT OF PERCUSSION PARTS

In the score, timpani are generally listed first among the percussion instruments. Then follow in any order the instruments of indefinite pitch and finally the mallet instruments, the celesta, and the piano (although few scores use all these instruments). Because the celesta and the piano are not usually played by members of the percussion section,[2] they are discussed, along with the harp, in Chapter 15.

Most professional orchestras have at least three percussion players (including the timpanist). The usual plan is to hire extra percussionists for works that require them, although the orchestra's budget unfortunately enters in here, and percussion parts have been known to go unplayed for financial reasons. With a little judicious planning, it is usually possible to arrange the percussion parts so that one player can play two or more instruments successively. For example, let us suppose that at a certain point the triangle must play a few notes; eight bars later there is a passage for snare drum, and sixteen bars after that the xylophone has a solo. Obviously the same player can handle all three instruments because he or she has time to move from one instrument to the next. Certain pairs of instruments can even be played at the same time by the same player if necessary: the percussionist can strike the triangle with one hand and shake the tambourine with the other or can play the bass drum with one hand and the gong with the other. It is also possible to arrange several percussion instruments so that the performer can rapidly play all of them within a single passage, as illustrated in Examples 14.4(m) and (o).

There is no hard and fast rule for the grouping of percussion instruments in either score or parts. Nor is there a standard method of distributing the instruments among the players. This is because each score presents individual problems of logistics to be solved. However, timpani parts are

---

[2]Nevertheless, many percussionists are able to perform celesta parts that are not too complex, and the celesta is sometimes listed as a member of the percussion section.

most often separate: that is, they have a staff to themselves in the score and a separate player's part.

Probably the most practical plan, especially if many percussion instruments are involved, is to arrange the percussion parts with a specific number of players in mind, assign each player a number that will be used to indicate his staff or line in both the score and the percussion part, and list all the instruments each player is responsible for at the beginning of the part and at the beginning of the score on the "instrumentation page." If a percussion part is highly complex, composers often include a diagram showing how the instruments should be set up.

Penderecki's *Fluorescences* calls for six percussionists, five of whose parts are shown in Example 14.5. The Roman numerals are used throughout the score to identify each percussion part. Arabic numerals are more common, though some composers (Pierre Boulez, for example) use capital letters.

EXAMPLE 14.5

Fluorescences

Krzysztof Penderecki

In this work, the timpani are included among half a dozen instruments played by percussionist V. (Note that definite pitches are not specified.) Because percussion is so extensively employed in many contemporary scores, the timpanist is sometimes expected to play other percussion instruments as well. In the above example, ♪ indicates the type of stick to be used, while variants of this symbol refer to methods of striking the instrument.

267

Arranging percussion parts in the way illustrated in Example 14.5 has many advantages. It solves in advance the problem of distributing the parts in a practical way among a given number of players, a problem that must otherwise be solved by the percussionists in rehearsal, often with a good deal of frenzied rushing from one instrument to another. It saves copying of several different percussion parts for the players if the following procedure is used: all the percussion parts (excluding the timpani in most cases) are written on the same sheet, and copies of that sheet—as many as needed for the players—are then made by a commercial reproduction process. (See Chapter 20.) Furthermore, all the percussionists have all the parts before them and can therefore relate their own parts to those of the other percussionists.

Whatever arrangement of percussion parts is used, the number of players required should be indicated at the beginning of the score, along with the list of instruments. In a few rare instances as many as six or seven percussion players are called for. An extreme example is Respighi's *Roman Festivals,* which lists fourteen percussion instruments, ten of which play at once at one point. But that sort of thing is obviously impractical as a general rule. It is, in fact, the kind of instrumentation that the aspiring composer had better not imitate if he expects to get his scores performed.

SYMBOL NOTATION AND PICTOGRAMS

Many contemporary scores require an enormous number of percussion instruments and beaters, and the identification of these in the course of a wok can be something of a problem. Abbreviations can be cumbersome and difficult for players and conductors to decipher quickly during rehearsal and performance. This is especially the case when a player performs on many different instruments in rapid succession. The problem is greatly compounded if the abbreviations are in a foreign language. In an attempt to solve this problem, many composers have taken to using *symbol notation* or *pictograms* in their scores. In symbol notation, a graphic representation or pictogram is devised for every percussion instrument and beater, and this symbol is used to identify a particular instrument and beater each time it appears in the score. The problem with this procedure is that there is no standard usage because composers tend to invent their own symbols, and conductors and percussionists are therefore forced to learn a new set of symbols for almost every new score. This is one reason why not all percussionists are enthusiastic about pictograms. Although the International Conference of New Musical Notation, convened in Ghent, Belgium, in 1974, set out to foster standardization by endorsing and recommending a uniform set of pictograms, these are by no means universally employed. (Example 14.4[o], for instance, uses symbol notation, yet none of the pictograms that appear in the example correspond to those given below. Henze provides a key that identifies the symbols at the beginning of the score.) The pictograms for several beaters, as well as the instruments discussed in this and the preceding chapter, are shown in Figures 14.2 and 14.3. Most of these symbols were approved by the Ghent conferees.

FIGURE 14.2

BEATERS

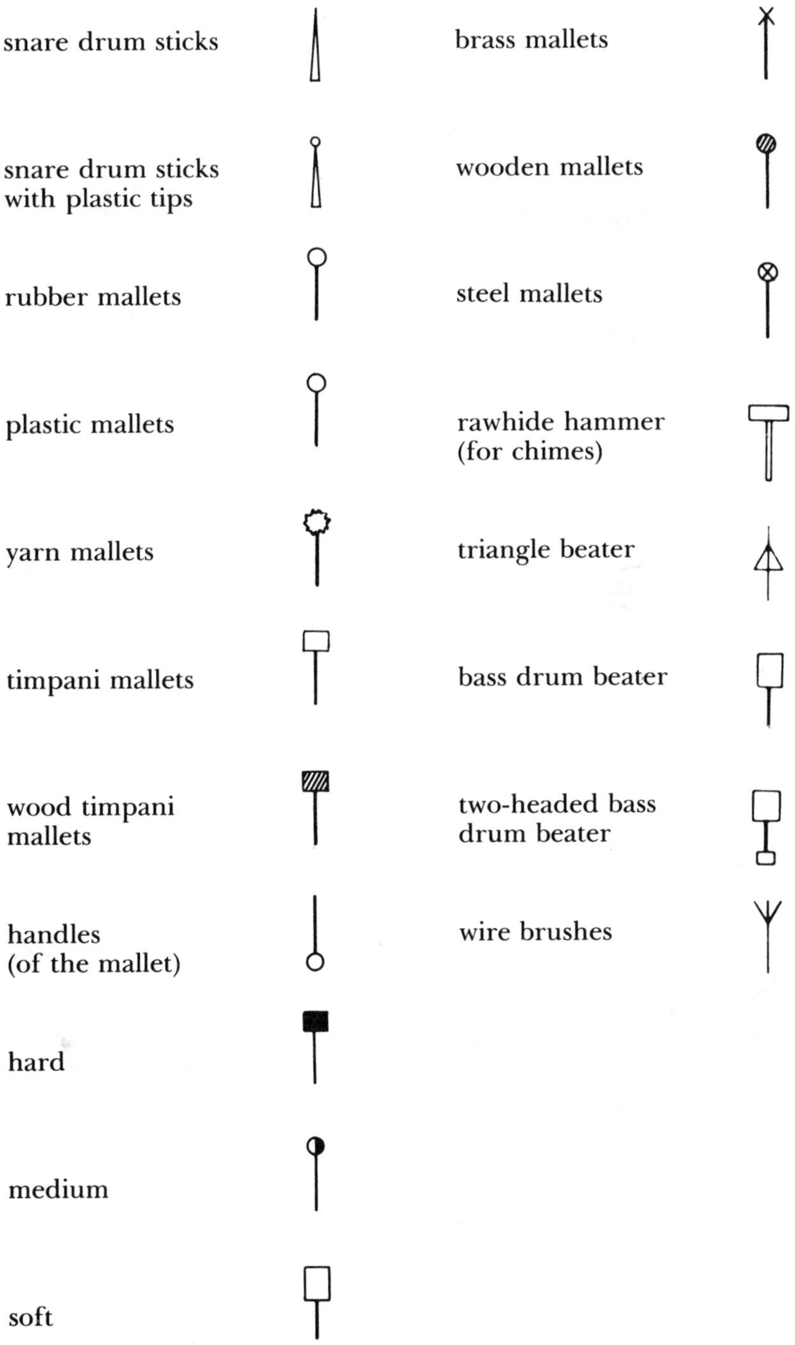

snare drum sticks		brass mallets	
snare drum sticks with plastic tips		wooden mallets	
rubber mallets		steel mallets	
plastic mallets		rawhide hammer (for chimes)	
yarn mallets		triangle beater	
timpani mallets		bass drum beater	
wood timpani mallets		two-headed bass drum beater	
handles (of the mallet)		wire brushes	
hard			
medium			
soft			

FIGURE 14.3

INSTRUMENTS

DEFINITE PITCH		INDEFINITE PITCH	
timpani		snare drum (with snares on)	
xylophone		(with snares off)	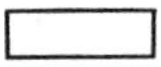
marimba		field drum *or* military drum with snares on	
glockenspiel *or* orchestra bells		tenor drum *or* military drum with snares off	
		tom-tom	
vibraphone		bass drum (upright)	
tubular bells (chimes)	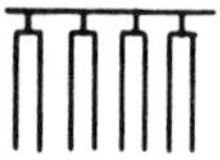	(on side)	
crotales		crash cymbals	
musical saw		suspended cymbal	
almglocken		sizzle cymbal	
anvil		finger cymbals	
flexatone		triangle	

INSTRUMENTS

DEFINITE PITCH		INDEFINITE PITCH	
tambourine		claves	
tam-tam		maracas	
gong		guïro	
castanets		bongo drums	
wood block		timbales	
temple block		conga drum	
glass wind chimes			

SUGGESTED ASSIGNMENTS

A. Be able to list the percussion instruments discussed here (except those in the Other Percussion Instruments section in this chapter), as well as to translate the foreign names for them into English.

B. Know:

1. the commonly used rudimental strokes.
2. the various ways of playing each instrument.
3. special capabilities of each of the instruments.
4. proper notation in each case.

C. Select a march tune and write parts for snare drum, bass drum, cymbals, and any other percussion instruments desired.

SUGGESTED LISTENING

Percussion (Including Instruments of Definite Pitch)

Rimsky-Korsakoff, *Capriccio Espagnol; Scheherazade.*
Debussy, *Ibéria.*
Ravel, *Daphnis and Chloe* Suite No. 2; *La Valse; Rapsodie Espagnole.*
Kodály, *Háry János* Suite.
Respighi, *Pines of Rome; Fountains of Rome; Roman Festivals.*
Stravinsky, *Les Noces; L'Histoire du Soldat; The Rite of Spring.*
Bartók, *Music for String Instruments, Percussion, and Celesta;* Concerto for Orchestra; *The Miraculous Mandarin.*
Hindemith, *Symphonic Metamorphosis of Themes by C. M. von Weber.*
Chávez, *Sinfonía India.*
Copland, *El Salón México; Appalachian Spring;* Third Symphony (especially 2nd and 4th movts.).
Shostakovich, Fifth Symphony.
Piston, Suite from the ballet, *The Incredible Flutist.*
Varèse, *Ionisation* for eleven percussion instruments; *Arcana; Amériques.*
Tippett, Third Symphony, Fourth Symphony.
Carter, *A Symphony of Three Orchestras.*
Brant, *Antiphony One.*
Messiaen, *Turangalîla-Symphonie; Chronochromie.*
Gerhard, Second Symphony (*Metamorphoses*); Third Symphony (*Collages*).
Schuller, *Seven Studies on Themes of Paul Klee.*
Rorem, *Air Music.*
Stockhausen, *Trans.*
Lutoslawski, *Mi-parti.*
Haubenstock-Ramati, *Tableau II; Tableau III.*
Boulez, *Pli Selon Pli* (I. don).
Hoddinott, Fifth Symphony.
Berio, *Sinfonia.*
Henze, Sixth Symphony; *Heliogabalus Imperator.*
Argento, *A Ring of Time.*
Davies, *Symphony; St. Thomas Wake.*
Penderecki, *Fluorescences.*

15

The Harp,
Celesta, and Piano

The harp, celesta, and piano have been allotted a special chapter because they do not belong to any of the four orchestral groups already discussed. Although the harp and the piano have strings, they are not classified as stringed instruments because their tone is not produced by bowing. The celesta is listed with the percussion group in some orchestration books, but it is not normally played by a member of the percussion section; most orchestras have a separate player who performs either celesta or piano parts as required.

THE HARP

Italian: Arpa   *French:* Harpe   *German:* Harfe

EXAMPLE 15.1

The harp (Figure 15.1) differs from other instruments in being built on a non-chromatic basis; that is, instead of having twelve strings (one for each

FIGURE 15.1

Studio Gilmore, Austin, Texas

Harp

semitone) within each octave, as might be expected, it has only seven. When the instrument is in its "home" key, these are tuned to the notes in the scale of C♭ major: C♭, D♭, E♭, F♭, G♭, A♭, and B♭. At the base of the harp are seven pedals, each one controlling all the strings of a particular letter name on the instrument and capable of raising those strings either a half step or a whole step in pitch. For example, if the appropriate pedal is pressed halfway down (where it can be secured in a notch), all the strings that formerly sounded C♭ will now sound C♮; if we depress the same pedal still further to a bottom notch, the same strings will sound C♯. Using another pedal, the D♭'s in all octaves can be raised to D♮'s or to D♯'s and so on with all the strings. It is obviously impossible to tune the strings of one pitch class differently in different octaves.[1] The reason for using the forbidding key of C♭ major as the basic key of the harp may now be apparent: it is the only one in which each pitch can be raised two semitones without the use of double sharps (or double flats to begin with); the three pitch possibilities of each string can be expressed by a flat, a natural, and a sharp.

---

[1]The only exceptions are the bottom C and D strings (and on some harps, the top G string as well). These are not controlled by the pedal mechanism and must be tuned independently by hand.

The pedals are arranged in semicircular fashion around the base of the harp, three on the left, four on the right, in the following sequence:

D C B | E F G A

The three on the left are operated by the harpist's left foot; the other four by the right foot. It takes only an instant to depress or release a pedal, and two pedals can be changed at the same time as long as they are on different sides of the instrument; for example, B and G, or D and A, or C and F. Harpists do occasionally take the E pedal with the left foot in cases when it is necessary to achieve a double change of pedals on the right side quickly. But the opposite arrangement (use of the right foot for pedals on the left side) is awkward and impractical. Fortunately these fine points need seldom be considered since it is usually possible to make pedal changes one at a time rather than simultaneously.

The setting of the pedals at the beginning of a work should be indicated in the harp part. This may be done in any one of the three ways shown here:

1.

⌈E♮ F♭ G♯ A♭
⌊B♭ C♯ D♭

2.

3.

D♭ C♯ B♭ E♮ F♭ G♯ A♭

The first method arranges the letters in a kind of radial fashion, with the pedal order starting from the right in the bottom row and then moving from left to right in the top row. The second (the one most often used by harpists) consists of a diagram that is a "picture" of the pedals; a horizontal line corresponds to the middle notch on all pedals, and small marks above, through, or below this line show whether the pedals are in the top, middle, or bottom notch, respectively. The third way simply lists the letters in the same order as that of the pedals.

Harp parts may be written either with or without a key signature. If the part is fairly diatonic, use of a key signature is the most sensible solution. But if the harp has a part that would require constant cancellations of the signature, then it may as well be written without a key signature, the accidentals being inserted. When there is a key signature and no pedal setting is shown, the harpist will normally assume that the pedals should be set according to the scale of the key involved.

Each pedal change needed in the course of the part should be shown beneath the bottom staff at the point where it occurs; the letter with the new accidental is sufficient. When two changes occur at the same time and when these involve pedals on different sides of the instrument (as is usually the case), the change for the pedal on the right should be shown *above* the one for the pedal at the left; for example: $\frac{G♮}{D♭}$. This standard placement (which conforms to the "radial" pattern given earlier) is an aid to the harpist in making pedal changes rapidly. There is often an advantage in indicating changes during rests that occur well in advance of the point where the new pitches will actually be needed, especially if a number of changes are involved. The pedal diagram is not normally used for showing pedal changes in the course of a work but is sometimes shown at the beginning of major sections.

To illustrate some points in connection with harp writing, let us suppose that the harp part in a given work starts in the thirteenth measure and involves the notes shown in Example 15.2.

EXAMPLE 15.2

Although the key is E♭ major, the pedal setting at the beginning includes an A♮ since the first time an A of any kind occurs it is in the natural form. The three pedal changes necessary are shown beneath the music. Such changes as these, occurring from time to time in a tempo that allows them to be made comfortably, are entirely reasonable and are considered part of the harpist's normal assignment. But constant pedal changes become overtaxing, especially if they must be made quickly. Consequently in highly chromatic music it is normally best either to omit the harp altogether or to give it a simplified part that eliminates some of the notes requiring changes. In the case of the example just given, for instance, the harp might play only on alternate beats (Example 15.3).

EXAMPLE 15.3

Another solution in such cases (one used by Debussy, Strauss, and others) is to write for two harps, letting them take turns at playing. Each harp will then have rests during which pedal changes can be made. A further advantage of this arrangement is that greater volume is available, in case that is wanted, from the two harps playing at once.

Two notes that sound the same but are spelled differently are spoken of as being enharmonic. If we think back to the possible tunings of each harp string, we will discover that there are many possibilities for enharmonic notes where the strings overlap in pitch. For example, if we have the B pedal in the middle notch so that the string will sound B♮ and the C pedal in the top notch to produce C♭, the two strings will give the same pitch. The only pitch classes that do not have enharmonic equivalents are D, G, and A.

The word *homophones* is sometimes used to describe these enharmonic tones on the harp. They are useful in various ways but most frequently in connection with glissandos.

In performing a glissando, the player draws the hand quickly across the strings, touching each string included within the compass notated. Because it is not possible to skip over any of the strings, each one must be tuned in such a way as to fit into the musical scheme at that point. The glissando may consist of a scale or a chord. If a scale is used, there is no particular problem since the strings can be adjusted to give any major or minor scale, each string sounding one note of the scale. But suppose that we want a chord, say a dominant 9th sound on C, to be played as a glissando. We could prepare C♮, E♮, G♮, B♭, and D♮ on the strings of those letter names. There is then the problem of what to do with the F and A strings. Can they be made to fit into the chord, and if so, how? By putting the F pedal in the top notch, the string can be made to sound F♭, equivalent to E♮ in pitch; by depressing the A pedal to the bottom, we can make that string sound A♯ or the same as B♭. Our complete pedal setting, then, would be: D♮, C♮, B♭, E♮, F♭, G♮, A♯. When the player's hand is drawn rapidly over the strings, the fact that certain pitches are sounded twice will not be apparent to the ear. The result will simply be a dominant 9th sound on C without any extraneous tones. To give another illustration, suppose we want a diminished 7th chord on F♯ to be played as a glissando.

The pedal setting in that case would be: F♯–G♭, A♮, B♯–C♮, D♯–E♭. (The letters have been listed here in such a way as to show the enharmonic pairs). Obviously not all chords can be played as glissandos. In the case of a G major triad, for example, the A string cannot possibly be raised to the enharmonic equivalent of B nor lowered to the enharmonic equivalent of G; likewise, the E and F strings cannot be made to fit into the chord. The only solution in such cases and one that is commonly used is to include extra notes. With the G major triad, the A string could be tuned to A♮, the E string to E♮, both extra; the C pedal would be tuned to C♭ (= B♮) and the F pedal to F♭ (= E♮). The notes played by the harp, then, would be: G♮, A♮, B♮, C♭, D♮, E♮, F♭. Although this is a more highly colored sound than the pure G major triad, the added notes would not sound as extraneous as might be expected. Of course another solution here would be simply to abandon the attempt at a chord glissando and use the notes of the G major scale as a glissando. Either way would give the requisite "splash."

Glissandos may be begun and ended anywhere on the harp, may be made in either direction—or in both directions at once—may be produced using either hand or both hands, and may cover as much of the instrument as desired. Various methods of notation have been used, but the clearest and most satisfactory one (as applied to) seems to be that shown in Example 15.4.

EXAMPLE 15.4

277

Here the half rests make it clear that the glissando is to last two beats. But in some instances there could well be ambiguity about the duration of the glissando, and that can be clarified in such cases by adding a note of the appropriate time value in the middle of a bracket below or above the glissando—for example,  . Of course the proper pedal settings must have been indicated previously. It is possible to play up to six notes (three in each hand) in an ascending glissando and up to eight notes in a descending glissando. Triple and quadruple glissandos are included in Example 15.5 (b) and (c).

EXAMPLE 15.5

(a) *Daphnis and Chloe* Suite No. 2

(b) *Amériques*   (c) *Firebird* Suite

Example 15.5 (b): Copyright 1929 and 1973 by Colfranc Music Publishing Corporation, New York. By courtesy of E. C. Kerby Ltd., Toronto, General Agent.

Notice that the actual notes (including enharmonic sounds) in glissandos need be written out for only one octave. If the strings are tuned to sound these pitches in one octave, they must sound them in all octaves. Consequently, it would be superfluous, as well as a great nuisance, to write out every note in the glissando. Sometimes even the written-out octave is dispensed with, as in Examples 15.5(b) and (c), where a pedal setting or a key signature suffices. In (c) no upward limit to each glissando is specified, the general effect being more important than exact notes.

The matter of time values in glissandos is not of any great importance; orchestrators seem to use anything from sixteenths to sixty-fourth notes. Usually there are so many notes that the actual mathematical values would be hard to notate accurately in any case.

There is no denying the fact that the glissando is basically one of the most intriguing and effective sounds in the harp's repertory. But it has been so overused (particularly in commercial scoring) that it has lost some of its freshness and charm; it is best employed sparingly nowadays.

Normally the harp's tones are allowed to ring after being plucked, and they have considerable sustaining power, especially in the lower portion of the instrument.[2] When sustained sounds would cause a blur or be inappropriate to the music, the player may be directed to damp the sound with the hands. For a series of notes or chords, each one to be damped immediately after it is played, the French expression *sons étouffés* ("damped sounds") is commonly employed. Sometimes the single word *étouffez* is placed at the end of a passage or after a glissando to show that the sound must not be allowed to ring.[3] The contrary direction is *laissez vibrer* (abbreviation, "l.v.") meaning "let vibrate."

As was intimated earlier, the harp is by nature more harmonic than melodic in feeling. As a rule, melodies played on it sound thin and ineffectual, though it occasionally doubles a slow melodic line for a special color effect. Arpeggios and chords are its most frequent assignments. Some typical and effective arpeggio figures are shown in Example 15.6.

EXAMPLE 15.6

(a)   *Prelude to The Afternoon of a Faun*

(b)   *The White Peacock*

Copyright renewal assigned, 1945, to G. Schirmer, Inc.

---

[2]It has been calculated that, assuming a dynamic curve of *ff* to *pp*, the sounding time of the harp's strings varies from 25 seconds for the lowest F on the instrument through nine seconds for the F just above middle C to three seconds for the F two octaves higher than that. This information comes from *Writing for the Pedal Harp* by Ruth K. Inglefield and Lou Anne Neill (Berkeley: University of California Press, 1985).

[3]A convenient symbol for "damp" (or "muffle") is ⊕ , which may be applied to individual notes, a specified group of notes, or an entire passage. This symbol circled ⊕ indicates that *all* notes at that point are to be muffled.

(c) *Requiem*

Because of the angle at which their hands engage the strings, harpists do not use the little finger of either hand in playing. That means that chords involving more than four notes to a hand cannot be played, except by using a very pronounced roll or arpeggio effect. Incidentally, the stretch of a 10th on the harp is roughly equivalent in difficulty to the stretch of an octave on the piano and may be considered a safe practical limit.

It is traditional to roll all chords slightly in harp playing; a vertical wavy line in front of a chord should be used only when a much more decided roll is wanted. If a chord is to be played without any roll whatever (that is, with all the tones starting at exactly the same time), a bracket the length of the chord should precede it (Example 15.7).

EXAMPLE 15.7

Double 3rds and 6ths are quite feasible, either harmonically or melodically performed (Example 15.8).

EXAMPLE 15.8

Rapid repeated notes on the same string are not very practical: a sudden return to the string only damps out the vibrations of the previous note before they have had a chance to get well started. Here is another case in which the enharmonic possibilities of the harp prove useful. By tuning two strings to the same sound and playing them alternately, we get the effect of a repeated note, but each string has twice as long to vibrate as it would if used by itself (Example 15.9).

EXAMPLE 15.9

Obviously two strings will produce more sound than one. It is for that reason that we sometimes find a single sound written for two enharmonically tuned strings (Example 15.10).

EXAMPLE 15.10

Daphnis and Chloe Suite No. 2

Although the changing of pedals is part of the harpist's business, it is only humane and reasonable to avoid unnecessary pedal changes. This can often be done by using an enharmonic spelling for certain notes. For instance, Example 15.11, as written, requires constant changing of the B pedal and a double change of the D and B pedals. (The double change is especially bad since both pedals are on the left side of the instrument.)

EXAMPLE 15.11

If the passage is written as in Example 15.12, different strings are involved and no pedal changes are necessary.

EXAMPLE 15.12

From the standpoint of harmonic spelling, the latter way is obviously incorrect. In fact, the whole system of false notation produces results that are often contrary to proper harmonic grammar. Nevertheless its use is justified in harp writing by the fact that it makes for greater ease in performance.

The bottom notes of the harp are dark and sonorous in quality, the middle register rich and warm. Although the higher strings do not have much volume or sustaining power, their dry, slightly percussive quality enables them to come through more clearly than might be expected. Remember, though, that whatever register the harp is playing in, it cannot compete with large masses of sound if it is to be heard prominently. Because harp strings are slightly more resonant in their "flat" position (in the top notch), flat keys should be chosen in preference to sharp keys where there is a choice and where maximum sonority is a consideration.

Special Effects

Harmonics can be produced on the harp (1) by touching the string lightly in the middle with the lower part of the left hand and plucking the string with the left thumb; or (2) by touching the string lightly in the middle with the knuckle of the index finger of the right hand and plucking the string with the right thumb. The note that results in each case is the first overtone, an octave higher than the normal pitch of the string. (Although harmonics involving higher overtones are possible, they are almost never used.) Harmonics have an attractive crystalline, bell-like quality; but because they have little volume, there is no point in using them except in passages where the background is extremely light. They are useful for single notes or, rarely, for short melodic lines that move slowly enough to allow for the special technique involved in playing the notes as harmonics. It is possible to play two harmonics at once with the left hand—even three or four if they are within the range of a 5th—but only one with the right hand. The middle register of the harp is much the best one for harmonics. As regards the notation of them, there are, unfortunately, two different systems in current use (1) the harmonic is written an octave lower than it is to sound, the pitch shown being that of the *string* used; or (2) it is written at the actual pitch. In both cases, a small circle above the note is the indication for a harmonic. The first way is the one most often seen, but in order to avoid ambiguity, harmonics should be accompanied by a note in the harp part telling which method is being used. In Example 15.13, the harmonics are intended to sound an octave higher than the written notes.

Example 15.13

(a) *Firebird* Suite

(b) *Prelude to The Afternoon of a Faun*

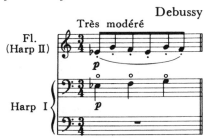

(c) *Daphnis and Chloe* Suite No. 2

Harmonics, like fundamentals, may be damped the instant they are played.

There is not space here to describe all the other special effects possible on the harp. Many of them have been widely used in solo music for the instrument (particularly in pieces by the eminent harpist Carlos Salzedo) but have been little exploited in symphonic music. One reason for this is that a number of them involve sounds too delicate to be clearly audible in the concert hall. However, others are quite usable, and descriptions of some of those follow:

Playing close to the soundboard, which produces a slightly nasal, guitarlike sound. The direction is *près de la table* (abbreviated "p.d.l.t.") or

just "table," or a horizontal "scalloped" line (〰〰〰〰) beneath the

passage.

Playing with the fingernails, which gives the tone a brittle, metallic quality. The symbol for this effect is a small crescent-shaped sign like a fingernail. The back of the nails may also be used in playing descending glissandos to give what Salzedo calls the "falling hail" effect.

Rapidly alternating two sounds (usually dyads or triads) between the hands in tremolo fashion (*bisbigliando,* meaning "whispering"). The notation is the same as for tremolos.

Producing a vibrato by plucking the string with one hand, then alternately pressing and releasing the left thumb against the string just below the tuning pin. The notation is a V-like symbol followed by a wavy line.

Muting one or more strings by placing the fingers of one hand lightly on the strings that are to be plucked by the other hand ("xylophonic" sounds). The most effective position for the muting hand is near the soundboard.

Tapping, knocking, or slapping the soundboard with the hand.

Playing a note in the normal manner, then moving the pedal for that string one notch so that a pitch a half-step higher or lower results ("pedal slide"). Even a slow pedal "trill" is possible by this same means.

Holding a pedal halfway between two notches, which results in a metallic, buzzing sound.

Striking the lower (wire) strings with the open left hand and letting them ring ("thunder effect") or damping them immediately ("dead slap").

Using the tuning key or a metal rod to produce a glissando, a vibrato, or a tremolo (the latter between two adjacent strings).

Using a drum beater, a wire jazz brush, a plectrum, or another object such as a coin, a chisel, or a pencil in any of the ways already described.

Tuning the strings in a nontraditional way (*scordatura*). This allows for the use of microtones as one possibility.

Threading a thin strip of paper, tinfoil, felt, or the like through the strings to alter the quality. With some materials the sound is akin to that of the harpsichord.

There are many subtle variants of the effects listed above, and at times two or more effects are combined—for example, a glissando played with the tuning key at the fingerboard.

Since it would be impractical to attempt to show the notation for all these effects here, the reader is referred to the books on the harp listed in the Bibliography.

Amplification of the harp is sometimes possible. It is employed mainly in the performance of commercial music or in outdoor concerts.

THE CELESTA

Italian: Celesta   *French:* Célesta   *German:* Celesta

EXAMPLE 15.14

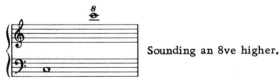

Sounding an 8ve higher.

In appearance the celesta is like a small piano (see Figure 15.2). It has a keyboard like the piano's (though much shorter) and a damper pedal that,

FIGURE 15.2

Dorf Photography, Austin, Texas

Celesta

when depressed, allows the tone to ring. In place of strings, the instrument is equipped with small steel bars, each one with its own wooden resonator. These give out a delicate, bell-like tone. Gordon Jacob remarks picturesquely that the tone of the celesta always reminds him of the taste of a ripe plum.[4] In spite of its charm, however, it has little power and is drowned out by anything but the lightest of backgrounds.

Apparently, there was at one time a celesta with a range that extended an octave below the one shown in Example 15.14. In the Berlioz-Strauss *Treatise on Instrumentation* Strauss refers to a five-octave celesta, and he wrote for that instrument in *Salome*. But it is not seen in the United States as far as we know.

The celesta is most often used to add a silvery edge to a melodic line. At other times it may merely provide "shimmer" via an arpeggio or some other figuration, as in Example 15.15(c). On rare occasions it may take a melody or a complete harmonic passage by itself, as in Example 15.15(a).

---

[4]Gordon Jacob, *Orchestral Technique*.

(Celesta sounding an octave higher)

EXAMPLE 15.15

(a) *Nutcracker* Suite

(b) *Schelomo*

Copyright renewal assigned, 1945, to G. Schirmer, Inc.

(c) *Daphnis and Chloe* Suite No. 2

(d) *Five Pieces for Orchestra,* II. "Vergangenes—Yesteryears"

Note: *This measure is repeated*
     nine times.

Copyright © 1952 by Henmar Press, Inc. (C. F. Peters Corporation). By permission.

THE PIANO

Italian: Pianoforte   *French:* Piano   *German:* Klavier

Example 15.16

The piano is not, strictly speaking, an orchestral instrument, but it is occasionally used in the orchestra for purposes of color or special effect. Its upper register can add sparkle or a bright clang, while the bottom notes are sometimes employed for their dark, faintly gonglike quality or to add percussive force and body to a bass line. The middle register, being more neutral in color, is less interesting in the orchestra. Furthermore, the use of the piano for middle-register harmony parts is apt to be unpleasantly reminiscent of small studio and salon orchestras, in which the piano must often take the place of missing horns, bassoons, and other instruments. Also to be avoided, as a rule, is the "fussy," rich-textured sort of writing that figures in piano concertos of the Romantic period. Something simple and striking is far more effective. In fact, parts for the piano as an orchestral instrument seem to be successful to the extent that they get away from overfamiliar solo-piano patterns.

A special effect calls for the strings of a grand piano to be struck with a soft stick (such as a gong beater or a marimba beater) or with a hard rubber stick. Another involves having an instrument play into the interior of a grand piano, causing sympathetic vibrations to sound.

The piano is by no means a regular member of the orchestra. When it is included, it is best used in small doses like other special orchestral colors. Excellent examples of its use in modern music can be found in Prokofieff's Fifth Symphony, Copland's Third Symphony, and Stravinsky's *Agon,* to mention only three instances.

EXAMPLE 15.17

(a) *Firebird* Suite

Stravinsky

(b) First Symphony

Shostakovich

(c) *Pines of Rome*

Respighi

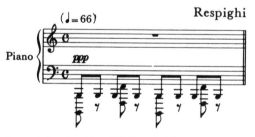

By permission of G. Ricordi & Co., copyright owners.

SUGGESTED ASSIGNMENTS

A. Know:

1. ranges of harp, celesta, and piano.
2. function of pedals on harp and order in which they are arranged.
3. enharmonic possibilities, false spelling.
4. proper notation of glissandos.
5. special effects on the harp.
6. transposition of celesta.
7. effective uses of celesta and piano in the orchestra.

B. (1) Give, in both letter form and diagram form, the pedal setting that would be used if each of the following harmonies were to be played as a glissando on the harp. If any of the chords are impossible as a glissando (without the addition of extra notes), indicate that opposite the appropriate number.

EXAMPLE 15.18

(2) List the dominant 7th chords possible as glissandos on the harp and show the pedal setting for each.

SUGGESTED LISTENING

Harp

Berlioz, *Fantastic Symphony*, 2nd movt. ("Un bal").
Wagner, "Love Death" from *Tristan und Isolde;* Immolation Scene from *Die Walküre.*
Franck, Symphony in D minor, 2nd movt.
Tchaikovsky, *Romeo and Juliet; Waltz of the Flowers* from the *Nutcracker* Suite.
Rimsky-Korsakoff, *Capriccio Espagnol,* near beginning of section IV (*Scena e Canto Gitano*).
Debussy, *Afternoon of a Faun; Nocturnes:* II. "Fêtes"; *Ibéria; La Mer.*
Ravel, *Introduction and Allegro; Daphnis and Chloe* Suite No. 2; *La Valse; Rapsodie Espagnole; Le Tombeau de Couperin; Pavane pour une Infante Défunte.*
Mahler, Symphonies; *Das Lied von der Erde.*
Stravinsky, *Firebird* Suite; *Orpheus,* First Scene and Third Scene.
Bartók, Concerto for Orchestra, particularly Section III ("Elegia") and latter part of Section II ("Giuoco delle Coppie"); *The Miraculous Mandarin.*
Dello Joio, Concerto for Harp and Orchestra.
Copland, Third Symphony, 3rd movt., figure 72, figure 83 (both involving two harps and celesta); 4th movt., beginning; figure 120 (two harps, celesta, piano).

Celesta

Tchaikovsky, "Dance of the Sugar Plum Fairy" from the *Nutcracker* Suite.
Strauss, *Der Rosenkavalier,* number 303 and following, other passages.
Debussy, *Ibéria,* Section II ("Les Parfums de la nuit").
Ravel, *Daphnis and Chloe* Suite No. 2; *Rapsodie Espagnole.*

Stravinsky, *Petrouchka* (celesta played 4-hands at figure 15).
Bloch, *Schelomo*.
Griffes, *The White Peacock*.
Bartók, *Music for String Instruments, Percussion, and Celesta*.
Shostakovich, Fifth Symphony, end of 1st movt., end of 3rd movt.; Sixth Symphony, 1st movt., at number 28.
Schönberg, *Variations for Orchestra*, Op. 31, Var. I, Var. VII; *Five Pieces for Orchestra*, Op. 16 (new version).
Webern, *Variations for Orchestra*, Op. 30; *Six Pieces*, Op. 6.
Copland, Third Symphony, 2nd movt., figure 40. See also the listings for the Copland Third Symphony under HARP, above.
Messiaen, *Turangalîla*—Symphonie.

Piano

Saint-Saëns, *The Carnival of Animals*.
Stravinsky, *Firebird* Suite; *Petrouchka; Symphony of Psalms;* Symphony in Three Movements; *Les Noces; Agon*.
Prokofieff, Fifth Symphony.
Respighi, *Pines of Rome; Roman Festivals*.
Shostakovich, First Symphony.
Bartók, *The Miraculous Mandarin*.
Copland, *Rodeo: El Salón México; Appalachian Spring;* Third Symphony.
Tippett, Third Symphony.
Messiaen, *Turangalîla*—Symphonie.

16

Scoring for Full Orchestra

The term *scoring for full orchestra* does not necessarily imply using all the instruments at once; an examination of a large number of scores would reveal that actual *tuttis* make up a relatively small portion of those scores. *Full orchestra* means only that all the instruments are on hand, to be selected as appropriate to the music being orchestrated. However, many of the examples in this chapter involve most of the instruments; they were chosen with the idea of illustrating techniques in scoring for large groups playing at once—a musical situation not encountered earlier in this book.

So far we have dealt principally with the scoring of chordal and homophonic music, reserving a full consideration of the scoring of purely polyphonic music until we had the entire orchestra to work with. In a sense, this last aspect of orchestration is one of the more difficult ones, for there are no harmonic masses that can be made to "sound" easily, and the relative weight of each line must be calculated with special care.

One of the main objectives in scoring linear music is to bring out the individual voices clearly. Here the orchestra has a certain advantage over the piano: whereas the piano has only one color to offer, the orchestra has many, and by allotting a different color to each voice we can give the lines a clarity and independence—a kind of three-dimensional feeling—that is impossible on the piano. For example, if three voices are involved, we might give one to oboe, one to clarinet, and one to bassoon. But it is not always necessary to use sharply contrasting colors. The three voices might be given instead to violins, violas, and cellos, respectively, in which case the differences of timbre, although less decided, would still afford a small color contrast between the parts. Although it is possible to use instruments of different sections on the various parts, one must be careful to choose instruments that can be made to balance properly. It is also possible to contrast one composite (mixed) color with another composite color or with a pure color.

Doublings of the top voice an octave (or even two octaves) higher and of the bottom voice an octave lower are useful and effective in arrangements of polyphonic music. But octave doublings of the inner voices are likely to be less successful, for they often involve a crossing of parts that may cause a muddled effect. When that happens, they had better be avoided.

Normally an instrument or group of instruments that begins a particular voice should follow through on that voice to the end of the phrase or musical thought. In fugues, for example, it is usual to retain the same instrument on each voice at least up to the point where all the voices have announced the subject. After that, changes in scoring on the various parts are decidedly in order at points where the structure of the music seems to warrant them. The reentrance of a voice will be doubly effective if it can be scored in a timbre that has not been heard for several bars. In other words, if an instrument is to make an important entrance, try to give it at least a few measures of rest beforehand.

With these brief remarks as a prelude, let us go on now to the fugue we are to use for our sample scoring. The first excerpt is the beginning or exposition of the fugue. Instead of including a separate example to show the actual orchestration, we have simply indicated here in the keyboard version the instruments that might be chosen. Since no dynamic markings or tempo indications are given in the original, we have had to supply our own. The third and fourth announcements of the subject have been marked a bit louder than the first two in order to make sure that they come through clearly against the upper voices.

EXAMPLE **16.1**

Fugue II (*The Well Tempered Clavier,* Vol. II)

292

Probably pure colors are best here at the beginning, with mixed tone reserved for later sections. Similarly, although it would be possible to give this opening section to brass instruments, it is much more effective to save them, or at least some of them, for the heavier, more emphatic announcements of the subject that occur later in the fugue.

Example 16.2 shows an ingenious *stretto* from about the middle of the fugue (in a *stretto* the subject overlaps itself). Here the subject appears in three different versions (1) in the original form; (2) in augmentation (with note values doubled); and (3) in inversion (with the direction of the intervals reversed). If the musical content of this passage is to be made clear, each voice must stand out sharply on its own; that effect, in turn, can best be achieved by using a different color on each voice. Here again, we have merely suggested one of the many possible ways in which the excerpt could be transcribed.

EXAMPLE 16.2

The third excerpt consists of the last five and one half bars of the fugue, again an impressive *stretto*. (Each entrance of the subject or a portion of it is marked with an "S" here.)

EXAMPLE 16.3

EXAMPLE 16.4

Fugue II (*The Well Tempered Clavier*, Vol. II)

Bach
(Arr. by K.W.K.)

Although this fugue is usually begun legato, a marcato effect seems appropriate or at least possible in this concluding section, and that interpretation has been used in the orchestral version in Example 16.4. The full orchestra, including brass, has been brought into play here. Since the voices seem to be about equally important and must therefore be balanced, it was necessary to distribute them among the brass instruments; strings and woodwinds were doubled with these parts either in unison or at the octave. However, instead of using the entire orchestra from the beginning of the passage, strings and woodwinds were added one or two at a time in order to accentuate each entrance of the subject and also to achieve a cumulative effect in leading to the *tutti*. It would have been possible to reverse the orchestration by starting the final *stretto* with strings and woodwinds and adding brass at each entry of the subject.

It must not be concluded from these comments that the brass should be included only in *fortissimo*, heavily scored passages or that all the brass instruments must play if one plays. At lower dynamic levels balance can often be maintained between a single brass instrument and a single woodwind or a string group.

Classes using this book as a text should discuss some of the questions pertinent to scoring situations such as those involved in Example 16.4—for instance: (1) Should one attempt to "sound like Bach"? (2) Is it *possible* to sound like Bach, even using instruments having the same names as the ones he used? (3) Considering the fact that natural horns and trumpets could not have played the fugue subject in Example 16.4, is that a valid reason for not giving it to modern horns and trumpets? (4) Are there limits, dictated by good taste, involved in using modern instruments for the scoring of Baroque music? For example, would roto-toms or vibraphone be acceptable? Are the answers to such questions purely a matter of individual, subjective judgment?

Example 16.5, from the Prelude to *Die Meistersinger*, combines three distinct musical ideas or elements. They are scored, respectively, as follows:

1. (consisting of three voices doubled at the octave): 2 flutes, 2 oboes, 1 clarinet, 3 horns (1 trumpet), violins II, violas;
2. 1 clarinet in unison with violins I; 1 horn in unison with cellos an octave lower;
3. 2 bassoons in unison with tuba; double basses an octave lower.

Although the greatest differentiation of the three elements could have been achieved by the use of sharply contrasting colors, Wagner chose to present each element in a composite tone color produced by at least one woodwind, one brass instrument, and one string group. Yet in performance the three elements stand out sufficiently from each other, partly because of the differences between the *composite* colors and partly for purely musical reasons—differences in articulation, note values, and registers.

Despite the fact that we move into a totally different musical world in Example 16.6, the principles of scoring discussed in connection with Example 16.4 are still valid: because of the high dynamic level, each of the lines involved must be included within the brass section if balance is to be achieved. Woodwinds and strings take unison or upper-octave doublings of them.

EXAMPLE 16.5

Prelude to *Die Meistersinger*

Wagner

EXAMPLE **16.6**

Third Symphony

Copland

The reverse of the approach seen in Examples 16.5 and 16.6 is demonstrated in Example 16.7, where each one of the musical elements is given a separate color and there is no mixing of timbres from different sections. In fact, except for some use of composite color *within* the woodwind section, the colors are pure, though produced in this case by more than one of each instrument. Even the two sections of violins differ from each other in quality since the first violins are unmuted and in a high, intense register, while the second violins are muted and playing bowed tremolos in a much less brilliant register.

EXAMPLE 16.7

Six Pieces for Orchestra, Op. 6, No. 1

Instead of making exclusive use of either composite colors (as in Examples 16.4–16.6) or pure colors (as, for the most part, in Example 16.7), the vast majority of contrapuntal scoring involves both. This is true in Example 16.8, though there is a preponderance of pure color there. In contemporary music that involves a complex linear fabric (as this passage does), considerable use of separate timbres is almost a necessity if the lines are to be kept distinct.

Example 16.8 illustrates certain tendencies in orchestration that are especially apparent in the works of serial composers:

1. There has been a reaction against the heavy, opaque, and often sumptuous scoring characteristic of late nineteenth-century orchestral music; composers today generally favor a leaner, more transparent sound. This does not necessarily mean, however, that a smaller orchestra is involved. A good many contemporary scores make use of a full orchestra but tend to employ the instruments consecutively more than simultaneously, so that for much of the time relatively few of them are playing at once. Changes in the orchestration are likely to occur frequently, and instruments are often treated in soloistic fashion. In Example 16.8 all the instruments play at some point; yet because of the somewhat fragmentary individual parts and the fact that one group often drops out when another enters, the total effect is not particularly heavy.

2. Octave doublings, so heavily relied upon in eighteenth- and nineteenth-century orchestration, are often avoided. In the case of Schönberg and his followers, this avoidance probably stemmed chiefly from their desire not to give any note or notes special importance that might have led to tonal implications, rather than from considerations of orchestration. But some nonserial composers also avoid octave doublings simply to achieve the particular clarity and uncluttered sound that result.

3. There has been an increasing use of "C scores." In some of these, all the instruments are written at concert pitch, as in Example 16.8, but the majority still employ the octave transposition for the piccolo, double bass, and other instruments that otherwise would need many ledger lines or an *8va* sign. In any case, the players' parts for transposing instruments must, of course, be written in transposed form.

EXAMPLE 16.8

Variations for Orchestra, Op. 31

Schönberg

Fragmentation, which stemmed chiefly from Webern's innovations[1] and which has been a major feature of much twentieth-century music, brought with it a parallel possibility in orchestration: melodic lines that formerly would have been taken by a single instrument are now sometimes divided among several. In serial music the row may even be fragmented to the point where each note is given to a separate instrument. In the Webern excerpt in Example 16.9, the individual passages are so brief (some only one note) and there is so little use of instruments simultaneously that the total effect is extremely delicate and transparent. But note that nearly every instrument of the orchestra is used at some point on that page.

Octave displacement, a frequent device in serial music, obviously contributes to fragmented scoring when applied in the orchestra. Whereas extremely wide leaps are entirely feasible on the piano, for example, they often present problems of range for individual instruments of the orchestra, with the result that the allotting of a melodic idea to several instruments in turn may become a necessity.

The term *pointillistic*, borrowed from a French school of painting that used small dots of unmixed color to achieve its effects, is sometimes applied to orchestration such as that in Example 16.9—as well as to highly fragmented lines themselves. Although it is an appropriate and convenient term, it has the slight disadvantage of having been associated on occasion with a very different style of scoring—the impressionistic variety that makes use of small touches of color and subtle effects (as in certain Debussy works). Today, however, it generally has the first connotation.

Schönberg's concept of a "melody" made up solely of changing colors (*Klangfarbenmelodie*, meaning literally "tone color melody") should be mentioned here, since it anticipated and undoubtedly encouraged the preoccupation with individual timbres that is seen in the music of Webern and his followers. It will be discussed briefly in Chapter 17.

Example 16.10, from the Passacaglia section of Hindemith's *Nobilissima Visione*, affords a chance to study four orchestral settings involving the same theme as basis but with that theme orchestrated in a different way each time and with different counterpoints surrounding it. Example (a) includes all six measures of one variation (the seventh appearance of the theme), plus the first two measures of the next; (b) and (c) show, respectively, the first two measures of the two variations that follow. Here, again, students will find it profitable to analyze the distribution of the instruments and to examine the weight of the passacaglia theme in relation to the other lines and the weight of those lines in relation to each other. Stylistic differences between the scoring here and in preceding examples should be observed, and the ways in which principles discussed earlier apply here should be considered.

---

[1]The fragmentation of lines is, in a sense, a return to the technique of "hocketing" employed in medieval polyphony.

EXAMPLE 16.9

Variations for Orchestra, Op. 30

Webern

Note: *All instruments are written here as they will actually sound.*

EXAMPLE 16.10

Nobilissima Visione, 3. Passacaglia

(a)

Hindemith

(b)

(c)

In *Melodien,* from which Example 16.11 is taken, Ligeti desired to project three different "planes of dynamics" that correlate in a general way to levels of rhythmic activity. In a brief preface to the score the composer states that the most important plane—the foreground—consists of melodies or short melodic patterns often marked *in relievo.* The middle ground consists of ostinatolike figurations, while the background is comprised of sustained tones. In this particular excerpt all strings except the double bass play middle-ground material and will be perceived as a rather wide "band" of sound against which the more important woodwind and brass figures will be heard "in relief." The middle ground is "painted with broad strokes" in which individual pitches really have little meaning other than to contribute to a highly complex "sound mass," as it is sometimes called. On the other hand, the foreground material is worked out in considerable detail, with a variety of instruments used to highlight, color, and accompany the most important continuous melodic lines. This sort of texture—and approach to composition—has much in common with electronic music.

Note the use of the oboe d'amore, plucked piano strings, extreme ranges of the trombone and bassoon, and the numerous special effects in the strings. (The score is notated as it will actually sound.)

EXAMPLE 16.11

Melodien

Gẏörgy Ligeti

*Horn 1, 2 bar 110: ▉ is equivalent to the previous ▤, so that the speed of the glissandi remains the same.
** Bassoon, bar 110: ⊔ is equivalent to the previous ⊔ ("doppio movimento"). *** Vln. A, B, Vla. bar
110: the speed of the figuration remains the same, as the ⊔⊔⊔ is equivalent to half of the former 12-
uplets, due to the doubling of the tempo (actual ♩ = former ♪). **** 'Cello, bar 110: the speed of the
figuration remains the same, as the ⊔⊔⊔ is equivalent to half of the former 10-uplet (actual ♩ =
former ♪). ***** Piano, bar 110: the strings to be plucked are to be identified beforehand. Plucking as
previously (see bar 98) but this time with the fingernails. (r.h.: index finger, l.h.: d: index finger, c:
thumb).*

As we turn to the scoring of chordal and homophonic music for the complete orchestra, there is little new in the way of general principles that need be added. If the music is chordal, we can apply the material learned in Chapter 10, the only difference being that a *succession* of chords is involved instead of a single isolated chord. The important question of voice-leading between the chord tones enters in here too.

Suppose that we had set out to score the Brahms Rhapsody in E♭ major (Op. 119, No. 4), the beginning of which is a good example of chordal music. The first two measures are shown in Example 16.12:

EXAMPLE 16.12

Rhapsody, Op. 119, No. 4

Although, as we have seen, scoring for orchestra does not necessarily involve making constant use of all the instruments on hand, this particular example seems to suggest the full orchestral *tutti*. It also suggests a fairly brilliant coloring. We shall want to fill in the gap between the two hands, of course. It would probably be wise to sketch the orchestration (for at least the first chord or two) before writing out the actual score. Such a sketch, showing the layout of each section, might look like this:

EXAMPLE 16.13

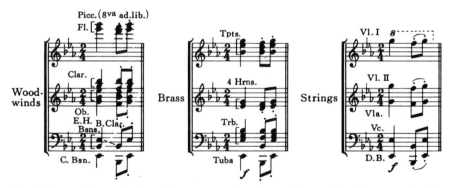

We would undoubtedly want to use timpani as well, either on the first beat of each measure

EXAMPLE 16.14

(a)

or on the complete rhythmic pattern:

(b)

Having set up this arrangement of instruments, our only problem during this opening portion involves letting each note progress to the appropriate note in the next chord so that good melodic lines will result for the individual instruments. Of course there will be different arrangements of the instruments as the musical structure changes. An excellent exercise would be to write out the first ten measures (or more) of this piece in full score, using the sketch given here as the basis for the beginning.

The excerpt from Strauss's *Death and Transfiguration* in Example 16.15 is a good example of primarily chordal music scored for full orchestra. Incidentally, it illustrates the fact that full scoring need not be reserved for very loud passages; in this case the dynamic marking is *pianissimo*.

Another example of chordal texture is the Mussorgsky-Ravel excerpt shown in Example 16.16. There the original piano version is included at the bottom for purposes of comparison and is not meant to be played in the orchestral version.

EXAMPLE 16.15

Death and Transfiguration

Strauss

EXAMPLE 16.16

"Promenade" (from *Pictures at an Exhibition*)

Mussorgsky - Ravel

The scoring of homophonic music was discussed in Chapter 12. There we used an orchestra consisting of woodwinds in pairs, horns, and strings. If a larger orchestra is involved, the situation is not altered as far as essential principles are concerned. The inclusion of additional woodwinds and of a full brass section merely gives us greater potential volume, increased range in the woodwind and brass sections, and new colors that may be used in a solo capacity. Some examples of homophonic music scored for full orchestra are shown next.

In Example 16.17 the chief melodic line in octaves is given to a doubling of woodwinds, brass, and strings, with harmonic background and moving bass also distributed among the three sections.

In Example 16.18, the most important melody is given to the strings, a countermelody to the woodwinds, and a second countermelody to the upper brass. Except for an E pedal point, which is shared by the lower brass and the double basses, this excerpt illustrates on a broad scale the principle we discussed in connection with polyphonic music: allotting a separate color to each voice to achieve the maximum distinctness and independence of line. Here we have not merely separate colors but also separate *sections* on the various parts. It might be argued that this example is actually polyphonic rather than homophonic in texture. The truth is probably that it lies somewhere between these two types; we are dealing in lines, to be sure, yet the countermelodies in woodwinds and brass seem to have the character more of ornamented harmony parts than of independent voices on a par with the melody in the strings.

This case brings up the point that music does not always fall exclusively into one of the three categories we have mentioned frequently in this book: chordal, homophonic, or polyphonic. We have used these categories in order to point out certain broad approaches to scoring, but hybrid types occur constantly. For example, we often have an important melodic line against a harmonic background (homophony), along with countermelodies that introduce a partially polyphonic effect. And some harmonic music consists of individual lines that move in an independent and musically interesting way so that a polyphonic element is present.

When countermelodies are involved, one must be careful to weight the principal idea strongly enough, either by dynamics or sheer number of instruments, so that it will not be eclipsed by the secondary counterpoints. In Example 16.18, the countermelody in the trumpets and horns is marked one degree softer than the woodwinds and strings in order to ensure that the greater power of the brass will not make that line too prominent.

In Example 16.19, the woodwinds and horns take the melody and its parallel harmonization, while the strings play a countermelody and the brass play subordinate parts.

Example 16.20 illustrates impressionistic scoring for a fairly large orchestra. Features characteristic of the impressionistic approach include the following: a sensitive (and often sensuous) use of color, such as the frequent division of string groups into numerous parts, the velvety richness of the lower strings in the last two measures, the unusual doubling involving horn with piccolos two octaves higher, and the delicate touches in the xylophone, celesta, harp, and tambourine; an avoidance of heavy masses of sound and of dynamic bombast; a constant concern for subtleties of dynamic nuance.

The distinction between the approach to color in this sort of scoring and in that of the Webern pointillistic school should be apparent from the examples given. In the first type, color has chiefly a decorative function, in the second, a constructional one. We will have more to say on this subject presently.

EXAMPLE 16.17

Symphony in D minor

EXAMPLE 16.18

Fifth Symphony

Tchaikovsky

Moderato assai molto maestoso

EXAMPLE 16.19

Les Préludes

Liszt

Example 16.20

Ibéria. II. "Les parfums de la nuit"

Debussy

318

SUGGESTED ASSIGNMENTS

A. The following are suitable as exercises in scoring for full orchestra (although not all of them call for consistently heavy scoring). If it is possible to have a school or local orchestra try out student projects in orchestration, the instrumentation of that orchestra should be learned in advance and used for the pieces to be played.

1. Bach, any of the chorale harmonizations.
2. Bach, Fugue XVI from *The Well Tempered Clavier*, Vol. I.
3. Bach, Fugue XXII from *The Well Tempered Clavier*, Vol. I.
4. Bach, Fugue in G minor from *Eight Little Preludes and Fugues* for the organ.
5. Beethoven, *Sonata Pathétique*, Op. 13 (beginning in particular).
6. Beethoven, Sonata, Op. 10, No. 3, 1st movt.
7. Beethoven, Sonata, Op. 101, beginning; 2nd movt., meas. 1–11.
8. Beethoven, Sonata, Op. 106, beginning; 2nd movt., meas. 1–46.
9. Schubert, Sonata, Op. 42, first movt.
10. Schubert, Sonata, Op. 143, 1st movt., exposition.
11. Schubert, Sonata in B♭ major, Op. Posth.
12. Chopin, Polonaise in A major, Op. 40, No. 1.
13. Schumann, *Carnaval*.
14. Schumann, *Fantasia*, Op. 17, 2nd movt., meas. 1–22.
15. Brahms, Sonata, Op. 1 (exposition).
16. Brahms, Variations and Fugue on a Theme of Handel, Op. 24.
17. Brahms, Rhapsody, Op. 79, No. 1.
18. Brahms, Rhapsody, Op. 79, No. 2.
19. Brahms, Rhapsody, Op. 119, No. 4.
20. Wolf, "Verborgenheit" (song).
21. Mussorgsky, "Ballet of the Chicks in their Shells" from *Pictures at an Exhibition*. (This offers a good chance for the use of special color effects: harp, celesta, percussion, etc.)
22. Mussorgsky, "The Great Gate of Kiev" from *Pictures at an Exhibition*.
23. Debussy, "The Engulfed Cathedral" from *Préludes*, Book I.
24. Rachmaninoff, Prelude in G minor.
25. Griffes, "The White Peacock" from *Roman Sketches*. (This lends itself well to impressionistic scoring.)
26. Griffes, Scherzo, Op. 6, No. 3.
27. Prokofieff, Gavotte, Op. 12, No. 2.
28. Prokofieff, March, Op. 12, No. 1.
29. Prokofieff, Seventh Sonata for piano, Op. 83, 1st movt.
30. Tcherepnine, (Alexandre), Bagatelle I from *Ten Bagatelles*.
31. Bartók, No. 1 from *Fifteen Hungarian Peasant Songs*.
32. Bartók, *Allegro Barbaro*.
33. Rochberg, *Twelve Bagatelles*.
34. Mennin, "Aria" from *Five Piano Pieces*.
35. Kennan, Prelude III from *Three Preludes*.
36. Kabalevsky, Prelude 24 from *24 Preludes*, meas. 33–39.

B. Certain interesting and useful exercises have not been mentioned before. One involves "deorchestrating"—that is, reducing an orchestral score for piano, or for piano four hands, or for two pianos. Almost any orchestral music may be chosen for this purpose, though for the first attempt it would probably be wise to select a relatively uncomplicated score, say a Mozart or Haydn symphony. This is an excellent way to achieve an intimate acquaintance with a score and with the composer's characteristic use of instruments.

Piano reductions of many scores are available commercially. Another exercise involves arranging such a reduction for the same orchestra that the composer originally used. The completed scoring can then be compared with the original orchestral version.

A somewhat similar exercise, mentioned earlier, is that of scoring a work that was written originally for piano (or another medium) and later issued in orchestral form. (A list of such works is given at the end of Chapter 11.) The student's version can then be compared with the published orchestral version.

Finally, there is score reading at the piano—or at two pianos, with one player taking the woodwind and brass parts and the other taking the string parts. In any case, it is wise to begin with fairly simple material and progress to more complex. (In this connection, *Music for Score Reading* by Robert A. Melcher and Willard F. Warch, Prentice-Hall, Inc., 1971, provides an excellent series of graded excerpts and is highly recommended.) Although this is a rather special technique that can be learned only by repeated practice over a period of time, a few hints may be of some help:

1. It will not always be possible to play all the notes; sometimes octave doublings, secondary counterpoints, and the like will have to be omitted.
2. In widely spaced chords, string figurations, and other passages that are awkward pianistically, some rearrangement of the notes will be necessary.
3. Try to keep going in spite of minor slips or omissions. It is more important to keep the music moving along at a steady pace (not necessarily up to tempo, however) and to aim at the general effect of the original than to worry too much about individual notes, although accuracy should be striven for, of course.

17

Special Devices

Special effects available on individual instruments were discussed in earlier portions of this book, notably Chapters 4 though 9. The purpose of the present chapter is to comment on special devices or considerations involved in scoring for orchestral groups in general.

EXTREME REGISTERS

Twentieth-century scores tend to make considerable use of the extreme registers of instruments, even extreme registers that were generally avoided in an earlier period because of difficulties in intonation, quality, or technique. This tendency does not, however, rule out the validity of a normal *tessitura* for each instrument. Nor does the fact that such exceptional passages are written mean that they are always successful; frequently they merely confirm in performance the reasons why the registers involved were avoided for so long.

UNUSUAL SPACING

The suggestions concerning spacing given in the course of this book apply chiefly to pre-twentieth-century music. Many contemporary scores achieve highly interesting effects precisely by departing from traditional patterns. In Example 17.1, for instance, a triad is placed at the very bottom (where intervals would normally be wider), whereas in the middle register there are numerous gaps instead of the usual closer spacing.

Agon, "Gailliarde"

With the special colors produced by harmonics in the flutes, harp, and solo double basses and by the rarely used mandolin, the total effect is fresh and highly distinctive despite the fact that little more than a C major triad is involved, harmonically speaking. Such exceptional spacing (and scoring) would of course be decidedly out of place in most music of earlier periods.

As a general principle, scoring that involves a wide gap in the middle register is likely to sound unsatisfactory and is normally avoided. Yet there are times when that very arrangement is employed for a particular effect. An instance is the following excerpt from Mahler's Ninth Symphony, where the two voices (one doubled at the lower octave) are separated by a vast distance. The passage is intensely affecting and dramatic to an extent it would not have been if it had been carefully "filled in" with octave doublings.

EXAMPLE 17.2

Ninth Symphony

Mahler

DIVISION OF THE ORCHESTRA INTO GROUPS

Since the earliest days of the orchestra, composers have occasionally used the device of dividing it into two or more parts; these may involve the same or different instrumentation. Such arrangements obviously suggest antiphonal effects and broad contrasts of weight or color. In contemporary usage they also lend themselves particularly to stimulating clashes between the groups, the clashes being either notated in the normal fashion or, in the case of aleatoric music, governed by chance.

Gabrieli's famous *Sonata pian' e forte,* which clearly reflects the divided-choir techniques of Venetian church music, is an example of an early venture into this genre. Mozart wrote a *Notturno* for four orchestras. Vaughan Williams' *Fantasia on a Theme by Thomas Tallis* and Bartók's *Music for String Instruments, Percussion and Celesta* both make use of a double string orchestra (plus a string quartet in the case of the Vaughan Williams work). In Stockhausen's *Gruppen,* three orchestras participate, as is the case in Elliott Carter's *A Symphony of Three Orchestras.* And Xenakis' *Strategy* involves two orchestras, each with its own conductor, that engage in a competition to see which one can produce the more interesting results under the same set of musical conditions, the winner being decided by judges.

SPECIAL DYNAMIC ARRANGEMENTS

In addition to the more usual possibilities in dynamic effects, there are some special ones that appear from time to time in orchestral scoring, including the following:

1. An instrument is introduced so softly that the listener is not aware of its entrance.[1] It then raises its dynamic level to that of the other instruments

---

[1] To indicate this effect some composers use an "*N*," which stands for *niente,* meaning "nothing" in Italian.

playing. In commercial arranging this device is known as the "sneak-in." It can be used effectively in building an orchestral crescendo, the instruments entering one or two at a time until all are playing. The reverse process, though seen less often, is also useful when a decrescendo is wanted; individual instruments make a diminuendo and drop out successively. Of course the process of adding or withdrawing instruments at an *audible* level for purposes of creating an orchestral crescendo or diminuendo is used frequently and thus is not in the "special" category.

2. *Contrapuntal dynamics* is a term sometimes applied to dynamic markings (including crescendos and diminuendos) that operate somewhat independently for the various parts. (This approach is the antithesis of the old "block dynamics" system that was the general rule during the Classical period.) Many composers of the Romantic era, including Wagner, Berlioz, Rimsky-Korsakoff, and Strauss, made considerable use of differing dynamic levels in the same passage, but it was in the works of Mahler that the "contrapuntal" aspect was first carried to great lengths. For instance, in the third measure of Example 17.3, six different dynamic levels are indicated, and at that point certain instruments are making a diminuendo, while others are making a crescendo. The whole example demonstrates Mahler's intense concern with the most minute dynamic subtleties. Incidentally, directions in this edition are given in *both* German and Italian, an unusual editorial procedure.

The simultaneous use of different dynamic levels in orchestral scoring stems in some cases from a desire to bring out a particular voice or tone color, in others from the need to compensate for inherent differences in weight between instruments. As examples of the latter situation, the brass section is sometimes marked one degree softer than the others in loud passages so that it will not overshadow them, and the harp, which tends to be easily covered, is often marked a degree louder.

3. The ultimate in independent dynamics occurs in certain serial music (especially the "totally organized" kind in which the dynamic pattern is one of the predetermined elements), where nearly every note has a separate indication. The levels indicated may vary widely and suddenly so that abrupt changes between extremes of soft and loud are common.

EXAMPLE 17.3

Fourth Symphony

Mahler

4. In order to produce a distant effect, instruments are sometimes directed to play offstage. This device has probably been applied most often to a solo trumpet (Beethoven, *Leonore* Overture No. 3) or to a group of trumpets (Strauss, *Ein Heldenleben;* Verdi, *Requiem;* Mahler, First Symphony). But it is also called for in woodwind parts on occasion. Two well-known instances (both involving the imitation of a shepherd's piping) are the passage for oboe, marked *lontano,* in Berlioz's *Fantastic Symphony* and the extended solo for English horn at the beginning of Act III of Wagner's *Tristan und Isolde.* The direction, in various languages, is as follows: Italian, *interna* or *dietra la scena* or *lontano;* French, *dans la coulisse* or *derrière la scène;* German, *auf der Bühne* or *in der Ferne* or *auf dem Theater.*

5. An instrument or a group of instruments that has been playing *forte* drops out, and as it does so, another instrument or group enters *piano* on the last note. Stravinsky appears to have been especially fond of this device; two examples from *Petrouchka* follow, and numerous others could be quoted, including one from *Agon* in which three double basses playing harmonics take soft sustained tones as the other instruments drop out—a magical effect.

EXAMPLE 17.4

Petrouchka

(All notes are actual pitches)

DIVISION OF A MUSICAL IDEA

A musical idea is sometimes divided between two instruments of the same kind. In certain instances this is done to ease a technical problem, such as fast passage work or awkward leaps or fast tonguing. This is the case in Example 17.5(a) and (b). At other times the same approach is applied to wind parts that continue for some time without rests; by having two or more instruments of a kind play alternately, each has plenty of time to breathe. This use is demonstrated in Example 17.5(c). (The passage continues in this fashion for another nine measures.)

EXAMPLE 17.5

Schelomo

In the excerpt quoted in Example 5.2(c) Brahms makes use of a similar alternating and overlapping arrangement in the flute parts to ensure that the melodic line will not be broken by even a brief retaking of breath.

THE CREATION OF PARTICULAR TONE QUALITIES THROUGH OVERTONE REINFORCEMENT

By having instruments softly play certain upper partials of a fundamental, it is possible to arrive at tone qualities not found in any one of the orchestral instruments. For example, in *Boléro,* Ravel in effect creates a new instrument by having the horn play the theme *mf* while two piccolos softly play partials 3 and 5 and a celesta plays partials 2 and 4. The resulting sound is striking and exotically colored.

EXAMPLE 17.6

Boléro

Ravel

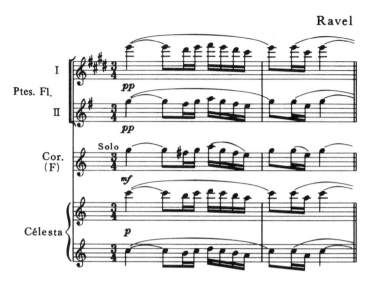

This general technique is most often used in making orchestral transcriptions of organ music from the Baroque period. Organ registration of that day was characterized by the use of stops that strongly reinforced some or all of the upper partials—through the sixth, sounding two octaves and a 5th higher than the fundamental. In the orchestra the sound of that sort of registration can be simulated by placing high woodwinds (or occasionally strings playing harmonics) on the upper partials. However, not all these partials need be included; even doubling a line softly a 12th higher or two octaves and a 5th higher begins to suggest the Baroque effect, and either doubling combined with one two octaves above the basic pitch is moderately effective for that purpose.

EMPHASIS ON INDIVIDUAL COLORS

In the remarks on pointillistic scoring made in Chapter 16, *Klangfarbenmelodie,* or "tone color melody," was mentioned. This concept forms the basis for the third of Schönberg's *Five Pieces for Orchestra,* Op. 16, entitled "Summer Morning by a Lake (Colors)." A concert sketch of the first few measures is shown in Example 17.7:

EXAMPLE 17.7

Harmonic and melodic activity have been reduced to nearly zero here, the chief "motion" being in the subtle shifting from one orchestral color to another. Although the *Klangfarbenmelodie* principle has not often been used in this particular fashion by other composers, it has been a major factor in music since Webern's day in the sense that there has been much emphasis on color as an actual compositional element rather than as a decorative feature. This approach has often been applied to melodic lines by assigning a different instrumental timbre to each note or to individual segments of a continuous melody. Although intriguing results can be produced in this way, there are certain inherent dangers. For one thing, there is a temptation to let color substitute for a strong and interesting melodic line; for another, a constantly changing orchestral palette can become just as monotonous as one that changes infrequently.[2]

Approached from another angle, orchestral colors can also be utilized in reinforcing the broad structural divisions of a composition—for example, mainly low brass for one section, string harmonics and high woodwinds for another, and so on.

EMPHASIS ON TEXTURE

Texture, like color, has come to be considered by many composers an important element to be planned carefully and even utilized for its own sake on occasion. This idea is, of course, not an entirely new one. For example, in *The Rite of Spring*, certain pages suggest that Stravinsky's chief purpose was to build up a complex fabric of sound (in which the listener is more aware of overall texture than of individual lines) by superimposing many instruments playing different parts.

---

[2]For a perceptive commentary on this whole subject, see Reginald Smith Brindle's book *Serial Composition* (Oxford University Press, London, 1966), Chapter 12: "Orchestration, Texture and Tone Colour."

Interestingly, a similar density of texture appears in a very different sort of work written by Stravinsky some fifty years later, the variations *Aldous Huxley in Memoriam.* The excerpt in Example 17.8 involves twelve-voice polyphony played by twelve solo violins *poco sul ponticello.* In speaking of the density of the work, Stravinsky remarked that this variation, which sounded to him like the sprinkling of very fine glass, pleased him most as timbre.

An intriguing montagelike texture can be created by having the players play out of phase with one another, as in Example 17.9. (Note the directions to some of the strings: "not together, even within sections.") The montage technique is also illustrated in Example 16.11.

Of course textural planning is often involved in music of a thinner nature in which individual lines come through clearly. Whatever the musical situation, texture is often a highly important factor in reinforcing such basic elements as unity, contrast, and climax.

Example 17.8

Variations

Stravinsky

Note: *Compare a passage of similar texture for woodwinds from the same work, shown in Example 6.15(d).*

ALEATORIC TEMPORAL ELEMENTS

Although temporal relationships do not, strictly speaking, come under the heading of orchestration, fresh approaches to them in some contemporary scores affect the sound of the scoring and often require new notational techniques.

The work quoted in Example 17.9 is a case in point. Certain instruments are directed to play "not together"; at those points the pitches are specified, but they are intentionally unsynchronized with the notes in the parts of other players. Also contributing to the free effect is the presence of numerous unmeasured bars. For these the conductor gives only a downbeat (for which the symbol ↓ is used in the score) and possibly a left-hand signal to a particular player (↴). At such times instruments are assigned passages to play repeatedly over a given number of seconds (one form of "proportional notation") or until a certain instrument completes its assigned passage or until the conductor gives the signal to go on. At some points in the work, strict and unmeasured tempos appear simultaneously; in these passages the symbol Ⓢ appears, an indication that the conductor is to give "a very clear sign at the place indicated to show the ad lib. players the beginning of their new bar." (The "ad lib. players" are those playing in unmeasured fashion.) At other places, one player gives a signal to another at the moment when the latter is to enter. In a reversal of the usual procedure, a player may even be asked to give a signal to the conductor at a specified point.

The ultimate in temporal freedom is the type of partly aleatoric music that supplies only basic pitches without rhythm and directs the player to improvise freely on them. The notation normally consists of the notes to be used enclosed in a square or rectangular box, along with the direction to improvise—usually for a given number of seconds.

EXAMPLE 17.9

Night Music

Thea Musgrave

* not together, even within section.

⊗ Stop playing immediately on sign.

Used by kind permission of J & W Chester/Edition Wilhelm Hansen London Ltd.

ALEATORIC PITCH ELEMENTS

In some orchestral music certain parts may involve the reverse of the situation just described: the rhythm is notated but the pitches are left up to the player. Although applicable to any instrument, this approach is perhaps most often seen in parts for the pitched percussion. Sometimes the general pitch curve is suggested by an appropriately shaped line or a graphic symbol; in other instances stems of different lengths are used to show relative pitch relationships, as in the example for wood chimes and marimba that follows:

EXAMPLE 17.10

Circles

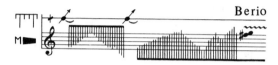

Occasionally several instruments or whole sections are asked to improvise at once, as in Donald Erb's Concerto for Percussion, where the percussion section is given that direction. At one point in Eugene Kurtz's *Ça . . .*, the orchestra is directed to tune and to play (scraps of pieces, exercises, or whatever they choose to) as they would before a rehearsal or a concert.

EXTENSIVE DIVISION OF THE STRING SECTION

Both Examples 17.8 and 17.9 illustrate a device seen frequently in contemporary scores, the division of a string group or the whole section into many parts. Example 17.8 involves only solo violins; Example 17.9 includes solo violins and violas, along with divided string groups.

Example 17.11, from a Penderecki score, makes use of a more extensive and complex division of the strings. It also includes some of the special effects cited in Chapter 4. The composer uses the following symbols to indicate these:

s. p. = *sul ponticello*

⬆ = *highest note of the instrument (no definite pitch)*

⋀ = *play between the bridge and the tailpiece*

⫲ = *arpeggio on four strings behind the bridge*

⊢ = *play on the tailpiece by bowing it at an angle of 90 degrees to its longer axis*

$\spadesuit$ = *bow the wood of the bridge at a right angle at its right side*

Z = *very rapid nonrhythmicized tremolo*

A much-used device in music of this genre is the tone cluster, a mass of sound in which the notes are bunched closely together, often a minor 2nd (or even a microtone) apart. The result is not as dissonant as might be expected, especially when higher registers and softer dynamic levels are involved. Various notations are employed. One, used mainly for sustained clusters, consists of a black band encompassing the width of the pitch area concerned. It appears at the top of Example 17.11. In this and other Penderecki works the notes to be played by the various string players are all shown in the score, designated by numbers; but only individual notes are shown in each player's part.

Another method of notating tone clusters involves writing out, in the score as well as the parts, the actual pitch to be played by each division. Of course clusters may be written for woodwinds, brass, or pitched percussion, as well as for strings. Those for strings often move in glissando fashion.

EXAMPLE 17.11

Threnody to the Victims of Hiroshima

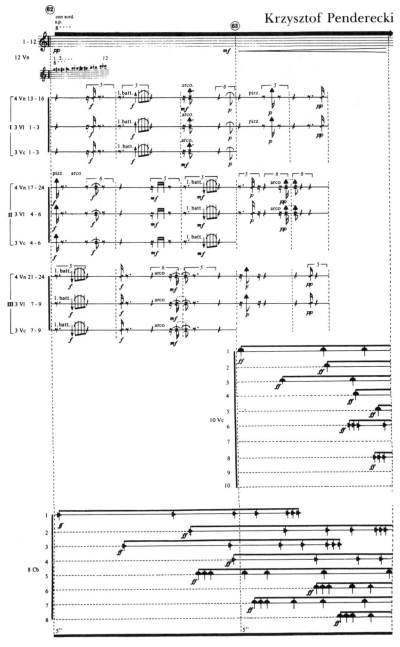

Krzysztof Penderecki

CUTOUT SCORES

Example 17.11 also illustrates the use of a "cutout" score, in which an instrument is given a staff only when it is playing; blank spaces are used in place of rests at other times. Proponents of this arrangement argue that it dispenses with needless clutter on the score page and allows the eye to concentrate on the points at which instruments are actually playing. Others maintain that not enough is gained by this format to justify the extra effort involved in setting up the score.

SPECIAL POSITIONING OF PLAYERS, AND OTHER ASSIGNMENTS

The well-known but still effective device of having an instrument played offstage was mentioned earlier. It appears in Example 17.9, where the first horn player is given the direction *move to position just off stage*. In recent years composers have specified other special positions or perambulations. Players may be asked to

1. stand as they play
2. move to a position elsewhere onstage or in the auditorium
3. play (from the start) at a given place in the auditorium
4. play while walking to a specified location or simply around the stage

(This last direction is obviously limited in terms of the players who can be asked to carry their instruments with them.)

In addition, contemporary performers must not be surprised if they are asked to make "vocalizations of one kind or another—speaking, shouting, screaming, whistling, hissing, grunting, muttering, laughing, whispering, singing, humming—either completely independent of instrumental playing or else combined with various methods of sound production on the instruments."[3] And in smaller groups especially, performers are sometimes called upon to play instruments other than their own; for example, a trombonist may be asked to play a few notes on a small percussion instrument at a point where all the percussionists are occupied with other parts.

---

[3]Gardner Read, *Contemporary Instrumental Techniques.*

18

Infrequently
Used Instruments

THE SAXOPHONES

Italian: Sassofono
Sassofoni

French: Saxophone
Saxophones

German: Saxophon
Saxophone

EXAMPLE 18.1

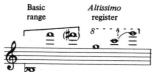

Eb Sopranino, sounding a minor 3rd higher
Bb Soprano, sounding a major 2nd lower.
Eb Alto, sounding a major 6th lower.
Bb Tenor, sounding a major 9th lower.
Eb Baritone, sounding an 8ve and a major 6th lower.
Bb Bass, sounding 2 8ves and a major 2nd lower.

With a few small exceptions,[1] all the saxophones have the same "basic" *written* range, but each size transposes differently. This arrangement will be illustrated shortly. First, however, a word needs to be said about the range chart in Example 18.1.

Until recently the top written note for the saxophones was generally given as f^3 (the first F above the staff). Today what might be called the basic range—that in which the usual fingering and tone production are employed—has been extended upward a half step by the addition of an F♯

---

[1]The exceptions: the sopranino saxophone, some older soprano saxophones, and most bass saxophones go only as high as (written) Eb; some baritone saxophones go down to a low (written) A.

key to some soprano, alto, and tenor saxophones. This key is optional; players specify whether they want it when they purchase the instrument. More important, players of these instruments have learned a special technique for producing notes in the *altissimo* (very high) register, thus further extending the range upward by an octave or more in some cases. But a word of warning is necessary: Although the bottom 4th of this register is playable by most professional and many advanced student saxophonists, the notes above the written C are extremely difficult and had better be reserved for players known to possess the capability of producing them. It may be, of course, that as these latter pitches are called for more frequently, more and more players will acquire the knack of achieving them. Because the sopranino and soprano saxophones can play relatively high notes by means of normal fingering, they generally have no need for *altissimo* notes, though virtuoso soloists report occasional use of them on the soprano instrument. (Incidentally, the sopranino saxophone is used considerably less often than the others—and very rarely in orchestral music, although that does not rule out the possible effectiveness of such scoring.) Because parts for the bass saxophone seldom exploit the upper portion of its compass, the *altissimo* register is for all practical purposes not involved in such parts. The E♭ contrabass saxophone (whose sounding range is an octave below that of the baritone saxophone) has not been included in the list above because so few exist that scoring for the instrument is normally impractical.

Let us return to the matter of individual transpositions. The written

note ![notation] would sound as follows on each of the saxophones:

EXAMPLE 18.2

Therefore, in terms of actual sound we have six different "basic" ranges.

EXAMPLE 18.3

Awkward as this system may seem at first, it has the advantage of enabling the player to use the same fingering on any one of the saxophones.

Suppose that we are scoring a piece for a combination that includes saxophones. We have decided that a particular melodic line lies comfortably within the range of the tenor saxophone and will sound well on that instrument. The part begins like this:

EXAMPLE 18.4

Actual
Sounds

In order to notate the passage correctly, we must transpose up a major 9th (an octave plus a major 2nd) and insert the appropriate key signature. The written part will then begin with these notes:

EXAMPLE 18.5

Tenor.
Sax.

To write a part for the baritone saxophone, we must think up an octave plus a major 6th from the actual sounds—and so on for the other saxophones.

The entire compass of the saxophone is usable. However, the bottom two or three semitones on the soprano, alto, and tenor instruments are full, thick, and difficult to play softly, while the top register of the baritone and bass saxophones is thinner and less characteristic. The instrument is remarkably agile technically. Almost every sort of figure is practical on it, but because it is a member of the single-reed family it is not ideally suited to playing rapid repeated notes.

In defense of the saxophone and its symphonic possibilities, a good saxophonist can produce a much more refined and sensitive sound than the one often heard in the performance of popular music. The soprano saxophone's quality is somewhat akin to that of a high oboe or English horn, the alto's "rounder" but bright; to some, the sound of the tenor instrument suggests an amalgam of bassoon, cello, and euphonium, while that of the bass saxophone is predictably darker and heavier in character. The saxophone is impressively versatile in terms of color variation and has the greatest dynamic power of any (unamplified) woodwind. Furthermore, it combines satisfactorily with the brass.

In the past, saxophones were used relatively rarely in the orchestra. Examples of their use are the parts for tenor, soprano, and sopranino (the latter part generally taken over by the soprano, however) in Ravel's *Boléro;* the wonderfully effective solo for alto saxophone in the same composer's orchestration of Mussorgsky's *Pictures at an Exhibition* in the section entitled "The Old Castle," and the part for alto saxophone in Britten's *Sinfonia da Requiem.*[2] In recent years saxophones seem to be appearing with increasing frequency, especially in music for chamber groups and small orchestra. Of

_____

[2]In *The Orchestral Saxophonist,* a collection of saxophone parts from orchestral literature (Cherry Hill, N.J.: Roncorp, Inc., 1978), Bruce Ronkin and Robert Frascotti mention the fact that there are over 2,500 orchestral works containing a part for saxophone; 138 of these parts are listed, of which forty-one by twenty-eight different composers are included. Representative composers and their works are the following: Berg, Violin Concerto; Roy Harris, Fifth Symphony; Prokofiev, *Alexander Nevsky, Lieutenant Kije, Romeo and Juliet;* Gunther Schuller, *Abstractions;* Vaughan Williams, Sixth and Ninth Symphonies; Walton, *Belshazzar's Feast, Façade.* Virtually all these parts are for alto or tenor saxophone.

course they are in constant use in commercial arranging. Their role in scores for high school orchestra is discussed in Chapter 19.

Example 18.6 shows a brief excerpt arranged for a quartet of saxophones—two altos, a tenor, and a baritone. (Other combinations of saxophones are possible in a quartet but less frequently employed.) The original key of D major has been changed to Db in order to allow for slightly better keys for the saxophones.

EXAMPLE 18.6

"Curious Story" from *Scenes from Childhood*

THE Eb FLUTE

Italian: Flauto terzino in Mib *French:* Flûte tierce *German:* Terzflöte

EXAMPLE 18.7

Presumably introduced in an effort to bridge the gap between the flute and the piccolo, the Eb flute can play, comfortably and without shrillness, notes that might be somewhat strained and harsh if given to the C flute in its extreme upper register. Its tone quality is, in fact, milder and gentler than that of the C flute throughout its compass (if therefore not very incisive in its bottom register). In spite of these virtues, the Eb flute has not so far found wide acceptance. It is sometimes used in flute choirs or in bands as a substitute for the small Eb clarinet; but it has not figured to any extent in orchestral scoring.

The Db flute and piccolo, sometimes employed in bands in an earlier day, are now virtually obsolete.

THE BASS FLUTE

Italian: Flauto basso   *French:* Flûte basse   *German:* Bassflöte

EXAMPLE 18.8

The bass flute differs from the other flutes in being bent back on itself in a U shape at the mouthpiece end. (Without this feature it would be too long to be manageable.) In spite of an intriguingly exotic tone quality, it involves some serious problems: it can be fatiguing to play, both because it requires an extraordinary amount of air and because it is uncomfortably heavy to hold for long periods of time; and even the finest players have difficulty in coaxing much sound out of the instrument. One reason it has been employed more in commercial arranging and in recording than elsewhere is that the amplification available in those settings builds the sound to a more effective level. In chamber groups, where the bass flute can be heard solo or pitted against only a quiet background, its unamplified sound may be adequate. And, of course, it is a valuable member of flute choirs—in the case of music departments or groups fortunate enough to own the instrument. Because of its rarity and the problems mentioned above, it is scarcely ever included in orchestral scores.

THE OBOE D'AMORE

Italian: Oboe d'Amore   *French:* Hautbois   *German:* Liebesoboe
                                          d'Amour

EXAMPLE 18.9

Used in Bach's day and revived by Strauss in his *Sinfonia Domestica,* the oboe d'amore is a rarity today. Perhaps the most widely known part for it is the extended one in Ravel's *Boléro.* It is like the oboe in fingering, but its tone is sweeter and less biting. Because it is midway in size between the oboe and the English horn, it is sometimes described as a mezzo-soprano oboe. In Bach's works, the part for it is written at actual pitch, but in modern scores the transposition given here is used.

THE HECKELPHONE

Italian: Heckelphon   *French:* Heckelphone   *German:* Heckelphon

EXAMPLE 18.10

Sounding an 8ve lower.

This instrument, invented by Heckel in 1904, is an oboe pitched an octave lower than the normal oboe. It is longer than the English horn and has a larger distension at the bell. Its tone quality is extremely reedy and full, particularly in the lower register. Except for Strauss (in *Salome*) and Delius, few composers have written for the heckelphone, but it is now finding some use in commercial orchestral arranging.

A baritone oboe in C, mentioned in some orchestration books, is such a rarity that writing for it is impractical. Its range differs from that of the heckelphone only to the extent that it lacks the bottom A and Bb.

Even rarer is the bass oboe, an instrument slightly different from the heckelphone but sharing the same range. The bass oboe was employed by Holst, Delius, and Bax in the early years of this century.

THE BASSET HORN

Italian: Corno di Bassetto   *French:* Cor de basset   *German:* Bassethorn

EXAMPLE 18.11

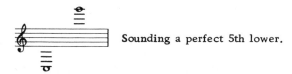

Sounding a perfect 5th lower.

This instrument was a smaller-bored forerunner of the Eb alto clarinet, mentioned next. A curious feature of early basset horns (not found on later ones) was a boxlike appendage that contained a portion of the tube coiled up so as not to increase the length of the instrument. Examples of parts for the basset horn can be found in Mozart's *Requiem* and several of his operas, as well as in Beethoven's *Prometheus*. Strauss revived the instrument for use in his operas *Elektra* and *Die Frau ohne Schatten*. In these works the part is sometimes written in the bass clef rather than in the usual treble, in which case it is intended to sound a perfect 4th higher instead of a perfect 5th lower. (Obviously this practice parallels the "old" bass-clef notation for the French horn in F.) Most major orchestras now have a basset horn available.

THE Eb ALTO CLARINET

Italian: Clarinetto contralto in Mib   *French:* Clarinette alto en Mib   *German:* Altklarinette

EXAMPLE 18.12

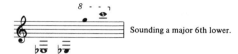

Sounding a major 6th lower.

Although by tradition the E♭ alto clarinet has primarily been a band instrument, there is no reason why it cannot prove valuable in the orchestra in a capacity similar to that of the bass clarinet. It is mentioned here chiefly because of its role as a substitute for the basset horn in orchestral music. Its sound is moderately dark and reedy—roughly midway between the B♭ or A clarinets and the bass clarinet in terms of tonal coloration.

Bands sometimes use an E♭ contra alto clarinet (often called E♭ contrabass) pitched an octave below the E♭ alto clarinet.

THE SARRUSOPHONE

EXAMPLE 18.13

Sounding an 8ve lower.

An invention of a French bandmaster named Sarrus, the sarrusophone is a double-reed instrument very similar to the bassoon in construction but made of metal instead of wood. It came originally in six sizes, pitched alternately in B♭ and E♭. Of these, the only one used in the orchestra was the largest, which sometimes substituted for the contrabassoon. So that the player could read from the contrabassoon part without having to transpose, a contrabass sarrusophone in C was introduced, and this instrument's range and transposition are given here. The sarrusophone in E♭ is still made today, however. Although the sarrusophone has had a considerable vogue in France, it appears only rarely in American orchestras. A part for it can be seen in Ravel's *Rapsodie Espagnole*.

THE CORNET

Italian: Cornetto   *French*: Cornet à pistons   *German*: Kornett
(*or* Cornetta)   (*or* Piston)

EXAMPLE 18.14

Sounding a major 2nd lower.

Some comments on the cornet were given earlier in the section on the trumpet in order to distinguish one instrument from the other. It was pointed out that the cornet, being different in shape, produces a slightly mellower, less incisive sound than the trumpet. But the difference in tone quality is far less marked today than it was at one time. The cornet speaks a bit more easily than the trumpet and is technically facile.

Parts for cornets in symphonic music can be seen principally in French scores of the late nineteenth century and early twentieth century. There are other instances, however, such as the important cornet parts in Stravinsky's *Petrouchka*.

At one time, the cornet, like the B♭ trumpet, had a slide by means of which the instrument could be pitched in A, but it is not included on cornets made today.

THE TRUMPET IN D

EXAMPLE 18.15

Sounding a major 2nd higher.

This valve instrument is somewhat smaller than the B♭ and C trumpets and only about half as large (in terms of tube length) as the natural trumpet in D used in the Baroque period. Its chief virtue is obviously its capability of playing parts that would be uncomfortably high for the larger trumpets. Consequently the lower register is likely to be little used. Parts for the D trumpet can be seen in Stravinsky's *The Rite of Spring* and Ravel's *Boléro*, among other works, and the instrument is often used to play the high trumpet parts in the music of Bach and his contemporaries.

THE TRUMPET IN E♭

This instrument, pitched in E♭, has the written range shown in Example 18.15 and sounds a minor 3rd higher than written.

THE PICCOLO TRUMPET IN B♭ OR A

EXAMPLE 18.16

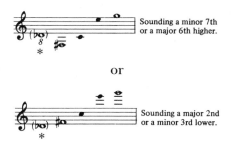

Sounding a minor 7th
or a major 6th higher.

or

Sounding a major 2nd
or a minor 3rd lower.

Notes down to the D♭ are possible if the instrument has four valves (as is usually the case), but these notes are generally of poor quality and difficult to play in tune.

The term *piccolo* is normally used to refer to this instrument in order to distinguish it from the larger, commonly used B♭ trumpet. It can be converted to A, a feature especially useful for playing in sharp keys. If the usual approach to the notation of transposing instruments is followed, it is written a minor 7th (or a major 6th if in A) lower than the sounds. However, some trumpeters prefer another system in which the notes are written a major 2nd (or a minor 3rd) higher than the concert pitches. (Obviously the greater proximity of written to sounding pitches seems more natural to players because of the parallel with the ordinary B♭ trumpet.) Given this choice of notation, there should be a note in the part indicating which one is being used. The piccolo trumpet in B♭–A is the instrument most likely to be chosen by players today for the performance of high Baroque trumpet parts both because it provides greater security in the upper register and because the smaller mouthpiece generally used facilitates the execution of such parts.

THE BASS TRUMPET

EXAMPLE 18.17

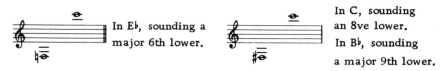

In E♭, sounding a major 6th lower.

In C, sounding an 8ve lower.
In B♭, sounding a major 9th lower.

The bass trumpet in E♭ is equipped with a fourth valve that allows it to go down to a written F♮, a half step lower than the trumpet's usual bottom written note (sounding the A♭ a major 6th below). Though the instrument is not often seen, parts for it, such as that at figure 139 in Stravinsky's *The Rite of Spring*, attest to its effectiveness, and Strauss also made notable use of it. Even when it does not go below the bottom limits possible on the B♭ and C trumpets, it has the great advantage of being capable of taking notes in the lower register with greater strength and security than those instruments.

Concerning the other bass trumpets listed here, Walter Piston says in his book *Orchestration:* "The bass trumpet, as written for by Wagner and Strauss, in the keys of 8-foot C and the B♭ below, is to all intents and purposes a valve trombone. It is played by trombonists, using the trombone mouthpiece."

There are one or two instances of trumpet in F basso (sounding a 5th lower) in the works of Wagner and Rimsky-Korsakoff.

THE FLÜGELHORN

Italian: Flicorno   *French:* Bugle   *German:* Flügelhorn

EXAMPLE 18.18

Sounding a major 2nd lower.

Once popular in bands but now seldom seen in this country, the flügelhorn resembles the cornet in construction and size but has a wider bore. Its tone has been described by some as being similar to that of the horn though more open and less mellow, by others as being midway between those of the cornet and the baritone.

Three of the very rare instances of parts for the flügelhorn in symphonic writing occur in Respighi's *Pines of Rome* (where *flicorni* are called for, obviously to suggest Roman horns), in Tippett's Third Symphony (an extended solo in the "Slow Blues" at figure 187), and in Stravinsky's *Threni.* In the last work the instrument is listed at the beginning of the score as "Contralto Bugle in B♭ (Fluegelhorn)." Although the range of the flügelhorn is theoretically the same as those of the cornet and the trumpet, the top 4th or so is not generally used.

Some jazz musicians have shown a fondness for the flügelhorn and perform with great virtuosity on it.

THE BARITONE AND THE EUPHONIUM (BOTH IN B♭)

EXAMPLE 18.19

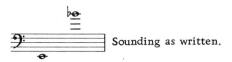

Sounding as written.

These two instruments are alike in general appearance and in range. They are built with either three or four valves; the current trend on the better instruments is toward four. They may have an upright bell or a "bell front." The tone is smooth and mellow, and great technical agility is characteristic. The euphonium is often made with a slightly larger bore, which results in a broader and darker sound than that of the baritone. But even this distinction does not always apply, and it is, in fact, difficult to cite any consistent difference between the two instruments. Consequently their names have become practically synonymous today.

The baritone and the euphonium are regular members of the band. They are mentioned here not because orchestral scores are likely to call for them by name but because they are often used to play orchestral parts labeled "tenor tuba" (as in Strauss's *Don Quixote* and Holst's *The Planets*).

Baritone players are frequently former cornet players, the fingering pattern on the two instruments being the same. For the benefit of those players who have not had occasion to become familiar enough with the bass clef to read parts written in it, publishers of band music generally print a treble-clef baritone part (in addition to the one in bass). Such parts are written a major 9th higher than the sounds; that is, when written in treble clef, the baritone becomes a transposing instrument using the same transposition as that used by the bass clarinet in treble clef and by the tenor saxophone. In *scores,* the bass clef is more or less standard for the baritone, however.

THE WAGNER "TUBAS"

EXAMPLE 18.20

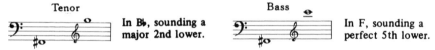

Wagner had these instruments constructed for use in his music dramas. It has frequently been pointed out that the name *tubas* is a misnomer inasmuch as they are really modified horns. They have been little used by other composers, though parts for them are included in Bruckner's Seventh, Eighth, and Ninth Symphonies and in Strauss's *Elektra.*

THE GUITAR

Italian: Chitarra   *French:* Guitare   *German:* Guitarre

EXAMPLE 18.21

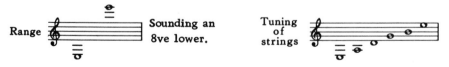

The guitar is of ancient Oriental origin and has appeared in various forms and under various names over the centuries. Unlike the lute, it has a flat back, and in its present form the sides curve inward. The neck is provided with frets (narrow strips of metal or wood attached to the fingerboard that mark the places where the strings are stopped by the left hand). The thumb and four fingers of the right hand are used in plucking the strings. In view of the unusual tuning of the instrument, a comment of Forsyth may be of interest: "Its tuning, a series of perfect fourths broken between the 2nd and 3rd strings by a major third, perpetuates the old vicious tradition of the irregular lute system." Another inheritance from the days of the lute is the "tablature" type of notation still used for the guitar in popular music. Instead of showing actual notes, that system employs a small diagram of the fingerboard, with dots marking the points at which the player is to put the fingers. Standard notation is used in serious guitar music, however.

The extremely rare appearances of the guitar in the symphony and opera orchestra seem to fall into three categories (1) those intended to provide a Spanish or Latin atmosphere; (2) those involving non-Spanish music in which the guitar contributes a folklike feeling through a simple strummed or arpeggiated background (e.g., Percy Grainger's accompaniments for English folk tunes); (3) those that use the guitar simply for the sake of its distinctive plucked sound. In addition to opera scores that contain parts for the instrument (*The Barber of Seville, Oberon*), the following symphonic works can be cited: Mahler's Seventh Symphony, Gould's *Latin-American Symphonette*, Thomson's orchestral suite from *The Plow That Broke the Plains*, and Schönberg's Serenade, Op. 24.

It should be added that the electric guitar, for which the sound can be amplified, has been used for many years in popular music.

THE MANDOLIN

Italian: Mandolino   *French:* Mandoline   *German:* Mandoline

Example 18.22

Smaller than the guitar and roughly pear-shaped, the mandolin has eight strings tuned in pairs to the same pitches as the open strings of the violin. It is played with a *plectrum,* or pick. Not only are single short notes possible, but the double strings allow for a rapid alternation between two of the same pitch so that a quasi-sustained effect with a kind of tremolo results. The fingerboard is fretted.

Like the guitar, the mandolin has occasionally been called for in the opera orchestra (Verdi's *Otello,* and Mozart's *Don Giovanni,* for example). The Mahler Seventh Symphony and the Schönberg Serenade, cited above as using the guitar, also contain parts for the mandolin, and the instrument is one of the many "extras" required for Respighi's *Roman Festivals.* A more recent instance of its use occurs in Stravinsky's *Agon.* (See Example 17.1.)

THE PIPE ORGAN

EXAMPLE 18.23

The organ is sometimes used in orchestral scores to supply added volume (generally at climactic points), liturgical atmosphere, or simply its own majestic tone quality. Occasionally the pedals alone, especially with 16-foot or 32-foot stops, are used to double the lower orchestral instruments for an extra-dark, ponderous effect.

Many timbres and textures are available through the stops. Eight-foot stops sound at the written pitch; four-foot stops sound an octave higher than the written pitch, 16-foot stops an octave lower, and so on. A system of couplers allows one manual to be linked with another or with the pedals. Music for the organ is written on three staves, the upper two for the manuals or keyboards, the bottom one for the pedals.

Although the organ was at one time a frequent member of the instrumental group used to accompany oratorios and cantatas of the Baroque period (where it realized the *basso continuo* part), it later relinquished that role. Parts for it in symphonic music did not appear until the late nineteenth century. Scores that contain organ parts include Saint-Saëns' Third Symphony, Scriabin's *Poem of Ecstasy*, Mahler's Second and Eighth Symphonies, Strauss's *Also sprach Zarathustra*, Respighi's *Pines of Rome* and *Roman Festivals*, Holst's *The Planets*, and Bartók's *The Miraculous Mandarin*.

THE HARMONIUM

EXAMPLE 18.24

This is a small keyboard instrument sometimes described as a reed organ. However, the "reeds" in this case are thin tongues of metal set into vibration by an air stream that is provided by a pair of bellows operated by the player's feet. The principle involved, that of the "free single reed," is one that does not figure in the workings of any of the regular orchestral instruments. Some variety of timbre is obtainable by means of stops.

Scores that contain parts for the harmonium include Tchaikovsky's *Manfred* Symphony, Mahler's Eighth Symphony, Strauss's *Ariadne auf Naxos*, Hindemith's *Kammermusik No. 1*, and Shostakovich's ballet suite *The Golden Age*.

THE HARPSICHORD

Italian: Clavicembalo   *French*: Clavecin   *German*: Cembalo
(*or* Cembalo)   (*or* Kielflügel)

EXAMPLE 18.25

Although the harpsichord was frequently used in combination with other instruments during the Baroque period (generally to supply the realized figured bass), its appearances in the modern orchestra have been few. One problem is the fact that its tone is so light as to be easily covered by other instruments and easily lost in a large hall. Even though many of the harpsichords built today are capable of producing more sound than their earlier counterparts, composers who use the harpsichord in an orchestral setting tend to make the orchestra a small one or to score relatively lightly for larger forces at points where the harpsichord sound must come through.

The instrument differs from the piano in that the string, instead of being struck by a hammer, is plucked by a plectrum made of crow quills or leather; this is attached to a jack which is set into motion when a key is pressed. Doublings at the upper or lower octave, coupling of the two manuals, and some variation in tone quality are all available through pedals. There is no sustaining pedal as on the piano and quite apart from that, the sustaining powers of the harpsichord are somewhat less than those of the piano. In writing for the instrument, one must remember that it cannot make differences in volume by means of a lighter or heavier touch.

The meager list of orchestral works that employ the harpsichord includes Strauss's *Dance Suite after Couperin*, Falla's *El Retablo de Maese Pedro* and Concerto for Harpsichord and Five Instruments, Poulenc's *Concert Champêtre* for harpsichord and orchestra, and Martin's *Petite Symphonie Concertante*. Effective use of the instrument has also been made in Elliott Carter's Sonata for Flute, Oboe, Cello, and Harpsichord.

THE ONDES MARTENOT

Invented in 1928 by a Frenchman named Martenot, this instrument produces its sound through electronic tone generation. It is played either by a keyboard (with approximately the same range as that of the piano keyboard) or by a ribbon attached to a ring on the player's finger. In the latter case, all pitches between those on the keyboard are also playable so that a "siren" effect is possible. The Ondes Martenot has been used chiefly by French composers, including Messiaen (*Turangalîla*), Honegger (*Jeanne d'Arc au Bûcher*), and Jolivet (Concerto for Ondes Martenot and Orchestra).

THE TAPE RECORDER

Some readers may have difficulty in accepting the tape recorder as an instrument. Nevertheless, it is the one natural purveyor of electronic music and *musique concrète,* and it has been used many times with orchestra, even to the point of being "soloist" in a concerto setting.

THE VIOLA D'AMORE

Italian: Viola d'Amore   *French:* Viole d'Amour   *German:* Liebesgeige

EXAMPLE 18.26

This curious instrument differs in several important respects from the ordinary viola. It is larger and heavier and has seven strings that are most often tuned as shown, although other tunings have often been used. Beneath each of these is another string that vibrates sympathetically with the one above (but which is not touched by the bow). A serious problem is the fact that the tuning of the strings usually centers so exclusively on the D major triad that passages which do not involve these notes are less resonant and effective. Also, the uneven spacing of the open pitches brings about some irregularities of fingering. Vivaldi, Bach, and Meyerbeer wrote for the viola d'amore; Charles Martin Loeffler included a part for it in *La Mort de Tintagiles,* and Hindemith even wrote a sonata for it, as well as *Chamber Music No. 6 for Viola d'Amore and Chamber Orchestra.*

SUGGESTED ASSIGNMENTS

A. Know:

1. written range of all the saxophones.
2. transposition of the various sizes.
3. general capabilities and limitations of saxophones.
4. transpositions of trumpets in D and E♭, and of piccolo trumpet in B♭

B. Score the first six bars of *America* for:

1. two alto and two tenor saxophones.
2. two alto, one tenor, and one baritone saxophone.
3. saxophone quartet (soprano, alto, tenor, baritone). Use other keys if you feel that the original key (F) is unsatisfactory.

19

Scoring for High School Orchestra

From time to time in the course of this book there have been brief comments on the subject of arranging for school orchestra. It may be helpful to gather together some of these remarks and expand on the problem as a whole.

There have been notable improvements in the state of high school orchestras during the last forty years or so: instrumentation has become much more nearly standardized, at least in senior high schools; the average performance ability of players has increased; the music used is of generally higher quality. Of course there are still differences in instrumentation, ability, and musical sophistication between the larger schools with highly active music programs and those schools less fortunate in terms of musical and material resources. But these differences are far less extreme than they once were.

Most published arrangements for senior high school orchestras make use of the following instrumentation:

1 piccolo (sometimes interchangeable with one of the flutes)
2 flutes
2 oboes
2 B♭ clarinets
2 bassoons
4 F horns
2 or 3 B♭ trumpets
2 or 3 trombones
(1 tuba)
timpani (normally 4)
other percussion
strings

Some scores also include parts for saxophones, usually two altos and a tenor. These are sometimes marked *ad libitum*—to be included or not at the discretion of the conductor. They are often duplications of the horn parts and can be used to replace or bolster the horns. The tenor saxophone can be helpful in doubling the bassoon and/or the cellos. A part for the bass clarinet is included more often than formerly—a laudable trend because the instrument is generally available and can be helpful in buttressing the bassoons and lower strings. Other instruments for which parts are occasionally included are the English horn, the harp, and (rarely) the celesta.

Some high school orchestras do not have players for all the instruments listed under the normal instrumentation. Second oboe, second bassoon, and third and fourth horns are the instruments most likely to be missing. Even when players are available, they may be inexperienced, and so it is normally unwise to give them parts that they must carry entirely on their own. Consequently parts for these instruments are frequently made "nonessential"; that is, the same notes are assigned to other instruments as well. This is largely true of viola parts also since some schools do not have enough violists to make up a section that can provide adequate strength and balance.

Partly because of the popularity of bands today, we find that most schools have plenty of performers on flute, clarinet, saxophone, trumpet, trombone, and percussion. But oboists and bassoonists sometimes present more of a problem. It is not merely a matter of training the players; the high cost of the instruments is also an obstacle, particularly in the case of the bassoon.

As a result of these considerations, important passages and even solos can be given to flute, clarinet, trumpet, or trombone with a reasonable assurance that players for these parts will be on hand. But solos for oboe, bassoon, or horn are often "cued" in another part so that the passage can be played by another instrument if necessary. Oboe solos may be cued for trumpet (usually muted) or for clarinet, flute, or violins, depending on which is convenient. Sometimes they are cued for two or more of these, in which case the conductor will decide which instrument is to do the substituting. Bassoon parts may be cued for trombone or cellos, and horn passages may be taken over by trombone, trumpet, or strings—or saxophones, if used.

However, solos are somewhat less frequent in scoring of this type than in actual symphonic orchestration. And there is likely to be more doubling between strings and winds, although today there seems to be a commendable tendency to break away from constant doubling of that sort and to introduce more use of pure colors and of individual sections.

What has been said so far applies chiefly to arrangements for the senior high school orchestra. Some junior high school orchestras are sufficiently well-staffed and proficient to use the same arrangements. Others with fewer and less-experienced players available use publications scored for the following more modest instrumentation:

1 or 2 flutes (one possibly interchangeable with piccolo)

1 oboe

2 B♭ clarinets

1 bassoon

2 F horns

2 B♭ trumpets

1 trombone

timpani (2–4)

other percussion

(piano)

strings

The piano part that is sometimes included may be placed either above the strings or at the bottom of the score page. It is usually a condensation of the score (or salient elements of it) and may be played or not, depending on whether it is needed to replace missing instruments, to reinforce weak instruments, or to reinforce the orchestra as a whole.

Some directors of junior high school orchestras use the following plan in making arrangements for their groups: each instrument has a part written for it throughout the piece, instruments being allotted according to a kind of "typecasting" system as shown in Table 19.1. When the time comes to play the arrangement and the availability of instruments is known; the conductor can cut out certain instruments wherever that is advisable in order to get away from a constantly heavy scoring and to introduce a lighter texture and pure colors. Although this system may seem at first to be roundabout and although it is certainly an unimaginative one, it has certain points in its favor. First, it ensures that there will at least be enough volume where volume is needed and that barring hopelessly deficient instrumentation, each voice will actually be played. Second, it eliminates the need for writing cues as such (the cues being "built in," so to speak), and it allows for the maximum number of possibilities in substitution. In the case of orchestras that vary radically in makeup from year to year, this type of arrangement may be more useful than one with only limited cross-cuing.

TABLE 19.1

MELODY	UPPER REGISTER HARMONY PARTS	MIDDLE REGISTER HARMONY PARTS	BASS
Flute	(1st Clarinet?)	Horns	Bassoon
Oboe	2nd Clarinet	2nd Violins	Trombone
1st Clarinet	(and/or 2nd Violins)	(and/or 2nd Clarinet)	Cellos
1st Trumpet	2nd Trumpet	Violas	Basses
1st Violins			

Third, arrangements made according to this plan can often be used for smaller instrumental ensembles, such as woodwind quartet or quintet, brass quartet, or small string group; that is, it is possible to plan the scoring so that certain groups of instruments playing by themselves will sound complete and satisfactory. And finally, in working with an orchestra, it is easier to delete parts than to add them. For example, the conductor who wishes to can simply tell a player not to play a particular passage; but if in rehearsal the conductor wants to add that instrument, it cannot be done without writing out a new part—assuming that the instrument is not cued at that point.

On the other hand, there are some serious disadvantages to this system. For one thing, it tends to involve much heavy doubling, which in turn brings about a constantly mixed tone that becomes monotonous. Also, because the arrangement must be contrived in such a way as to sound satisfactory whether it is played by a large or a small group, instruments are often not used in the most interesting or effective way. This whole method is one born of practical necessity rather than artistic choice; obviously there is no point in adopting it in the case of orchestras that have more or less complete and constant instrumentations.

Of course there is nothing hard and fast about the allotment of instruments to various voices in Table 19.1. In the first place, it applies, as given here, chiefly to homophonic music, and even within that category it would have to be altered from piece to piece to fit the individual structure of each. If a countermelody were present, that might involve changes in the distribution of the voices, and if the music were entirely contrapuntal, a different approach to the labeling of the musical elements would be needed.

Some technical points to keep in mind in scoring for school orchestra are given next, arranged by section.

WOODWINDS

In writing for senior high school woodwind players, a good axiom is to stay within the "practical" woodwind ranges given earlier. However, in the case of the bassoon, the top note had better be G or at most A. A safe top note for the clarinet is a written E above the staff; anything higher than that tends to be shrill and out of tune. With junior high school groups, it is advisable to work within upper woodwind ranges that are about a 3rd lower than the usual practical ranges.

Be sure to give the flute and oboe sufficient rests (though not necessarily extended ones). This is a good principle to follow even in writing for seasoned players, and it is doubly important in the case of young performers, whose breathing powers are not fully developed. Remember that the flute is by nature weak in its bottom octave and must be written higher if it is to add anything in a *tutti* or to come through any but the lightest background in a solo.

Whereas in symphonic scores bassoon parts that go relatively high are customarily written in the tenor clef, this is less often the case in school-score parts. Consistent avoidance of the tenor clef is a debatable practice, as players who go on to more advanced work are then unprepared to read passages in that clef, which they are certain to encounter. The same situation pertains to tenor trombone parts.

BRASS

Horn parts should be kept within a written range of about .

Notes above the F are risky, and passages that go below A or G are more difficult for young players—unless they are performing on a double horn. Happily, the chances of having a full horn section (four players) are better now than formerly. But even when four players are available, it sometimes happens that one or more of them is too inexperienced to manage a separate part, and in such cases a frequent solution is to use only two horn parts (I and II as a rule) with two players to each part. Probably the safest approach to horn writing for school use is to score for four horns but to plan their parts in such a way that the music will sound satisfactory if only the parts for Horns I and II are played.

High school trumpet players, on the other hand, are apt to be quite proficient, and the same is true to a slightly lesser degree of the trombonists. In fact, few limitations apply to writing for these players—apart from the natural limitations of the instruments themselves, which have already been discussed. Remember especially that entrances on high notes should be avoided. Trombone parts use the bass clef as a rule.

PERCUSSION

Most high schools now own four timpani, and some schools may even have five. Remember that it is unreasonable to demand extremely fast changes or a great number of changes in quick succession from an inexperienced student player, though a tuning gauge helps with more accurate and rapid tuning.

Thanks to the band, there is rarely a shortage of percussionists. Today these student performers receive comprehensive instruction that prepares them to perform on any of the percussion instruments, including the "mallet"—or "keyboard percussion"—instruments (xylophone, marimba, glockenspiel, and vibraphone). The concept of the specialist seems to be fading. Many school orchestras include a set of chimes, a glockenspiel, and a xylophone (or a marimba). Vibraphones are considerably scarcer, however.

An unfortunate tendency in arrangements for high school orchestra has been the inclusion of inappropriate percussion parts (for example, snare drum rolls in a Bach chorale transcription) simply to keep the players busy. Stylistic appropriateness and good taste should be the primary considerations.

HARP, CELESTA, AND PIANO

Some scores now contain parts for the harp, and in recent years the number of high schools that own harps and have student harpists available has been increasing.

Although parts for the celesta appear occasionally, they are most often played on the piano since few schools own a celesta.

The role of the piano in arrangements for junior high school orchestras has already been mentioned. It is chiefly a utilitarian role, rather than a coloristic one as in symphonic scoring.

STRINGS

At one time many scores for school use subdivided the violins into three parts labeled A, B, and C or I, II, and III. The third part was generally a simple one designed for beginning players, and it often involved the same notes as the viola part to the extent that the difference in ranges permitted. That format is seldom seen today in the literature for more advanced high school players. The strings are most often listed in the usual symphonic format: Violin I, Violin II, Violas, Cellos, Double Basses.

All the string groups may be written with safety as high as the third position, and the use of fifth position is by no means uncommon in the case of the first violins and the cellos (especially in advanced-level arrangements). The following notes may be considered safe upward limits for high school players of average ability:

EXAMPLE 19.1

| Violin | Viola | Cello | Double Bass |

If higher notes are required in the first violin part and there are doubts as to whether all the players in that group can manage them, the part can be written in octaves, *divisi*, so that the less experienced players can take the lower octave. Another solution used in some scores is the inclusion of an "advanced violin" part that is placed above the other violin parts and is a bit more demanding than those, especially in terms of passages that go higher than the third position.

The tenor clef, once avoided in cello parts, is now used frequently.

Only the easier multiple stops should be called for, preferably those making considerable use of open strings, especially in the case of triple and quadruple stops.

Harmonics are seldom seen in school scoring, although the natural harmonics on the E string of the violin may occasionally prove useful for color effects or for very high notes that would be too difficult if played in the ordinary way.

Because the string groups are likely to be small, the players inexperienced, and the instruments of generally inferior quality, *divisi* passages should be used sparingly (and not at all for the violas). Division into more than two parts had better be ruled out altogether, unless the string section is well above average in size.

As to the size of string sections, a word should be added about the number of string parts included in published arrangements. Some publishers make a practice of including only one of each string part, any additional parts being ordered separately. Others classify their arrangements in three sets of different sizes, according to the number of string parts contained in each. One leading publisher uses the proportions shown in Table 19.2.

TABLE 19.2

	SET A	SET B	SET C
1ST VIOLINS	2	5	8
2ND VIOLINS	2	5	8
VIOLAS	1	3	5
CELLOS	1	3	5
BASSES	1	3	5

These figures represent parts, and because two string players normally read off the same stand the number of string players will be roughly twice as large as the number of string parts.

GENERAL

Sets A, B, and C also include one of each woodwind, brass, and percussion part, a full score, and a "piano-conductor" score. The latter is a condensed version of the music on two or three staves, with general indications as to what instruments are taking the respective musical ideas. Although such scores can be used to conduct from, they have the disadvantage of not showing the exact part for each instrument as specifically as the full score does. They are not actually played at the piano except, perhaps, in the case of junior high orchestras with deficient instrumentation, which occasionally use them (in the absence of an actual piano part) to supply missing parts.

Arrangements for high school orchestra should be made with an eye to providing individual parts that will be grateful and enjoyable for the players, parts that will be challenging enough to be interesting yet not so difficult as to be impractical. In general it is wise to choose the easier keys, preferably those involving no more than three sharps or four flats. Remember that a concert key of three sharps will put the B♭ instruments in five sharps, while a concert key of four sharps means six sharps (or six flats) for them.

CONCERNING THE EXAMPLES THAT FOLLOW

Examples 19.2 through 19.4 are excerpts from works written or arranged by American composers for high school orchestras. Example 19.2 (from *Vignettes* by Theron Kirk) gives a good idea of normal cross-cuing for the instruments that are sometimes missing; the third and fourth horn parts are cued for the trumpets in the first measure, and the oboe and bassoon parts are cued for the clarinets and trombones, respectively, in the last two measures.

Example 19.3, an arrangement of one of a set of dances by Mozart, provides further examples of cuing. Other points to note are the inclusion of saxophones, the "advanced violin" part, and the optional piano part.

Example 19.4 ("Rustic Dance" from *Three Miniatures* by David Ward-Steinman) shows an excerpt from a piano piece and an arrangement of the music made by the composer especially for school orchestras. All the voices have been doubled at the octave in the orchestral version for greater fullness and brilliance. Bowing indications have been carefully marked. The multiple stops are easy and provide great resonance.

EXAMPLE 19.2

Vignettes

Theron Kirk

EXAMPLE 19.3

The Sleigh Ride

Mozart (K. 605)
arr. by Phillip Gordon

EXAMPLE 19.4

Three Miniatures for School Orchestras, I. "Rustic Dance"

David
Ward-Steinman

SUGGESTED ASSIGNMENTS

A. Know:

    1. ranges practical for (a) senior high school orchestras; (b) junior high school orchestras.

    2. the instrumentation generally used in published arrangements for (a) senior high school orchestras; (b) junior high school orchestras.

    3. which instruments are most likely to be missing or weak in high school orchestras.

    4. how to write cues, including those involving a transposition; for example, an oboe part cued for muted trumpet or a horn part cued for clarinet (the latter involving a double transposition). See Chapter 20 for more explicit directions.

    5. the written range of the saxophones and the transposition used by each (if not learned earlier).

B. Make an arrangement for high school orchestra of one of the following, keeping in mind the points discussed in this chapter and including cross-cues wherever advisable.

    1. A short piano piece, e.g., Debussy's "Golliwogg's Cake Walk," (from *The Children's Corner*), first two pages (in ORCHESTRATION WORKBOOK III).

    2. A short piece written originally for a small instrumental group.

    3. A song from a school song book.

    4. A work written originally for symphony orchestra that lends itself to an arrangement playable by high school orchestras.

20

Writing Score and Parts

Because most student orchestrators cannot afford to hire a professional copyist, they are faced with the task of writing out their own scores and parts. Although this aspect of orchestration may appear to be mere hackwork requiring no special knowledge, it actually involves a number of matters that students have seldom had occasion to learn before. Therefore, some pointers on the subject seem in order.

CONCERNING THE SCORE

Composers and orchestrators nearly always need more than one copy of a work they have scored. For example, composers may wish to make the score available to several conductors at the same time or to have an extra copy of it on hand as the work is being rehearsed. Two different processes are available to accomplish this end: (1) the music is written, preferably in ink, on thin "vellum" ("onionskin") paper (printed with as many staves as needed) and then duplicated by the Blackline Diazo or Ozalid process; or (2) the music is written on ordinary music paper (or vellum if preferred) and duplicated by a xerographic machine large enough to accommodate orchestra-size pages. Ideally, the score should be reproduced "back-to-back"—that is, with music on both sides of each page—in order to minimize bulkiness. But not all photocopiers are equipped to produce back-to-back copies, and as an alternative it is possible to attach single-sided sheets back-to-back with adhesive or tape. (The use of single-sided pages in a score is not recommended because of the excessive amount of page-turning involved.) For a long time, the first of these two copying processes was the one in standard use, but photocopying is finding increasing favor today.

Although ink was recommended above, it is possible to reproduce a legible score written in pencil on either onionskin or ordinary music paper, provided that (1) a good grade of pencil (such as an IBM or a Staedtler "Mars-Lumograph F") with fairly dark lead is used; (2) the pencil point is kept sharpened; and (3) the completed master sheets are sprayed with a fixative to avoid possible smudging. Writing in pencil makes erasures easier and precludes the possibility of spills and blots. Some composers use ink for notes (in the interest of making them as sharply defined as possible) and pencil for stems, bar lines, and so on. In any case, a trial printing of a sample page is recommended before the entire score is written out.

The vellum master sheets, which are available in a variety of sizes and formats designed for various combinations of instruments, can be bought from numerous firms, including these four:

Associated Music Copy
Service Corp.
333 West 52nd St.
New York, N.Y. 10019
(212) 265-2400

Judy Green Music Co.
1634 Cahuenga Blvd.
Hollywood, CA 90028
(213) 466-2491

Circle Blue Print Co.
225 West 57th St.
New York, N.Y. 10019
(212) 265-3674

Huey Co.
19 South Wabash Ave.
Chicago, IL 60603
(312) 782-2226

These same firms can make copies of the sheets, by either of the processes previously mentioned, and can also supply cardboard covers and spiral binding, or "saddle-stitch" binding for scores of only a few pages. Although many blueprint companies in other parts of the country are equipped to make reproductions, few sell the blank master sheets or handle covers and bindings. Specially prepared music pens and much other equipment for music copying are available through Associated Music Copy Service Corp. and Judy Green Music Co., included in the preceding list.

As explained earlier, dynamics must be shown beneath each part, in the score, but it is usually sufficient to show tempo indications in only two places on the page, at the top and just above the violins.

Meter signatures may be written in each part, or two or three meter signatures written in large elongated figures may be used instead. The latter system is preferable in certain modern music where the meter changes frequently, for the larger figures are more easily visible to the conductor. In cases where there is a change on the first measure of a new page, the new meter signature is generally shown in advance at the end of the preceding page as well.

In order to save time in student scoring, it is possible to omit whole rests and to leave the measures blank instead. But rests of a *fraction* of a measure must always be shown. Whole rests are included in printed scores and in most manuscript scores intended for professional use.

When a single melodic line appears on a staff that is shared by two woodwind or brass instruments, there must be an indication as to whether the passage is to be played by both instruments or by the first or by the second ("a 2." or "1." or "2.").

When only a portion of the orchestra is playing, either one of two approaches may be used: (1) all the instruments are listed on each page, with rests (or blanks) for those that are not actually playing; or (2) some or all of the instruments that are resting are omitted from the listing on the page. Since fewer staves are required this second way, it is sometimes possible to put on one page what would have taken up two full pages under the other method; that is, the page is divided into an upper system and a lower system with "slash marks" (two short diagonal bars) between the systems at the left-hand side to call attention to the division (as in Example 12.8). Although this method saves paper, it has the disadvantage of not keeping the instruments in the same relative places on the page and therefore makes score reading a bit more difficult. In any case, the *first* page of a score generally shows all the instruments to be used. If this is not the case, the complete instrumentation should be listed on a facing page preceding the first page of music.

The sections of the orchestra can be more clearly distinguished from one another on the score page if there is a gap in the bar lines between them. The horns may have a separate bar line or be grouped with the other brass instruments.

Rehearsal numbers or letters must be included in both score and parts so that the conductor can tell the orchestra where to start when particular passages are to be rehearsed. If numbers are used, it is recommended that they be measure numbers in order that measures preceding or following can easily be identified numerically. In the score, rehearsal numbers should be placed above the top instrument on the page (at the beginning of the measure) and above the strings, every five or ten bars. (Some scores number every measure.) If letters are employed, each should be enclosed in a square or a circle so that it can be found readily. Rehearsal letters are most often placed at likely starting points throughout the score. One possible disadvantage of letters is that works of considerable length may exhaust the twenty-six letters of the alphabet, requiring the use of *AA, BB,* and so on. On the other hand, measure numbers have the following disadvantage: If after copying a work one decides on revisions that entail the addition or deletion of measures, *all* measures must be renumbered in the score and parts from the point of revision. Of course it is possible to use both numbers (at frequent intervals) and letters spaced farther apart at probable starting points.

CONCERNING THE PLAYERS' PARTS

Ten-stave manuscript paper should be used[1]—except perhaps in the case of instruments that use two staves, such as the harp, the piano, and the celesta, for which twelve-line paper is satisfactory.

---

[1]Some music reproduction firms carry nine-stave 8½ × 11-inch manuscript paper, a size that can be easily and inexpensively duplicated on ordinary photocopiers.

As with the writing of scores, black ink is preferable. However, if experimentation proves that fully legible parts can be produced via the pencil method mentioned earlier, that is an acceptable alternative. Be sure to make the notes large enough. Also, allow enough room so that they are not crowded. Ledger lines should be the same distance apart as the lines in the staff. Although a vertical line is used at the beginning of the staves when two or more instruments are involved (as in a score), a single staff should be left open at the start—that is, without a "beginning bar line."

Ordinarily the part for each wind instrument is written on a separate sheet. However, when it might be helpful for each player of a pair to see the other's part, the two parts can be written on the same sheet with a separate staff for each part; each of the two players is then given a copy of this double part. This is the usual approach in the case of horn parts, I and II generally being written on one part, III and IV on another. In rare cases where two instruments play "a 2" much of the time or have very similar parts, it may be practical to write the parts for both on the same *staff*. (In such a situation, horns I and III and II and IV might be paired.) Again, each player should have his or her own part.

For directions on writing percussion parts, see the final portion of Chapter 14.

In planning string parts, remember that you will need only half as many parts as there are players because two players read from each part. Copies of the master part for each string group can be made via the Blackline Diazo process or by photocopying. The latter permits the use of regular music paper (instead of vellum) for the masters.

It is wise to have in reserve a master set of parts that can be used to provide replacements for missing parts if need be. A further reason is the possible need for a duplicate set of parts—for example, if performances of a work are to occur in two different places at the same time.

Each part must include indications for tempo, dynamics, expression, phrasing, slurring, bowing, and muting—in short, every direction that is necessary in telling the player exactly how the part should sound.

Rehearsal letters or numbers, described in the section on the score, must be shown in each part.

Rests of more than one or two measures are indicated in the manner shown in Example 20.1.

EXAMPLE 20.1

Notice that when a rehearsal letter occurs in the middle of a rest of two or more measures, the rest must be divided to show the number of measures before and after the rehearsal letter. Rests of only one measure are often shown by simply putting a whole rest in the measure.

The expression *tacet* (literally translated, "it is silent") in a part indicates that the instrument in question does not play for a specified length of time. For example, if the tuba had nothing to play in the second movement of a particular symphony, we might write, "2nd Movement, tacet" in the part. Or if it played at the beginning of the movement but had nothing to play for the last 200 bars, we could write, "Tacet to end of movement (200 bars)," rather than bothering to enumerate the separate rests and rehearsal letters.

Example 20.1 illustrates the use of cues in parts, in this case the fragment of the trombone part included in the trumpet part. Cues help players to keep their places, and players have a right to expect them. They are most often included just before an entrance after a rest of some length, but they are also useful as "landmarks" in the middle of very long rests. (Cues that may have to be *played* obviously serve an additional function, which will be discussed presently.) One or two bars are usually sufficient for a cue, though longer cues are common. Be sure to select an important voice that can be easily heard and not a minor part that is apt to be covered up by other instruments. Cues are written in small notes, generally with stems up—unless the part goes well above the staff. They should be written in the key of the instrument whose part contains the cue. For example, if one were using a portion of an oboe part as a cue in a B♭ clarinet part, the cued notes would be a major 2nd higher than the oboe notes (the clarinet's key signature taking care of sharps or flats, except for accidentals). If one were using a portion of a horn part as a cue in a B♭ trumpet part, the cued notes would be a perfect 4th lower than the horn notes. (The horn will sound a perfect 5th lower than written, and those notes must then be written a major 2nd higher for the B♭ trumpet.) That particular cuing situation appears in Example 19.2. Of course if a nontransposing instrument is cued for another nontransposing instrument (as in Example 20.1), no transposition is involved.

Examples 19.2 and 19.3 illustrate a point mentioned earlier: in some scores—especially those designed for performance by high school orchestras—passages for instruments that may be missing or weak are often cued in the parts of other instruments that are certain to be present, the idea being that the cue can actually be played if necessary. The same approach is occasionally seen in scores intended for professional orchestras. For example, a low B for flute in Bartók's *Concerto for Orchestra* is cued for bassoon because not all flutes have the low B; and a solo for E♭ clarinet in Copland's *El Salón México* is cued for B♭ clarinet so that it can be played if the E♭ instrument is not available.

In writing the players' parts, label each part carefully, centering the name of the composition at the top of the page, placing the names of the composer and the arranger in the upper right-hand corner, and placing the name of the instrument that is to play the part (for example, "Clarinet II in B♭") in the upper left-hand corner.

If page turning is involved, copy the part in such a way that at the bottom of the page there will be a rest of sufficient length to allow for the turn. (Sometimes it is necessary to leave a staff or more unused at the bottom of the page in order to allow for a turn during a rest.) This is more important in wind parts than in string parts since one of each pair of string players can turn the page while the other continues to play, if necessary. Even in cases involving two players, however, that arrangement is better avoided.

21

Nonorchestral
Instrumental Groups

Although this book is concerned primarily with the orchestra, some supplementary information on other instrumental groups may be helpful, especially to students whose program of study does not include a course in band arranging.

THE CONCERT (SYMPHONIC) BAND
AND THE WIND ENSEMBLE

During the past forty years or so, concert bands have flourished in the United States, particularly in colleges and universities but also at the secondary-school level. They fulfill a valuable function in providing musical training and performance experience for the large number of students interested in playing a woodwind, brass, or percussion instrument. Obviously, school orchestras can absorb only a small percentage of those students; and in some schools a shortage of string players may even rule out an orchestra, in which case the role of the band becomes an even more crucial and important one.

A smaller version of the concert band is the wind ensemble, in which each part is most often performed by only one or two players. Such groups are able to achieve a lightness and transparency of sound not possible with larger bands, where heavy doubling and mixed colors are often involved.

Table 21.1 shows the number of players that might be used on each part in a college-level concert band and wind ensemble, respectively. There is no "standard" number of performers for either group, and the figures for these vary from school to school, depending on the availability of instruments and players, the level of performance ability, and the preferences of the conductor, among other things.

It can be seen from Table 21.1 that the concert band differs from the

TABLE 21.1
**Number of Players in College-Level Concert Bands
and Wind Ensembles**

	CONCERT BAND	WIND ENSEMBLE
PICCOLO	1–2 (alt. with flute)	1 (alt. with flute)
FLUTE I	1–8	1–2
FLUTE II	1–8	1–2
OBOE I	1–2	1
OBOE II	1–2	1
*ENGLISH HORN	0–1 (alt. with oboe)	0–1 (alt. with oboe)
E♭ CLARINET	1	0–1
B♭ CLARINET I	4–8	1–2
B♭ CLARINET II	6–10	1–2
B♭ CLARINET III	8–12	1–2
E♭ ALTO CLARINET	1–4	0–2
B♭ BASS CLARINET	2–6	1
† { *E♭ CONTRA ALTO CLARINET*	0–3	0–1
B♭ CONTRABASS CLARINET	0–3	0–1
BASSOON I	1–3	1
BASSOON II	1–3	1
*CONTRABASSOON	0–1 (alt. with bsn.)	0–1 (alt. with bsn.)
ALTO SAXOPHONE I	1–2	0–1
ALTO SAXOPHONE II	1–2	0–1
TENOR SAXOPHONE	1–2	0–1
BARITONE SAXOPHONE	1	0–1
*BASS SAXOPHONE (little used)	0–1	0
‡ { *CORNET I*	2–3	0
CORNET II	2–3	0
CORNET III	2–3	0
TRUMPET I	1–2	1
TRUMPET II	1–2	1
TRUMPET III	0	1
HORN I	1–3	1
HORN II	1–3	1
HORN III	1–3	1
HORN IV	1–3	1
TROMBONE I	1–3	1
TROMBONE II	1–3	1
TROMBONE III (BASS)	1–3	1
BARITONES (EUPHONIUMS)	2–4	1
TUBAS	2–8	1
*STRING BASS	0–1	0–1
TIMPANI	1	1
PERCUSSION	4–6	3–4
*HARP	0–2	0–1
*KEYBOARD	0–2	0–1
	62–151	25–37

*These instruments are included only as needed.

†In many bands, only one of these two instruments is used.

‡Some recent scores include no parts for cornets but instead make use of four trumpets (and four trombones).

orchestra in several respects: (1) It includes no strings—except for the possible addition of a double bass; (2) although it includes all the wind instruments used in the orchestra, many of these (notably flutes and clarinets) are employed in whole *sections* rather than only in pairs or threes; (3) it makes use of certain instruments *not* normally found in the orchestra—the E♭ alto clarinet, the E♭ contra alto and/or the B♭ contrabass clarinets, saxophones (four sizes), cornets (especially in older scores), and baritones (euphoniums); (4) the instruments are listed on the page in an order slightly different from that seen in orchestral scores: the trumpets—and cornets, if used—are generally placed *above* the horns, while the percussion is shown at the bottom of the page. Saxophones may be put either just below the bassoons or below the bottom bass clarinet, preferably the former. In older scores one sometimes finds the bassoon part written just below the oboe.

A note of explanation may be in order concerning the number of players for the respective clarinet parts shown in the table. Although some conductors allot players equally for the three parts, the figures here reflect another practice often followed: Clarinets II and III are weighted more heavily than Clarinet I—and III more heavily than II. The reasoning is that the Clarinet-I part is normally in a higher register and will therefore come through more clearly, whereas Clarinets II and III generally play in a lower, less penetrating register of the instrument and will balance better if reinforced. Then, too, there may be fewer intonation problems if the number of players on the Clarinet-I part is kept small—and confined to the better players.

Scoring for the concert band involves a few special problems.[1] First, no real equivalent of the orchestra's violins is available; flutes are too limited in terms of power, and clarinets tend to become shrill and out of tune if taken high. Furthermore, neither instrument can equal the particular *espressivo* quality of the violin.

A parallel—though less crucial—situation exists at the other end of the pitch spectrum: nothing in the band is as satisfactory on the bass as cellos and double basses are in the orchestra. Tubas and/or bass trombones often prove inappropriate, and in that case the only other possibilities are the bass clarinet, baritone saxophone, bassoons, and a string bass if one is included.

Also, bands—particularly those at pre-college levels—often encounter the same situation faced by high school orchestras: players for certain instruments—such as oboe, bassoon, and contrabass clarinet—may not be available or may be inexperienced. Composers and arrangers for the band, being unsure exactly what instrumentation can be counted on, tend to make much use of cuing and cross-scoring (duplication of parts in different sections) to insure that all notes will be played. Although this approach is undoubtedly necessary from a practical standpoint, it results in a heavy, opaque sound that palls easily. Obviously the uncertainty concerning in-

---

[1] In John Cacavas's book *Music Arranging and Orchestration* (see the Bibliography), the eminent composer-arranger has this to say: "I insist there is no ensemble more difficult to write for than a symphonic or concert band," and he goes on to explain that statement by enumerating the sorts of problems mentioned here.

strumentation works against sensitive and imaginative scoring. This point is less likely to apply to the wind ensemble, where the instrumentation is more predictable.

Despite these challenges in scoring for the concert band, writing effectively for it is quite possible, as evidenced by the many successful twentieth-century works in that medium. The problem seems to lie chiefly in attempting to transcribe orchestral works containing features (notably high violin parts) that simply cannot be rendered satisfactorily in band terms. Yet because the concert band is a relative newcomer to the musical scene and does not boast a body of pre-twentieth-century literature comparable to that of the orchestra, it must depend to some degree on transcriptions. The solution, according to Cacavas, is to transcribe "only those works which *lend* themselves to the band medium."

As examples of successful transcriptions, the following are cited:

Malcolm Arnold, *Four Scottish Dances,* trans. by Keith Wilson.

J. S. Bach, Passacaglia and Fugue in C minor, trans. by Donald Hunsberger.

Leonard Bernstein, Overture to *Candide,* trans. by Walter Beeler.

Aaron Copland, *El Salón México,* trans. by Mark Hindsley.

Paul Hindemith, *Symphonic Metamorphosis of Themes by C. M. von Weber,* trans. by John Paynter.

Gustav Holst, "Jupiter" and "Mars" from *The Planets,* trans. by the composer.

Ralph Vaughan Williams, *Folk Song Suite,* trans. by Gordon Jacob.

Of course the ideal situation is to compose music conceived specifically for the concert band—or the wind ensemble. Some of the more effective works of this sort that come to mind are the following:

Ingolf Dahl, Sinfonietta.

Paul Hindemith, Symphony in B♭ for Concert Band.

Karel Husa, *Music for Prague; Apotheosis of this Earth.*

Darius Milhaud, *Suite Française.*

Vincent Persichetti, *Masquerade;* Symphony for Band.

William Schuman, *George Washington Bridge.*

Joseph Schwantner, *. . . and the mountains rising nowhere* (wind ensemble).

The example that follows shows an excerpt from a Husa work listed above.

EXAMPLE 21.1

Music for Prague 1968, for Concert Band

Karel Husa

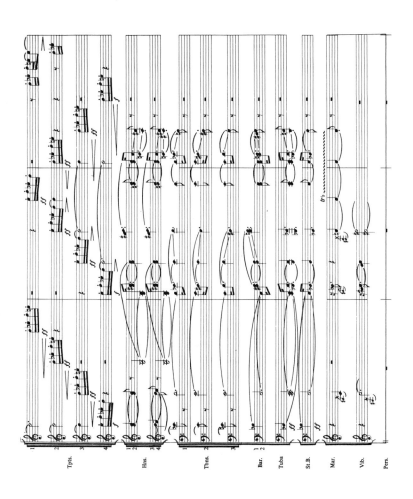

THE MARCHING BAND

The size of marching bands varies greatly—from 30 or so players to as many as 300, though most often at least 60—as does the makeup of these groups. With all of them, however, there is necessarily an emphasis on instruments whose sound will carry well outdoors: the brasses (particularly trumpets and cornets), saxophones, B♭ clarinets, piccolos, and keyboard percussion such as marching orchestra bells (replacing the bell lyre) and the marching xylophone. The oboe, bassoon, and baritone and bass saxophones, which are awkward to play on the march, are seldom included. Because the sound of flutes tends to be lost in the open, some band directors elect not to use them and may substitute piccolos. Alto and bass clarinets, being better suited to concert music, are also likely to be excluded.

Experience has shown that band arrangements intended for outdoor use are best kept simple. Elaborate passagework that makes a brilliant effect in the concert hall may be all but lost on the football field, for example. In general, it is best to rely on fewer parts and to use more unison doublings.

THE JAZZ BAND

The term *jazz band* has been applied to groups of widely varying size.

The largest of these is the big band or stage band, which typically consists of the following: five saxophones (two altos, two tenors, and a baritone), four trumpets, four trombones, and a rhythm section consisting of piano (or other keyboards), string bass, drums, and guitar. Other instruments sometimes included are: auxiliary percussion such as vibraphone and conga drums, (French) horn, and tuba. Further scoring possibilities are opened up by the fact that many saxophonists are able to double on flute or clarinet.

At the other end of the size scale are small jazz "combos" consisting, for example, of trumpet and/or saxophone, piano, string bass, and drums.

PRACTICAL APPLICATION OF THIS MATERIAL

Readers who are interested in learning how to score for any of the groups mentioned so far in this chapter are referred to the books listed in the appropriate sections of the Bibliography.

SMALLER (CHAMBER MUSIC) INSTRUMENTAL GROUPS

Listed next are some of the more frequently used chamber-music groups involving three to six players. Septets, octets, nonets, and so on are seen less often. The larger of these groups begin to suggest a small orchestra. Of course there are many other possible combinations of instruments in addition to those shown here—particularly when mixed strings, woodwinds, and piano are considered.

String trio: violin, viola, cello

String quartet: two violins, viola, cello

String quintet: two violins, viola, two cellos

Piano trio: violin, cello, piano

Piano quartet: string trio, piano

Piano quintet: string quartet, piano

Piano sextet: string quartet, double bass, piano

Woodwind trio: oboe, clarinet, bassoon; or flute, clarinet, bassoon; or flute, oboe, clarinet; or flute, oboe, bassoon

Woodwind quartet: flute, oboe, clarinet, bassoon; or oboe, clarinet, bassoon, horn*

Woodwind quintet: flute, oboe, clarinet, bassoon, horn*

*The horn is sometimes listed *above* the bassoon in the score.

As with the strings, piano may be added to any of these woodwind groups to form a quartet, quintet, or sextet. And strings may combine with woodwinds (with or without piano) to form groups such as: oboe, violin, viola, cello; or clarinet, cello, piano.

Brass trio: trumpet, horn, trombone

Brass quartet: two trumpets, two trombones; or two trumpets, horn, trombone; or two trumpets, baritone, trombone

Brass quintet: two trumpets, horn, tenor trombone, bass trombone; or two trumpets, horn, trombone, tuba

Brass sextet: two trumpets, horn, two trombones, tuba; or two trumpets, horn, trombone, baritone, tuba

Percussion ensemble: two or more percussionists

List of Foreign Names for Instruments and Orchestral Terms

Unless one has taken the trouble to learn the Italian, French, and German names for instruments and the abbreviations for those names, score reading is likely to degenerate into a kind of guessing game. It is easy enough to guess correctly that *Klarinette* means clarinet in German. But it is also easy to guess *incorrectly* that *cors* means cornets (instead of horns) or that *trbe.* stands for trombone (instead of trumpets—in the Italian plural form). And how is one to decipher such names as *Posaunen* (trombones in German) or *piatti* (cymbals in Italian)?

Students who have covered the material in this book have learned a good many of the foreign names as they went along. The complete list (given on the following pages) is for purposes of reference and study. Also given are the foreign equivalents of some important terms commonly found in orchestral scores. The blanks in the latter list reflect the fact that some of the terms are seldom or never used in certain of the languages. Also, there are cases in which the Italian term is used even in French and German scores. For example, one finds *sul ponticello* and *con sordino* in German scores, and such terms as *arco* and *pizzicato* are universal.

Names of Instruments

ENGLISH	ITALIAN	FRENCH	GERMAN
WOODWINDS	LEGNI (or FIATI)	BOIS	HOLZBLÄSER
Piccolo	Flauto Piccolo (or Ottavino)	Petite Flûte	Kleine Flöte
Flute	Flauto	Flûte	Flöte
Alto flute	Flauto contralto	Flûte alto en sol	Altflöte
Oboe	Oboe	Hautbois	Oboe (or Hoboe)
English Horn	Corno Inglese	Cor Anglais	Englisch Horn
Eb Clarinet	Clarinetto piccolo in mib	Clarinette en mib	Es Klarinette
Clarinet	Clarinetto	Clarinette	Klarinette
Bass Clarinet	Clarinetto Basso	Clarinette Basse	Bassklarinette
Bassoon	Fagotto	Basson	Fagott
Contrabassoon	Contrafagotto	Contre-basson	Kontrafagott
BRASS(ES)	OTTONI	CUIVRES	BLECH-INSTRUMENTE
Horn	Corno	Cor	Horn
Trumpet	Tromba	Trompette	Trompete
Trombone	Trombone	Trombone	Posaune
Tuba	Tuba	Tuba	Tuba (or Basstuba)
PERCUSSION	PERCUSSIONE (or BATTERIA)	BATTERIE	SCHLAGZEUG
Timpani (or Kettle Drums)	Timpani	Timbales	Pauken
Xylophone	Silofono (or Xilofono)	Xylophone	Xylophon
Marimba	Marimba	Marimba	Marimbaphon
Glockenspiel (or Orchestra Bells)	Campanelli	Jeu de Timbres (or Carillon)	Glockenspiel
Vibraphone	Vibrafono	Vibraphone	Vibraphon
Tubular Bells (or Chimes)	Campane Tubolari	(Tubes de) Cloches	Glocken
Antique Cymbals (or Crotales)	Crotali	Cymbales Antiques (or Crotales)	(Antike) Zimbeln (or Crotales)
Musical Saw	Sega Cantante	Scie Musicale	Spielsäge
Almglocken	Campane da pastore	Sonnailles de troupeau	Almglocken
Anvil	Incudine	Enclume	Amboss
Flexatone	Flessatono	Flexatone	Flexaton
Snare Drum (or Side Drum)	Tamburo (Militare)	Tambour (Militaire) (or Caisse Claire)	Kleine Trommel
Field Drum	Tamburo (Militare)	Tambour	Rührtrommel

Names of Instruments (*Continued*)

ENGLISH	ITALIAN	FRENCH	GERMAN
PERCUSSION	PERCUSSIONE (*or* BATTERIA)	BATTERIE	SCHLAGZEUG
Tenor Drum	Tamburo Rullante	Caisse Roulante	Rührtrommel
Tom-toms	Tom-toms	Tom-toms	Tom-toms
Tabor	Tamburo	Tambour de Provence (*or* Tambourin)	Tambourin
Bass Drum	(Gran) Cassa	Grosse Caisse	Grosse Trommel
Cymbals	Piatti	Cymbales	Becken
Suspended Cymbal	Piatto Sospeso	Cymbale Suspendue	Hängendes Becken (*or* Becken frei)
Finger Cymbals	Cimbalini	Cymbales Digitales	Fingerzimbeln
Triangle	Triangolo	Triangle	Triangel
Tambourine	Tamburino (*or* Tamburo Basco)	Tambour (de) Basque	Schellentrommel (*or* Tambourin)
Gong	Gong	Gong	Gong
Tam-tam	Tamtam	Tam-tam	Tamtam
Castanets	Castagnette	Castagnettes	Kastagnetten
Rattle (*or* Ratchet)	Raganella	Crécelle	Ratsche
Wood Block	Cassettina (*or* Blocco di Legno)	Wood Bloc (*or* Bloc de Bois)	Holzblock
Temple Blocks	Blocchi di Legno Coreani (*or* Blocchi Cinesi)	Temple-blocks	Tempelblöcke
Wind Chimes:			
Bamboo	Tubi di bambu	Bambou suspendu	Bambusrohre
Wood	Bacchette di legno sospese	Baguettes de bois suspendues	Holz-Windglocken
Glass	Bacchette di vetro sospese	Baguettes de verre	Glas-Windglocken
Metal	Bacchette di metallo sospese	Baguettes métalliques suspendues	Metall-Windglocken
Shell	Bacchette di conchiglia sospese	Baguettes de coquille suspendues	Muschel-Windglocken
Claves	Claves	Claves	Claves (*or* Holzstab)
Maracas	Maracas	Maracas	Maracas
Guiro	Guiro	Güiro	Guiro
Bongo Drums	Bongos (*or* Bonghi)	Bongos	Bongos
Timbales	Timpanetti (*or* Timbales Latino-Americani)	Timbales Cubaines (*or* Créoles)	Kuba-pauken

Names of Instruments   (Continued)

ENGLISH	ITALIAN	FRENCH	GERMAN
PERCUSSION	PERCUSSIONE (or BATTERIA)	BATTERIE	SCHLAGZEUG
Conga Drums	Tumbas	Congas	Congas
Cowbells	Campanelli di Vacca (or Campanacci)	Cloches de Vache (or Gencerros)	(Heerdenglocken (or Kuhglocken) (or Viehschellen)
Sleighbells	Sonagli	Grelots	(Roll)schellen
Slapstick (or Whip)	Frusta	Fouet	Peitsche
Celesta	Celesta	Célesta	Celesta
Harp	Arpa	Harpe	Harfe
STRINGS	ARCHI	CORDES	STREICH-INSTRUMENTE
Violin	Violino	Violon	Violine (or Geige)
Viola	Viola	Alto	Bratsche
(Violon)cello	Violoncello	Violoncelle	Violoncell
Double Bass	Contrabasso	Contre Basse	Kontrabass

Orchestral Terms

ENGLISH	ITALIAN	FRENCH	GERMAN
muted	{ con sordino [1] { con sordini	sourdine(s)	mit Dämpfer (or gedämpft, in horns)
take off mutes	via sordini	enlevez les sourdines	Dämpfern weg
without mute	senza sordino	sans sourdine	ohne Dämpfer
divided	divisi (div.)	divisé(e)s (div.)	geteilt (get.)
divided in 3 parts	div. a 3	div. à 3	dreifach
divided in 4 parts	div. a 4	div. à 4	vierfach
in unison	unisono (unis.)	unis	zusammen (or einfach)
a 2	a 2	à 2	zu 2
at (near) the bridge	sul ponticello	sur le chevalet (or près du chevalet)	sul ponticello (or am Steg)
over the fingerboard	sul tasto (or sulla tastiera)	sur la touche	am Griffbrett
with the wood of the bow	col legno	avec le bois	col legno (or mit Holz)
at the point of the bow	punta d'arco	(de la) pointe	Spitze
at the frog	al tallone	du talon	am Frosch

---

[1] May also be spelled *sordina*, in which case the plural is *sordine*.

Orchestral Terms   (*Continued*)

ENGLISH	ITALIAN	FRENCH	GERMAN
bells in the air	campane in aria	pavillons en l'air	Schalltrichter auf
half (a string group)	la metà	la moitié	die Hälfte
stopped (horns)	chiuso (chiusi)	bouché(s)	gestopft
brassy		cuivré(s)	schmetternd
open	aperto (aperti)	ouvert(s)	offen
soft sticks	bacchette molli (*or* bacchette mor- bide)	baguettes molles (*or* baguettes douces)	mit weichen Schlegeln
hard sticks	bacchette dure	baguettes dures	mit harten Schlegeln
wooden sticks	bacchette di legno	baguettes en bois	mit Holzschlegeln
change G to F♯	sol muta in fa♯	changez sol en fa♯	G nach Fis um- stimmen
near the sound- ing board (harp)		près de la table	
desk or stand	leggio	pupitre	Pult
in the ordinary way (after *sul pont.*, etc.)	modo ordinario (ord.)	mode ordinaire	gewöhnlich
string	corda	corde	Saite
the others (the rest of a string group)	gli atri, le altre	les autres	die Andere

appendix B

Ranges of Instruments

In each case the limits of the extreme possible range are shown in open notes, the limits of the practical or commonly used range in black notes. These are written ranges.

INSTRUMENT	WRITTEN RANGE	ACTUAL SOUND	INSTRUMENT	WRITTEN RANGE	ACTUAL SOUND
WOODWINDS					
Piccolo		8ve higher	Eb Clarinet		minor 3rd higher
Flute		as written	Clarinet in Bb		major 2nd lower
Alto Flute		perfect 4th lower	Clarinet in A		minor 3rd lower
Oboe		as written	Bass Clarinet		major 9th lower
English Horn		perfect 5th lower			

For notation of bass clarinet in bass clef, see text.

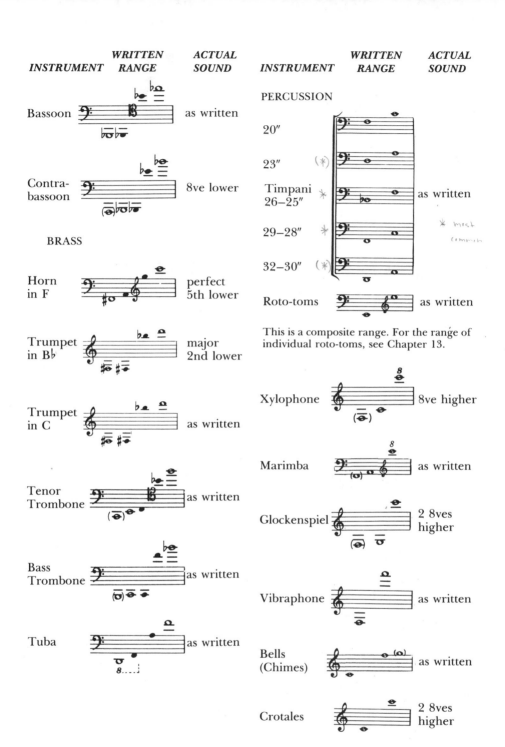

This is a composite range. For the range of individual roto-toms, see Chapter 13.

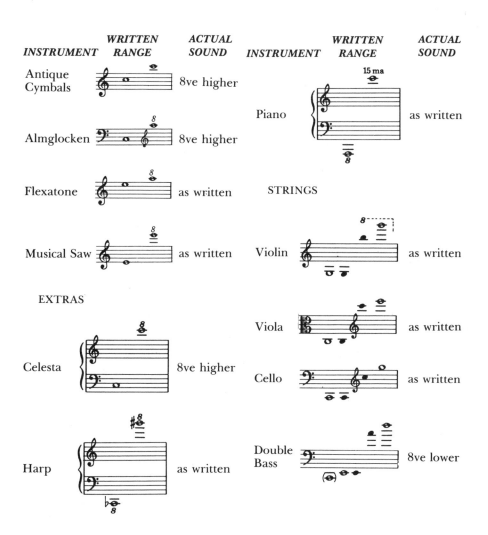

INSTRUMENT	WRITTEN RANGE	ACTUAL SOUND	INSTRUMENT	WRITTEN RANGE	ACTUAL SOUND
Antique Cymbals		8ve higher	Piano		as written
Almglocken		8ve higher			
Flexatone		as written	STRINGS		
Musical Saw		as written	Violin		as written
EXTRAS			Viola		as written
Celesta		8ve higher	Cello		as written
Harp		as written	Double Bass		8ve lower

Infrequently Used Instruments

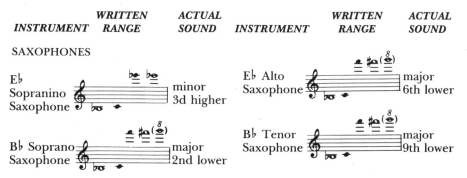

INSTRUMENT	WRITTEN RANGE	ACTUAL SOUND	INSTRUMENT	WRITTEN RANGE	ACTUAL SOUND
SAXOPHONES					
Eb Sopranino Saxophone		minor 3d higher	Eb Alto Saxophone		major 6th lower
Bb Soprano Saxophone		major 2nd lower	Bb Tenor Saxophone		major 9th lower

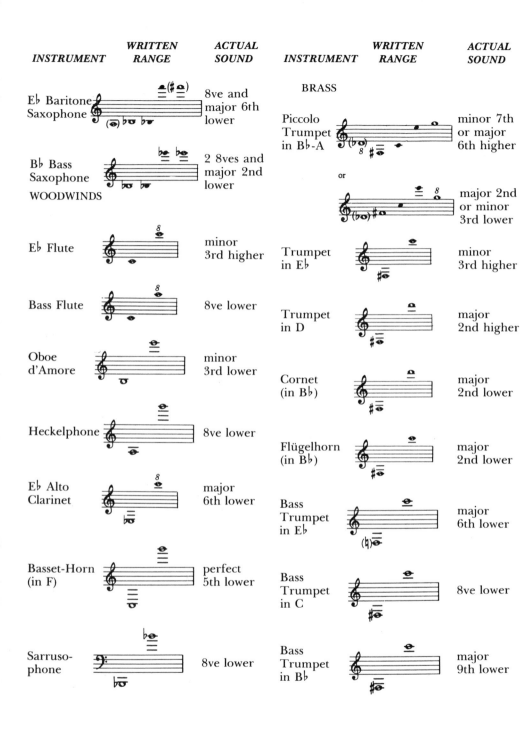

INSTRUMENT	WRITTEN RANGE	ACTUAL SOUND	INSTRUMENT	WRITTEN RANGE	ACTUAL SOUND
E♭ Baritone Saxophone		8ve and major 6th lower	BRASS		
			Piccolo Trumpet in B♭-A		minor 7th or major 6th higher
B♭ Bass Saxophone		2 8ves and major 2nd lower	or		
WOODWINDS					major 2nd or minor 3rd lower
E♭ Flute		minor 3rd higher	Trumpet in E♭		minor 3rd higher
Bass Flute		8ve lower	Trumpet in D		major 2nd higher
Oboe d'Amore		minor 3rd lower	Cornet (in B♭)		major 2nd lower
Heckelphone		8ve lower	Flügelhorn (in B♭)		major 2nd lower
E♭ Alto Clarinet		major 6th lower	Bass Trumpet in E♭		major 6th lower
Basset-Horn (in F)		perfect 5th lower	Bass Trumpet in C		8ve lower
Sarruso-phone		8ve lower	Bass Trumpet in B♭		major 9th lower

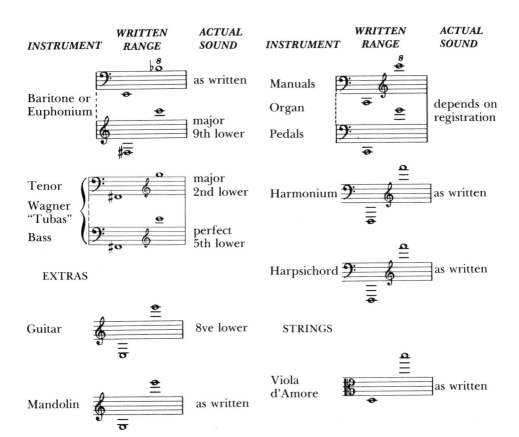

INSTRUMENT	WRITTEN RANGE	ACTUAL SOUND
Baritone or Euphonium		as written
		major 9th lower
Tenor Wagner "Tubas" Bass		major 2nd lower
		perfect 5th lower

EXTRAS

Guitar		8ve lower
Mandolin		as written

INSTRUMENT	WRITTEN RANGE	ACTUAL SOUND
Manuals Organ Pedals		depends on registration
Harmonium		as written
Harpsichord		as written

STRINGS

Viola d'Amore		as written

Bibliography

BOOKS ON ORCHESTRATION

1.   Relatively recent books designed primarily as texts:

ADLER, SAMUEL. *The Study of Orchestration.* 2nd ed. New York: W. W. Norton & Company, Inc., 1989. There is a workbook to accompany the text, as well as recordings of all the examples in the text on compact discs.

BLATTER, ALFRED. *Instrumentation/Orchestration.* New York: Longman, Inc., 1980.

BURTON, STEPHEN DOUGLAS. *Orchestration.* Englewood Cliffs: NJ: Prentice Hall, Inc., 1982.

JACOB, GORDON. *The Elements of Orchestration.* Original English publication, 1931. Reprint. Westport, CT: Greenwood Press, 1976.

PISTON, WALTER. *Orchestration.* New York: W. W. Norton & Company, Inc., 1955.

WAGNER, JOSEPH. *Orchestration: A Practical Handbook.* New York: McGraw-Hill Book Company, 1959. Out of print.

2.   Other books of value to the student of orchestration:

BARTOLOZZI, BRUNO. *New Sounds for Woodwind.* Translated by Reginald Smith Brindle. 2nd ed. New York: Oxford University Press, 1981. A compendium of monophonic and multiphonic possibilities for individual woodwind instruments, with fingerings and other directions for producing the sounds. A recording is included.

BRINDLE, REGINALD SMITH. *Contemporary Percussion.* New York: Oxford University Press, 1970. An admirable storehouse of useful information concerning the potentialities and notation of percussion instruments today. Excellent pictures and a recording are included. Out of print.

CASELLA, ALFREDO. *La Tecnica dell'Orchestra Contemporanea.* Edited by Virgilio Mortari. Milan, Italy: S. A. Ricordi, 1948, 1974. Also published in French: *La Technique de l'orchestre contemporain.* Translated by Pierre Petit: S. A. Ricordi, 1958. Notable for the inclusion of numerous examples from contemporary music. Even for persons with a limited knowledge of Italian or French, this book is not difficult to follow.

DEL MAR, NORMAN. *Anatomy of the Orchestra.* Berkeley, CA: University of California Press, 1984. A large and engagingly written book containing a vast amount of practical information about individual instruments and orchestral techniques. Oriented to some degree around English practice.

INGLEFIELD, RUTH K., AND LOU ANNE NEILL. *Writing for the Pedal Harp: A Standardized Manual for Composers and Harpists.* Berkeley, CA: University of California Press, 1985. A commentary on effective harp writing and on special devices found in contemporary music. A recording is included.

LEIBOWITZ, RENÉ, AND JAN MAGUIRE. *Thinking for Orchestra.* New York: G. Schirmer, Inc., 1960. A book consisting of two parts: (1) reductions of excerpts from orchestral scores, which the student is to orchestrate; (2) the excerpts in their original form, to be studied and compared to the student's version. There are accompanying comments on various styles of orchestration. Out of print.

READ, GARDNER. *Contemporary Instrumental Techniques.* New York: Schirmer Books, a division of Macmillan, Inc., 1976. An invaluable commentary on current performance practice. Out of print.

_____. *Style and Orchestration.* New York: Schirmer Books, a division of Macmillan, Inc., 1979. A welcome and expert treatise on a neglected aspect of orchestration.

_____. *Thesaurus of Orchestral Devices.* 1953. Reprint. Westport, CT: Greenwood Press Inc., 1969. New York: Pitman Publishing Corp., 1953. An encyclopedic compendium of possibilities in the use of orchestral instruments, with listings of the places in orchestral literature where each device can be found. Foreign terms are included. Out of print.

REHFELDT, PHILLIP. *New Directions for Clarinet.* Berkeley, CA: University of California Press, 1978. A recording is included.

SALZEDO, CARLOS. *Modern Study of the Harp.* New York: G. Schirmer, Inc., 1948. Contains material on special effects for the harp and on their notation.

SCHNEIDER, JOHN. *The Contemporary Guitar.* Berkeley, CA: University of California Press, 1958. A detailed treatise on possibilities in writing for the guitar and on newer devices. A recording is included.

STILLER, ANDREW. *Handbook of Instrumentation.* Berkeley, CA: University of California Press, 1985. A massive volume designed to serve as "a guide to the potentials and limitations of every instrument currently in use for the performance of classical and popular music in North America." Explanations of the operation, acoustical properties, and fingering of instruments (including many early ones); also material on voices.

TURETZKY, BERTRAM. *The Contemporary Contrabass.* Berkeley, CA: University of California Press, 1974.

YAMPOLSKY, I. M. *Principles of Violin Fingering.* Translated by Alan Lumsden. New York: Oxford University Press, 1967.

3. Books that are outmoded in some respects but contain much material that is still valid and have historical interest as important early treatises on orchestration:

BERLIOZ-STRAUSS. *Treatise on Instrumentation.* Translated by Theodore Front. First issued in German in 1904. Reprint, New York: Edwin F. Kalmus, Inc., 1948.

FORSYTH, CECIL. *Orchestration.* New York: Macmillan Company, 1st ed. 1914; 2nd ed. 1935. Reprint, New York: Dover Publications, 1982.

RIMSKY-KORSAKOV, NICOLAI. *Principles of Orchestration.* First published in Europe, 1922. Reprint, New York: Dover Publications, Inc., 1964.

BOOKS ON THE HISTORY OF INSTRUMENTS OR OF THE ORCHESTRA

BAINES, ANTHONY. *Woodwind Instruments and Their History.* 3rd ed. New York: W. W. Norton & Company, Inc., 1967. Out of print.

CARSE, ADAM. *The History of Orchestration.* New York: Dover Publications, Inc., 1964. Reissue of 1925 ed.

———. *Musical Wind Instruments.* New York: Da Capo Press, 1966. Reissue of 1939 ed.

———. *The Orchestra from Beethoven to Berlioz.* New York: Broude Bros., 1949. Reissue of original ed.

———. *The Orchestra in the XVIIIth Century.* New York: Broude Bros., 1969. Reissue of original ed.

COERNE, LOUIS ADOLPHE. *The Evolution of Modern Orchestration.* New York: AMS Press, Inc., 1979. Reissue of 1908 ed.

GEIRINGER, KARL. *Instruments in the History of Western Music.* 3rd ed. New York: Oxford University Press, 1978.

LANGWILL, LYNDESAY G. *The Bassoon and Contrabassoon.* Rev. ed. New York: W. W. Norton & Company, Inc., 1965. Out of print.

MORLEY-PEGGE, REGINALD. *The French Horn.* 2nd ed. New York: W. W. Norton & Company, Inc., 1973.

NELSON, SHEILA M. *The Violin and Viola.* New York: W. W. Norton & Company, Inc., 1972. Out of print.

TOFF, NANCY. *The Development of the Modern Flute.* New York: Taplinger Publishing Co., Inc., 1979. Includes a ten-page index, Avant-Garde Notation.

DICTIONARIES OF MUSICAL INSTRUMENTS

ADATO, JOSEPH, AND GEORGE JUDY. *Percussionists' Dictionary.* Melville, NY: Belwin-Mills Publishing Corporation, 1984.

LANG, MORRIS, AND HARRY SPIVACK. *Dictionary of Percussion Terms.* Rev. ed. New York: Lang Percussion Co. [635 Broadway], 1988.

MARCUSE, SYBIL. *Musical Instruments: A Comprehensive Dictionary.* New York: W. W. Norton & Company, Inc., 1975. Out of print.

BOOKS ON BAND SCORING

LANG, PHILIP J. *Scoring for the Band.* New York: Mills Music, Inc., 1950. There is a workbook to accompany the text.

WAGNER, JOSEPH. *Band Scoring.* New York: McGraw-Hill Book Company, 1960. Out of print.

BOOKS ON COMMERCIAL ARRANGING

BENNETT, ROBERT RUSSELL. *Instrumentally Speaking.* Melville, NY: Belwin-Mills Publishing Corp., 1975. Out of print.

CACAVAS, JOHN. *Music Arranging and Orchestration.* Melville, NY: Belwin-Mills Publishing Corp., 1975.

MANCINI, HENRY. *Sounds and Scores: A Practical Guide to Professional Orchestration.* Northridge Music Co., Inc., 1962. Distributed exclusively by Cherry Lane Music Co., Inc., Greenwich, CT. A record is included. Out of print.

PRENDERGAST, ROY. *Film Music, A Neglected Art.* New York: W. W. Norton & Company, Inc., 1978.

SEBESKY, DON. *The Contemporary Arranger.* New York: Alfred Publishing Company, 1975. On orchestrating for recording.

SKINNER, FRANK. *Underscore.* Hollywood, CA: Criterion Music, 1960. First published in 1950. On writing music for films.

BOOKS ON NOTATION OR COPYING

HARDER, PAUL O. *Music Manuscript Techniques: A Programmed Approach,* Part I, Part II. Rockleigh, NJ: Allyn and Bacon, Inc., 1983.

HEUSSENSTAMM, GEORGE. *The Norton Manual of Music Notation.* New York: W. W. Norton & Company, Inc., 1987.

KARKOSHKA, ERHARD. *Notation in New Music.* Translated by Ruth Koenig. New York: Praeger Publishers, 1972. Out of print.

READ, GARDNER. *Music Notation.* 2nd ed. Boston: Crescendo Publishers, 1969.

_____. *Modern Rhythmic Notation.* Bloomington, IN: Indiana University Press, 1978.

STONE, KURT. *Music Notation in the Twentieth Century.* New York: W. W. Norton & Company, Inc., 1980.

Index

Beethoven, Ludwig van:
Eighth Symphony, for
bowing, 57
Fifth Symphony
for bassoon, 98
for cello, 26
chords for orchestra,
182–83
for double bass, 28
for horn effect, 134
for strings, 41
tenor trombone in, 152
First Symphony, for bow-
ing, 54
Fourth Symphony, for *dé-
taché* bowing, 56
Leonore Overture No. 3,
for trumpet, 145
Ninth Symphony, for tim-
pani, 232
Prometheus, basset horn in,
343
Seventh Symphony
for oboe, 84
string chords, 180
Sixth Symphony, for
bowed tremolo, 63
Sonata, Op. 22, 195
Sonata, Op. 27, No. 2
(*Moonlight*) 191, 213–
15
contrasting sections, use
of, 213–15
Third Symphony (*Eroica*)
for cello, 26
for classical trumpet,
141
for flute, 78
for oboe, 84
for violin, 18
Bells. *See* Glockenspiel; Orchestra bells; Tubular
bells
"Bells in the air" (horns), 134
Bell tree, 249, 259
Berg, Alban, Violin Concerto, saxophone in,
340fn
Berio, Luciano:
Chemins IIb, for bass trombone, 155
Circles, for wood chimes
and marimba, 334
Berlioz, Hector:
anvil used by, 245
Fantastic Symphony
for bowed tremolo, 63
for E♭ clarinet, 92, 93
offstage trumpet in, 326
timpani used in, 228
ophicleide used by, 159

Romeo and Juliet, antique
cymbals in, 243
Bernstein, Leonard, Over-
ture to *Candide*, tran-
scribed for concert
band, 373
Bizet, Georges, *Carmen*, for
percussion, 262
Bloch, Ernest:
Schelomo
for celesta, 286
for division of musical
idea, 327
Bongo drums, 249, 259, 271
Boulez, Pierre, *Pli Selon Pli*,
for E♭ clarinet, 93
Bowing, 52–61
definition of, 52
off-the-string, 58–61
jeté (richochet, saltando,
sautillé), 59–60
spiccato, 58–59
staccato volante (flying
staccato), 59
successive down-bows,
60
successive up-bows, 60–
61
on-the-string, 55–58
détaché, 56
legato, 55–56
louré (*portato*, brush
strokes), 58
martelé (*martellato*), 56–57
slurred staccato, 55, 57–
58
plotting, 53–55
types of, 55–61
Brahms, Johannes:
First Symphony
for trombones, 154
for clarinet, 92
for flute, 78
violin G string, 9
Fourth Symphony
for bowing, 57
for cello, 26
for strings, 41
Intermezzo, Op. 119, No.
2, scoring for wood-
winds, horns, and
strings, 208
Requiem, for harp, 280–81
Rhapsody, Op. 119, No. 4,
scoring for full or-
chestra, 309–10
Third Symphony, horn in
solo capacity, 131
*Variations on a Theme of
Haydn*, Var. III, scor-
ing for woodwinds,

horns, and strings,
218
Brake drums, 246
Brass mutes, 158
Brass section, 162–72
chords, scoring, 177–78
instruments. *See* Bass
trombone; Horn; Ten-
or trombone; Trum-
pet; Tuba
school orchestra, scoring
for, 357
special effects, 169–70
Breath tones, woodwinds,
112
Bridge, violin, 11–12
Brindle, Reginald Smith,
250
Britten, Benjamin:
Serenade ("Elegy"), for
horn effect, 135
Sinfonia da Requiem, saxophone in, 340
*The Young Person's Guide to
the Orchestra*, for xy-
lophone, 236
Sinfonietta, III. Tarantella,
scoring for wood-
winds, horns, and
strings, 222
Bruckner, Anton, Wagner
"tubas" in, 348
Brush pizzicato, 67
Buzz pizzicato, 67

Carse, Adam, 85fn, 132fn
Carter, Elliott:
Sonata for Flute, Oboe,
Cello, and Harpsi-
chord, harpsichord in,
351
*A Symphony of Three
Orchestras*
division, technique of,
323
for timpani, 234
for trumpet, 147
Castanets, 249, 257, 262
Celesta, 284–86, 358
school orchestra, scoring
for, 358
Cello, 3, 24–27
Chalumeau register, 90, 113
Chamber music groups,
376–77
Chimes, 241–43. *See also* Tubular bells; Wind
chimes
Chopin, Frédéric, *Nocturne*,
for transcribing piano
music, 189–90